ULTIMATE
MIND GAMES

First published 2015 by Parragon Books, Ltd.
Copyright © 2018 Cottage Door Press, LLC
5005 Newport Drive, Rolling Meadows, Illinois 60008
All Rights Reserved

ISBN 978-1-68052-471-0

Parragon Books is an imprint of Cottage Door Press, LLC.
Parragon Books® and the Parragon® logo are
registered trademarks of Cottage Door Press, LLC.

ULTIMATE
MIND GAMES

PaRragon.

Contents

Sudoku
Puzzles

No 1

		7					1	5
			3	9	7			
	6	2		1		4		9
	2				1	5	4	3
7			4		9			1
4	8	1	2				6	
9		6		2		7	3	
			9	8	4			
1	5					2		

No 2

		1	5	3				
6						7	1	8
	8	2	7				9	
3		4		5	1			9
		7	2		4	6		
5			3	8		2		1
	9				5	3	2	
7	4	5						6
				6	9	1		

No 3

2	5					8		
			3	1	8			
	1	6		2		9		4
6	3	5			2			9
	2		6		1		8	
4			9			2	6	7
3		8		9		4	1	
			1	7	6			
		9					2	5

No 4

	9	8					7	5
				8	6	4		1
		5		1			3	2
	2		3					9
	3	4	8		1	5	2	
7					4		6	
2	1			3		7		
5		3	6	9				
6	4					9	8	

No 5

8	9			3		5		6
	7	1						3
			9	2	4			
		3			7	4	5	1
	6		4		9		7	
7	4	2	3			8		
			5	9	6			
6						7	1	
3		8		7			9	4

No 6

		1		3		4		
5		2		8		9		3
	4		2		7		5	
3		7	6		5	8		2
	2		1		3		6	
6		4	8		2	3		1
	9		7		6		3	
2		5		1		6		9
		6		2		7		

No 7

		9			4		7	2
8					9		5	
		3	6	5		4	9	
4		8		1			3	
2			8		7			1
	7			2		9		6
	4	1		6	8	7		
	6		2					4
5	8		7			3		

No 8

2			6				4	
	8	9	7			6	5	
		6	2	5	1	3		
	9				2			7
	6	5				4	2	
4			3				1	
		2	1	4	9	8		
	7	8			6	1	3	
	1				3			9

No 9

	7		8			6		4
	3	6			5		1	
		5	1	4				2
3	6	9		7	8			
		2				5		
			4	6		3	9	8
7				3	1	9		
	9		2			1	8	
5		4			7		6	

No 10

2				1		6	3	4
4			8	7	6			
9			2		3			
	9		3		7	4		
3		7				1		5
		4	1		9		8	
			5		8			1
			6	2	4			8
8	5	6		9				2

12

No 11

			2			5	4	8
2	8				4		7	
		7		1	3			6
8		6		9			3	
	3		1		6		5	
	9			8		4		7
5			7	6		9		
	1		9				2	4
9	7	3			8			

No 12

		9			8			
		1		3		2	6	8
		5	1	6				
5	9		4		7		8	1
4		6				7		2
8	2		9		6		3	5
				4	1	5		
1	7	2		9		8		
			7			3		

1	9	8
3	5	2
4	6	7

No 13

7				6				4
9	6			8			2	1
		2	5		1	7		
6	4		1		8		3	7
		3	6		4	1		
8	1		2		3		6	5
		6	3		5	9		
3	9			4			1	2
5				1				3

No 14

				5	6			4
			2					9
7	6	2		1				3
	3	7	1		8	9	4	
8	5						7	2
	4	1	5		2	3	6	
6				9		8	3	7
1					3			
4			6	8				

5	1	4
8	3	6
9	2	7

No 15

4					1		7	3	2
8						7			
5			3	6					
	5	8	9		1		2	4	
7	2							6	9
	3	4	7			6	1	5	
				9	3				5
			4						1
2	4	9			8				3

No 16

4		3	2		9	1		6
6			8		7			9
	9			4			5	
	3		4	7	2		8	
7		8				9		2
	4		5	9	8		3	
	6			8			1	
8			9		4			5
5		4	3		1	7		8

6		5				2		
9			5		6			8
3				8	2	1	6	
	7	3		2	1			
	1		7		9		8	
			6	4		7	5	
	6	2	4	3				7
8			1		7			3
		9				5		4

		1	3				6	
9				6	7		3	5
3			5			8	4	
	4			8		7		3
		8	4		1	2		
1		5		2			9	
	1	6			4			9
2	5		1	7				4
	7				8	5		

No 19

7		8			5	9		
5			9	3			2	
		6	1				3	7
			3	7		4	1	8
2								5
4	8	7		6	1			
3	5				6	7		
	6			8	9			4
		4	2			1		9

No 20

			6	5	7			
9	8			2		5		4
6						1	2	
	9		2			7	4	1
		6	5		4	2		
2	3	4			9		8	
	1	2						9
8		5		9			7	6
			4	3	5			

No 21

5		3	8	4				
4			2		7	8		
		2	5			9		1
	9		4	3			2	
	3	4				1	6	
	8			2	1		3	
9		1			4	7		
		7	1		6			5
				9	2	3		4

No 22

			7	3		2		
	6		1			4	8	
8	2	1						5
6				7	2	9		3
		5	4		9	1		
2		4	3	8				7
5						7	9	1
	4	3			7		6	
		2		5	6			

No 23

9				4	2			
	8					9	1	7
6		1			7	5		
	2			1	4		9	6
7			3		6			8
3	4		9	2			5	
		5	2			6		4
2	7	3					8	
			5	8				9

No 24

7		3	6			8		5
	2	5			3	9	7	
		1		5		3		
3	6		4	1				
2								9
				7	2		3	8
		6		8		1		
	1	8	5			7	4	
4		2			9	5		6

No 25

			4	3	5	8		
6	4	8		1		3		
			6		8	9		
1			2		7		5	
	7	2				6	9	
	5		9		1			8
		1	3		2			
		3		9		5	4	2
		5	8	7	4			

No 26

		9	1		5	8		
3	7			6			9	5
5				7				1
4	5		2		7		6	8
		7	6		8	5		
1	8		5		3		7	2
6				8				4
7	3			2			8	9
		4	7		1	3		

No 27

4	1		3			5		
		6	1					
2				7	9		4	6
9	5		6				2	1
		2		9		8		
1	7				4		3	9
8	4		5	2				7
					7	4		
		7			8		6	3

No 28

6		2		3		9		8
5	7			9	8			6
			4				2	
9	1	8			2	7		
		4				3		
		7	1			2	9	5
	8				5			
1			7	2			4	3
7		6		4		1		9

No 29

	9		1		5	2	6	
		7		8				4
	4		2		3	9		
5		2			9		7	
	6			1			3	
	1		4			8		6
		5	6		7		4	
9				3		6		
	3	4	5		1		8	

No 30

			8			4	9	5
	6			2	7	3		
4		8			5			6
1				4		6	5	
7			2		3			9
	3	4		1				7
2			1			5		8
		9	6	3			1	
6	7	1			4			

No 31

		2	4	7	1	3		
8		3			5	4		9
4					9		1	
	7		9					4
5		6				7		2
1					2		8	
	2		5					7
3		1	8			5		6
		5	2	6	4	9		

No 32

5	6	9			3			
2		8	5	4		1		
	4			8		7		8
	9		4	7				
4	1						7	2
				2	8		9	
3		1		6			8	
		7		5	9	3		4
			1			6	2	5

No 33

		6	4	7		3	1	
3					5			
	5	1			9			2
	2	4			3	5	6	
6				4				8
	7	5	1			4	9	
7			8			9	3	
			7					1
	1	8		6	2	7		

No 34

	3			2			8	
	6	9		1		2	4	
8			5		6			9
	8	7	6		1	3	2	
6			2		3			7
	5	2	9		7	6	1	
4			7		5			2
	9	6		3		4	7	
	7			6			5	

No 35

3		2		7		5		6
6				2				1
	5		1		6		8	
1		8	6		3	2		4
	2		7		8		6	
9		6	4		2	7		8
	9		2		1		3	
7				8				9
2		3		4		8		5

No 36

7		3		1	2			4
	6	2	4					9
		1	5				3	
		4		5			1	8
	5		2		4		7	
2	3			7		9		
	2				8	6		
8					3	4	5	
9			1	6		8		3

25

No 37

1		9	5	2				4
					8		1	
	6				7	8		9
8		4			1	6		5
	3			5			4	
5		7	9			2		8
7		1	3				2	
	9		2					
2				4	6	9		3

No 38

	3				8	6		2
5					9	4		
	8		6	4		5	7	
		3		7			6	5
7			8		6			9
4	1			9		8		
	5	1		2	4		3	
		2	1					6
9		8	5				1	

26

785
296
431

No 39

		9	8		7	3		
	7						6	
2			6		1			4
8	3		4		5		9	1
6	9		2		8		5	7
9			5		6			3
	1						4	
		8	7		4	2		

No 40

5		2				7		9
	3						8	
	8		9		7		4	
		6		1		3		
	1		5		3		2	
		5		2		8		
	7		4		9		6	
	6						5	
9		4				1		3

27

468
317
592

No 41

					5		4	
8		2		6				
		1	2	4				6
			4				9	
		6		1		2		
	7				3			
5				3	8	7		
				2		8		1
	3		9					

No 42

		9	8		5	4		
5			2		4			6
	2			3			1	
3	8						7	5
		1				8		
6	4						3	1
	1			2			5	
7			9		3			2
		5	1		6	7		

28

No 43

3								6
9		6	7		3	1		4
			6	4	9			
8		5	4		6	9		2
		4				5		
6		9	2		1	4		8
			5	1	8			
1		8	3		4	6		5
7								1

No 44

6		2	7	3				
7		4						
	3		5				8	
					8		4	
3				7				6
	9		1					
	1				4		6	
						4		9
				6	5	7		2

29

No 45

	5		1				2	
				2		7		4
						8		9
	9	3			6			
		7		4		2		
			5			4	3	
9		4						
1		8		7				
	7				9		6	

No 46

3		2		4				
		5			2			
			7		5		1	
					6	5	8	
		4		5		9		
	7	8	1					
	6		5		3			
			6			2		
				9		4		5

No 47

2			6		3			9
		9				6		
	1		7		9		4	
3		6	5		2	1		8
4		1	8		6	5		3
	3		9		8		5	
		7				2		
5			4		1			7

No 48

						3		
4	1			3	9		2	6
			8	4				
		7		6			5	
	2		3		7		6	
	5			4		2		
			8	7				
8	6		5	1			9	7
		5						

1 9 8
3 5 2
4 6 7

No 49

2	6	7		8		4		
				2	4	9		
			6			1		
	4							1
	7	5				2	3	
8							6	
		8			5			
		9	4	3				
		6		1		7	4	5

No 50

3		8	7		9	5		6
7			3	4	2			9
5	7		1		4		2	8
	4						6	
8	3		6		7		9	4
6			4	2	3			7
4		7	9		1	6		2

5 1 4
8 3 6
9 2 7

No 51

5				7				6
	2		3		8		5	
		7	4		9	1		
3	8						4	5
		1				8		
7	6						1	9
		5	8		2	7		
	1		7		5		3	
2				9				4

No 52

			6		1	3		
5	1			9				
7					3			
1		2	3					
9				1				5
					4	8		2
			7					1
				5			6	7
		4	1		8			

33

No 53

			7					4
		1						
	3	8	1	5				
6			2				3	1
		5		1		8		
1	2				4			9
				8	7	3	1	
						6		
2					9			

No 54

5			6		4			3
		3				6		
4	9						7	5
	4			3			6	
9			4		2			1
	6			8			5	
1	3						9	6
		8				2		
2			1		6			7

No 55

	9	5				6	2	
			9		6			
1		2				9		4
6			3		5			8
			7		1			
4			8		2			9
5		9				3		6
			4		7			
	4	3				1	7	

No 56

	7		3			6		
	8	1						3
3			7				9	5
	9				7			
		2				4		
			4				5	
5	2				6			8
6						1	3	
		7			9		2	

No 57

	3			5				
7		5			6			
8		9	1		7			
1		3	2		4	8		5
	9						3	
5		6	7		3	9		4
			5		1	3		6
			6			2		9
				2			1	

No 58

9			8		3			2
	3						1	
1	7						9	6
		4	9	2	6	8		
		3	7	4	5	1		
7	2						8	1
	4						6	
8			5		1			3

36

No 59

				7		8		
			3		2		6	7
			9		5		2	4
1	4		5		7			8
		9				6		
8			6		1		4	9
3	1		8		9			
2	9		7		4			
		7		2				

No 60

	3			5	9			
	4		2					
	7			1		2	3	8
3						9		
5	2						6	1
		4						3
8	9	6		4			7	
					6		1	
			3	7			9	

No 61

			7	5				4
					8			2
4	8	3		9				5
		7					4	
6		1				2		8
	9					7		
5				2		3	6	7
9			6					
7				1	4			

No 62

3				9				6
		6	1		4	5		
	7		8		2		9	
6		8				4		1
	4						7	
2		7				3		9
	9		4		5		6	
		1	9		6	7		
8				2				5

38

No 63

6			3	4				
3				1		4	8	2
9					8			
	8					1		
4	5						2	7
		9					3	
			7					1
2	3	7		9				8
				5	3			6

No 64

			5				4	9
		1			6	5		
							3	7
				1	2	9		
	4			9			5	
	2	7	8					
7	9							
		4	7			8		
6	3			4				

No 65

4		8				3		1
	5						2	
		7	8		3	5		
8				1				9
		3	5		9	4		
6				2				8
		1	9		8	6		
	8						1	
7		6				9		4

No 66

			5	6	7			
		7		8		3		
	8	5	2		3	6	4	
	6						7	
		1				2		
	5						3	
	3	9	1		2	4	5	
		2		5		1		
			4	9	8			

40

No 67

7	8		4		9			
1	9		6		2			
		3		7				
6	1		8		5			3
		8				6		
3			2		7		1	5
				9		7		
			3		6		5	4
			7		1		6	9

No 68

9			6	4	5			7
3		8	9		7	1		5
1	6		4		2		7	8
	3						4	
4	9		7		3		5	1
6		3	2		9	7		4
7			5	6	4			3

41

No 69

		1			2	3		9
2					1		5	
8	7					1		
9			2					
	4						6	
					6			3
		5					7	1
	2		9					4
4		3	5			8		

No 70

								5
	9	3	1	5		7	6	
			9	4				
2				6		8		
		7	2		5	6		
		8		9				7
				2	4			
	4	6		3	8	1	2	
8								

42

No 71

		2	1		3	5		
	4		8		6		7	
9								1
7	2		6		1		9	4
4	8		2		5		3	6
3								8
	5		9		8		1	
		4	3		2	7		

No 72

		6	8		2	7		
				9				
4			7		6			2
9		1	5		8	3		7
	5			4			9	
7		4	1		9	5		6
1			6		5			3
				3				
		5	2		1	8		

43

No 73

			5	9	1			
	7	1	4		2	9	3	
		2		7		4		
	8						6	
		4				2		
	3						7	
		3		5		8		
	1	6	3		4	7	5	
			8	6	7			

No 74

	3		9		1		2	
1			3		2			5
				4				
2	8		7		4		5	3
		4		5		8		
3	6		8		9		7	4
				6				
6			2		8			7
	9		1		7		8	

44

No 75

				2		7	4	
6					5			
		3	4	6			8	
					9			5
	1			7			2	
8			6					
	7			9	2	1		
			3					9
	2	4		1				

No 76

1					5	8		6
		5			1		7	
	9	3						1
		8	5					
	2						4	
				4	6			
7						1	9	
	5		8			2		
6		2	7					3

45

1 9 8	
3 5 2	
4 6 7	

No 77

	3		7		8		2	
6			5		9			3
		5		2		6		
	9	1				8	5	
5								4
	8	4				3	6	
		2		8		5		
7			4		6			1
	6		2		1		9	

No 78

6			7		9			1
		7				2		
2		8				6		5
	7		3	4	8		2	
	4		5	1	6		9	
8		1				9		2
		4				5		
9			2		3			7

5 1 4	
8 3 6	
9 2 7	

No 79

	8	1				6	5	
		5				3		
	2		7		3		1	
5			6	9	4			3
7			1	2	8			9
	3		4		5		7	
		8				9		
	5	7				2	6	

No 80

		8				1		
6			3		7			8
	9		2		5		6	
7		3	4		2	6		9
9		4	1		6	3		2
	3		5		8		7	
1			9		4			5
		5				4		

No 81

				4	7	9		
	5	9					4	
	8	7			2		5	
			2			5		
5		8				1		4
		6			4			
	6		4			8	1	
	4					2	7	
		3	9	7				

No 82

						7		
				4	7	1	6	
5					2			
3			5				9	7
		1		7		4		
7	6				9			8
			3					9
	7	6	2	1				
		8						

48

No 83

6			8			3		7
9						4		6
		4	3	9				
		6			8			
	9	1				7	6	
			9			5		
				3	4	2		
3		8						9
1		7			9			5

No 84

4	8							9
		6		2			3	
1			4			5	8	
					7	1		6
7		8	2					
	9	7			1			5
	3			5		7		
8							6	4

No 85

1			2		5			8
2		3				7		5
	9						1	
		5		9		4		
7			6		1			2
		6		3		5		
	3						5	
6		7				8		4
4			5		6			3

No 86

	5						3	
	8		3		7		1	
4		7		2		6		9
8				3				5
			1		2			
5				6				4
7		3		1		9		8
	2		9		6		4	
	6						5	

50

No 87

7	9						2	3
3		5		4		8		6
	5		2		3		6	
2								1
	4		8		1		3	
9		4		3		6		2
8	1						9	5

No 88

3			6	5				
7				2		1	6	4
8					1			
		8					7	
1	4						5	9
	6					2		
			7					2
4	7	9		8				6
				9	6			3

No 89

			8	9				
8	4		3	6			2	9
		3						
	3			7		1		
	1		5		9		4	
		9		4			3	
						5		
7	6			5	2		1	4
				8	7			

No 90

2	9				7		1	
				3	2			5
5	1						3	
8					3			
9		1				3		4
			7					1
	3						2	7
6			5	2				
	8		3				4	9

No 91

	7		2		6		9	
		3	8		4	7		
1								3
4		6	7		1	9		5
7		9	6		5	8		4
5								2
		2	5		9	1		
	8		3		2		4	

No 92

				3				
	9		6		4		5	
		1	5		9	4		
	1	5	2		3	9	7	
7				1				3
	2	3	7		6	5	8	
		2	9		7	8		
	7		4		2		6	
				8				

No 93

9							5	
				6			2	1
		7	3					
		8			4			2
7	9			5			6	4
6			7			3		
					1	4		
5	6			9				
	2							8

No 94

	1		6		2		9	
	2						4	
5		3		7		8		6
		4		2		9		
			7		1			
		8		5		4		
3		9		1		6		2
	4						5	
	8		5		3		7	

No 95

4		3					1	
	1				8	6	9	
		8			1			7
		6	8					
2								5
					5	9		
8			6			2		
	9	2	7				3	
	7					1		4

No 96

	9	3		8	2	1	7	
				6	3			
								8
5				1			4	
	7		8		5		1	
	4			3				7
4								
			6	5				
	1	6	4	9		5	2	

No 97

3	8		5		1		9	4
1				9				5
			4	3	2			
	7						6	
5								1
	9						8	
			9	7	6			
6				2				8
9	2		1		8		4	7

No 98

9				3				1
			7	4	1			
4	2		6		9		3	7
	9						7	
6								8
	1						4	
2	7		8		6		9	5
			2	5	3			
8				7				6

No 99

		1		7		2		
	3						4	
2			6		9			3
	1	4	9		7	8	3	
			1		4			
	7	9	2		8	1	6	
1			8		6			5
	6						8	
		5		4		9		

No 100

6	7			4			5	1
		2				7		
	3		7		5		6	
7				2				8
		1		9				
4				8				7
	1		8		7		3	
		9				1		
2	4			3			8	5

57

No 101

				2			7	8
		4	3			2		
							9	6
			4			5		7
8				7				2
5		9			1			
7	9							
		8			9	1		
6	3			8				

No 102

6	7			3			4	8
	2		1		8		7	
	6	7				2	3	
2		5				4		9
	3	9				1	8	
	8		4		2		9	
3	5			6			2	1

58

No 103

			2	7				
4								
	5	2	4	3		7	9	
7				5			4	
	8		6		7		5	
	4			1				8
	3	1		6	9	5	8	
								6
				2	1			

No 104

9				1	6	3	4	
				5				
	5	6				1	2	
					4	5		9
5								2
2		4	5					
	6	3				7	5	
				6				
	9	2	7	3				8

No 105

	4	1		6				
6			5					9
	7	8						
					2	3		7
		6		4		1		
3		4	9					
						4	7	
2					7			1
				1		8	5	

No 106

		3	1		7			
					3			2
				4			7	9
			3			8		7
9				7				4
8		6			5			
2	1			9				
7			2					
			7		6	5		

No 107

	2		9	5				6
		5			3			
			7				4	9
		6	5					
1				4				7
				8	3			
7	9			1				
		2				8		
4				8	7		1	

No 108

	9				3			
3			4	8				5
8								6
5		7		6				
9		2	8		7	6		1
				9		2		4
7								2
1				3	4			8
			6				4	

No 109

		6	7				5	3
3				6			4	
	1	9				8		
7		1	3					
					2	3		8
		5				9	8	
	4			2				1
6	8				9	7		

No 110

	9	2		7		6	3	
	8		9		5		4	
9	6						7	1
5		8				9		3
2	4						6	8
	1		4		2		9	
	5	4		6		7	1	

No 111

		7	9		2	1		
	1	2		6		9	3	
5								2
	6			4			2	
		8		3				
	2			5			4	
8								3
	5	6		7		4	9	
		3	2		4	7		

No 112

	3						9	
	8	4		1		7	5	
		5	3		9	6		
			8		6			
	9						8	
			1		7			
		1	2		8	5		
	2	8		6		3	1	
	7						2	

63

No 113

6		8				3		5
4		9		6	5		7	
				8				
1	4				3			
	3						4	
			1				9	3
				3				
	9		8	2		1		6
8		3				4		2

No 114

		4	1	2				
			9					
						3		
5	3							7
2				8				1
6							9	4
		1						
					5			
				7	3	6		

No 115

	4				3	7	1	
		6	5					4
			8					6
	9	4		7	8			
			6	5		2	9	
9					5			
4					9	8		
	7	8	3				5	

No 116

	9	8			3	2		
4			6					
2			5				4	
				9	6	1	2	
	7	1	4	5				
	6				1			2
					5			1
		5	3			9	6	

No 117

					5			
		4					3	6
			8	4			5	
1				3			6	
2			9		4			7
	4			2				9
	2			7	8			
3	6					7		
			1					

No 118

6		5						7
			1		8	2		
8	3							
	1			3				
		7	6		2	4		
				1			3	
							2	6
		2	9		7			
4						5		8

66

No 119

8	6	5						
4			9		6			
	9			8	7			
			8	3			2	
		6				1		
	3			9	5			
			7	4			1	
			1		2			8
						7	9	5

No 120

	9		3				6	
6	1		9			7		
8				7	5			
3	5							
		8				9		
							2	4
		6	8					5
		9			5		7	2
	7				3		1	

No 121

	9				5		4	
		6	2					1
		7			1		9	8
5	1							
		2				7		
							8	3
6	4		7			9		
2					9	1		
	7		5				6	

No 122

		5			6			3
6	4							
		2			4	6		
4	1				5	8		
			1		2			
		8	3				5	1
		1	4			9		
							3	6
5			7			2		

68

No 123

	6		7					
		8		4		2		5
4						1		
	8		2		6			
		2		1		4		
			9		4		3	
		3						7
1		5		2		3		
					8		9	

No 124

	2				7			
3	1				9			6
		5		3			4	
			1			4	6	
4								3
	8	2			5			
	7			6		1		
5			9				8	4
			8				5	

No 125

	6	4		5				
					1	6	5	
2					7	3		4
	5					4		1
1		7					2	
3		2	8					6
	7	8	9					
				4		2	7	

No 126

	4	6	9					8
	1			3			2	
2			6					
	5	8	2					
1								7
					4	9	5	
					3			4
	7			1			3	
3					7	2	9	

No 127

							3	8
			9			7		5
				5				2
	6		2			4	5	
		3	7		9	8		
	1	4			8		7	
4				1				
7		1			6			
2	8							

No 128

	4				7			
	9	7		8		2		
					2		1	4
	6				1		3	7
5								2
7	2		8				4	
8	5		6					
		6		1		9	8	
			3				7	

No 129

1		8	4					9
		9	8					
	3			6		2		
					9	8	7	
5								1
	1	6	3					
		1		5			9	
					2	7		
6					4	3		5

No 130

				3		8		
					9	3	4	
						7		5
6	2		7					4
	5		9		4		7	
1					8		2	3
7		8						
	6	4	1					
		2		6				

No 131

4				9	3			
1	6					9		
		4						
	2			5				9
	7		9		2		5	
6				1			8	
					8			
		7					1	6
			3	7				5

No 132

	9			8				5
		4	6					
	1	2					3	
6				1				7
			4		6			
2				5				8
	8					1	2	
					4	5		
5				3			9	

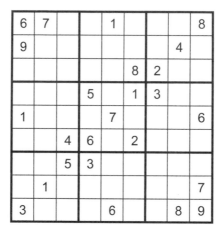

No 133

6	7			1				8
9							4	
					8	2		
			5		1	3		
1				7				6
		4	6		2			
		5	3					
	1							7
3				6			8	9

No 134

	8			5				4
					2	8		
3						1		6
	9			1			7	
			2		9			
	6			8			3	
1		6						5
		2	9					
4				3			8	

No 135

		6		2		3		
7		9			5		8	
	3				7			
8		1			3			
	6						4	
			9			1		5
			2				9	
	2		4			5		3
		4		6		2		

No 136

5							8	
			4	7	9			
					3			
						9		3
7				2				6
8		1						
			1					
			5	8	6			
	3							4

No 137

9			5	6				
7	2	5						
		1	9		7			
			5	8				3
	7						4	
8				9	2			
			4		3	5		
						2	6	9
			6	1				4

No 138

	5							2
4	9			3			5	
			8			7		
			1		7	5		
	3			4			1	
		8	6		3			
		6			2			
	8			1			3	9
1							4	

No 139

1			9		8	3	6	
		5				4		
8			6	5				
					3		9	2
		3				1		
5	6		1					
				7	6			3
		6				2		
	8	4	2		5			7

No 140

	7	9			8		3	
				5		9		4
4		8			6			
2						5	1	
	1	4						9
			1			3		2
3		5		2				
	9		4			7	5	

No 141

	2	3						
			8		3			4
9		7				5		
	8			2				
5			7		4			6
				8			2	
		6				3		9
4			1		5			
						7	4	

No 142

			3		5		7	
						8	9	4
			1	4	5			
		2	9	8				
6								5
				2	7	3		
		8	4	7				
9	7	6						
	1		6		8			

No 143

	8	3				6		
5		9						
			7		2		5	
4				1				
	6		5		9		7	
				4				1
	5		3		1			
						3		4
		7				9	8	

No 144

			3					
	5							
			4	9			7	
3		7				2		
		4		1		9		
		6				8		5
	2			6	5			
							4	
					8			

No 145

	2			6				7
			1				3	
		9	4			6	5	
2	9				5			
		6				2		
			7				8	3
	8	2			4	7		
	7				8			
5				9			1	

No 146

1			9	6				
					3			
7	2					6		
	3			2				7
	1		8		4		6	
8				1			4	
		8					7	2
			5					
				8	9			5

No 147

2					5			6
	9				2			8
						5	2	
3					8	7	5	
			7		6			
	7	8	9					3
	2	9						
6			1				8	
4			5					7

No 148

					6		5	
3		9		8				6
7						4		
			1		8		2	
8				7				4
	6		4		5			
		2						3
9				4		7		8
	1		9					

No 149

2		4	8					
7				4				
6	9							
	4	7	9				2	
		3	5		2	9		
	8				6	7	1	
							3	9
				1				6
					5	2		1

No 150

			5					
	2					8		
			1	7	9			
3	8							
	7			4			6	
							5	1
			6	8	2			
		5					9	
					3			

Wordsearch Puzzles

Musicals

```
Q K L Y M M O T M O R C I W E
V S E L B A R E S I M S E L Y
A G S L N O G I A S S S I M D
Z C U O P L H M N W T F L A O
E H O D T H O J N S A K T M U
F I R O W H E P I M F I A M K
G C A L A C E D E U Y S O A S
R A C L H F E K N L T S B M Z
Y G K E J S L N I A T M W I P
N O S H T X Y O C N G E O A K
L S W O E F N U Z Q G K H F O
Y B R E A K I N G G L A S S B
I Y I C I C A B A R E T N F F
U L E N Z G X A T I V E A D G
H L G O D S P E L L M C P E I
```

ANNIE	HELLO DOLLY
BREAKING GLASS	KISS ME KATE
CABARET	LES MISERABLES
CAROUSEL	LION KING
CATS	MAMMA MIA!
CHESS	MISS SAIGON
CHICAGO	OKLAHOMA!
EVITA	SHOWBOAT
FAME	THE KING AND I
FUNNY FACE	TOMMY
GODSPELL	WEST SIDE STORY

No 2
What a Gas!

```
E W Z C R S F Z C R Z Q R M N
O I M A E A C E T Y L E N E R
G X D R N C J P F E E I I T X
C O E B A O H L R M T B T H H
N T G O P P U L G R N I R A I
F Y B N O O G Z O O C O O N N
Y I V D R I P U X R Z P G E K
Q A M I P D S Y N K I O E R T
X E N O N O G A E O A N N P A
Z E K X X E H N G N T L E E Q
I O D I N E A U O L I P Z Y U
C I D D Y T L N R R A M Y H J
J E W E U E O U D T K O O R Y
G Y L B A E N Y Y N D F C R K
R U U D N R H N H E L I U M B
```

ACETYLENE	IODINE
ARGON	KRYPTON
BROMINE	METHANE
BUTANE	NEON
CARBON DIOXIDE	NITROGEN
CHLORINE	NITROUS OXIDE
COAL GAS	OXYGEN
FLUORINE	OZONE
HALON	PROPANE
HELIUM	RADON
HYDROGEN	XENON

Greek Deities

```
T S Q S M A A V J O R H Q I D
M G U H I U R Z L A G K C M M
A R L E X W R L W R L O B L A
Q S G Z H X O R E T E M E D E
T Y U U W P S E L E N E X O T
H N G I A K R S S M J A S B A
E Q X A P H R O D I T E Z I C
M K L K I A T S M S M G T R E
I C D L Z A L T K R R S O K H
S E E K N E W U E O E N B H A
P R I A P U S H C H U T Y E S
Q I H R R R A R W S X M H B Y
S T N E V H L Q U M E R O S P
T M B S U E Z D A N A A J A P
O B X V P M G W V P K E O V A
```

AESCULAPIUS	HERMES
APHRODITE	HESTIA
APOLLO	HYGEIA
ARES	HYMEN
ARTEMIS	MORPHEUS
CRONUS	PRIAPUS
DEMETER	RHEA
EOS	SELENE
EROS	THANATOS
GAIA	THEMIS
HECATE	ZEUS

Moons of the Solar System

```
T S O M I E D Z Z W F X R K U
C M T S S O B O H P J W F L U
O L R V P U S H B L L K E N O
V L I X Z Y D D G E T I O O U
Z O T S I L L A C D R I Y R S
W H O N V E N A L A R O Z E P
T P N F I Y N S C E Z P I B J
J T P R M K Y Z P H C A A O Q
A E B E O H P Y F T E N P R U
N M D T T W H V M L H D E R O
U E N E E U R O P A T O T E M
S N T A D N A R I M D R U A S
T O Z F T D A T L A S A S H I
X M W U Z I K V X M R O W Q U
M F A X F S T D M E Y W U Y P
```

AMALTHEA	JANUS
ARIEL	LEDA
ATLAS	MIRANDA
CALLISTO	OBERON
CALYPSO	PANDORA
DEIMOS	PHOBOS
ENCELADUS	PHOEBE
EUROPA	TETHYS
GANYMEDE	TITAN
HYPERION	TRITON
IAPETUS	UMBRIEL

Sauces

```
A C S E N A T T U P B G K B C
R S D E S P A G N O L E O L W
E L W I A I W W K V O L H B U
V L B E N I A C I R O M R A B
A D R U E O I D R G L A Z R L
M G A Q Y T G R N P T R Q B A
I B E E A Q A E E A E M B E N
R E R R N R S N I P L T L C Q
P C V G R E G B D D I L I U U
W H I A O S B U N S Y R O E E
V A O L M A R I E R O S E H T
Y M P A R N I T A R G U A P T
N E U R U S A L S A V E R D E
B L A C K B E A N I A R H O O
I X R I B R U E S S A H C J A
```

A LA GREQUE	CHASSEUR
ARMORICAINE	ESPAGNOLE
ARRABBIATA	HOLLANDAISE
AU GRATIN	MARIE ROSE
AU POIVRE	MORNAY
BARBECUE	PERI PERI
BECHAMEL	PRIMAVERA
BLACK BEAN	PUTTANESCA
BLANQUETTE	SALSA VERDE
BOLOGNESE	SWEET AND SOUR

Shipping Lines

```
A F K G B D X T R F A P F Q A
P C N M D E T B R J O Y F L I
T O I T A F R E S L F R K A D
H S L R H E D G I F E Z C U N
T T A Y E O R S E N X U C R I
W A E N L M H S C N N C I O H
H L S S V O A H K A L U H L S
I I E C C U L D R B V I P I I
T N V E S I R D N A H C N N T
E E A U N I O N C A S T L E I
S N A E B B I R A C L A Y O R
T H N S W E A S H E L L N O B
A U E L I C A W P A N D O T Z
R Z T H X L L I V A S W A H S
G Z S C R A T S D E R T F N U
```

BERGEN LINE	MAERSK
BRITISH INDIA	P AND O
CHANDRIS	POLISH OCEAN
COSTA LINE	RED STAR
CUNARD	ROYAL CARIBBEAN
DFDS	SEALINK
FRED OLSEN	SHAW SAVILL
FRENCH LINE	SHELL
FYFFES	STENA
HOLLAND AMERICA	UNION CASTLE
LAURO LINE	WHITE STAR

Down the Hatch!

```
U I M L R D Y W T M T B Y V Z
Q B B I D D N M L T W N B Q V
B R E A N M O C V V H F C E P
Z U E A O E B E O O I D H J M
F M R E Z Z R G G C S Q A H O
T B U C C M U A D H K U M C J
T D H Q O O O O L S Y T P S B
M W C U G Y B J C W G S A R D
S P T V N Z C H I I A T G I W
K H O M A A N H N W T T N K L
L I C F C A B S I N T H E V Q
D S S B P N G N T A X Y W R S
U P V P Z B E O R E N Y T W F
P N S I V O D K A V H T R O P
L M U M T R J O M B S T I U R
```

ABSINTHE	MEAD
BEER	MINERAL WATER
BOURBON	OUZO
BRANDY	PORT
CHAMPAGNE	RUM
CHIANTI	SCHNAPPS
COCKTAIL	SCOTCH
COGNAC	VERMOUTH
GIN	VODKA
KIRSCH	WHISKY
MARTINI	WINE

Fabrics

```
J T F G D A P A Q C R H G A Y
H U L R I A H O M E Z H N M H
G W K Q K N R C K P P G M I C
T F E O B I G C J Z O U B C V
L Q N N Y K U H N R S E A J U
M E T I Q S D R A L O N M X J
W D O R R K E D I M V I S G B
X E W E F C G N S A D M L R J
P U E M E U N U S E R R T N U
N S L E V B T V E L V E T G O
O I L S K I N W H Z V P S W X
L F I L G N T A C W U R J F Q
Y Z N O T T O C O D I A L P D
N I G O H U A U S L U N G P F
D R B W E C I Q K I A G Q T Z
```

ANGORA	MOHAIR
BUCKSKIN	MUSLIN
CANVAS	NYLON
COTTON	OILSKIN
DRALON	PLAID
ERMINE	SEERSUCKER
FLEECE	SUEDE
GAUZE	TOWELLING
GINGHAM	TWEED
HESSIAN	VELVET
MERINO	WOOL

Airy

```
A E N R G E H T A E R B B O N
T E E X E P T N P M T B U A E
C K F T Z E C A R G W U B D W
F N T V E E A A L R V O B L S
F R S S E N T H G I L Y L S R
M Z N R R R S H P J T A E B L
Z E E M B E E T E Y C N K A Z
J P G K R M U H N R N C E L G
V H Y F E B E F P E E Y P V D
G Y X L E J U L P S R A G V G
S R O O D T U O P Y O R L W Y
E D D N G J J W M R C M U O X
Y N I Q N A I R T I G H T C S
P W R Q C O R N K A E N I A X
S B C M Y U G Z L W L N Q L J
```

AIRTIGHT	FRESH
AIRY	GRACE
ATMOSPHERE	LIGHTNESS
BLOW	MELODY
BREATHE	OPENNESS
BREEZE	OUTDOORS
BUBBLE	OXYGEN
BUOYANCY	TUBE
CURRENT	VENTILATE
ETHEREAL	WIND
FLOW	ZEPHYR

Distance and Area

```
N O I T A C O L P M U I D G P
M J C T H A S E F E A N C D Y
R U Q X H I U T L A G F G T M
K H O L Z G C M K S J I I M M
G M G E A H I K D U V N N Q Y
M E F E U L J E N R R I E Z I
E M L X E V S N H E F T C Y E
Y E C V I N M H T J S Y A R D
X R W O A C R E A G E S P C T
G T G P T S H C T E R T S B V
I X X L E N G T H T H E K Y R
X E O G H P Z A I O T O O F V
L A I N Y H Y R W M D P W Y K
N P N S R E T E M E I F A F P
U G F A H S N L C R W L E X R
```

ACREAGE	LOCATION
ETERNITY	MEASURE
EXPANSE	METER
EXTREME	MILE
FOOT	REMOTE
HECTARE	SIZE
HEIGHT	SPACE
INFINITY	STRETCH
LEAGUE	THICKNESS
LENGTH	WIDTH
LIMIT	YARD

Headgear

```
C P D R O R E R B M O S H B G
W R E B R A I N H A T Q A J T
D H A M A C R E L O K T T A M
P R Q S T L C L V F H X H Q Q
B A E P H K A E L I D X Y L J
E T P K Y H P C N B O W L E R
F E I H L I E G L B D E R B Y
T E T M P A C L L A B E S A B
S A H E I A T L M B V J K L L
T N H O P E I S I E R A U L I
E A E P M P V E R R T D L I R
T B L N O B Y S D E O A L T T
S R M P R T U O R T E G C N R
O U E F E D O R A B H D A A P
N T T M R H K I G A B J P M N
```

BALACLAVA	MANTILLA
BASEBALL CAP	PILLBOX HAT
BATHING CAP	PITH HELMET
BERET	RAIN HAT
BOWLER	SKULLCAP
CRASH HELMET	SOMBRERO
DEERSTALKER	STETSON
DERBY	STOVEPIPE HAT
FEDORA	TOP HAT
HOMBURG	TRILBY
HOOD	TURBAN

Girls' Names

```
Y R E F Y N R M K U D E C V N
G V D O R O T H Y T S R I K Z
F T O W E K E V E J M Z A P U
F F W N A N L N A R A B R A B
F L E I N M I I I R M C J U D
A E L H N E N C A L O O U L S
E L I O L G A Y N G O M I I E
M I N E T N R M R A I R R N R
S Z D G D W X I P A R B A E E
B A A I K U S F D Q M F A C N
M B C V G E G A S E R E T F A
T E N I L E U Q C A J N S K Q
Z T Y D N E W U K T T T B O R
R H A I R O T C I V X L Q K R
Y W I I V W Y A N E D V Y O F
```

ABIGAIL	KIRSTY
BARBARA	LINDA
CANDICE	MADELEINE
CAROLINE	PAULINE
DOROTHY	ROSEMARY
ELIZABETH	SERENA
FRANCINE	TERESA
GRISELDA	VICTORIA
HERMOINE	WENDY
INGRID	YVONNE
JACQUELINE	ZARA

Geographical Features

```
X Q F R U G H N S G O T S U D
C A J E S Y P W Z R X D W N M
E G N K D X A S N O Y N A C T
P U G A I M I C A N A L T D A
J E W L P S M S V P D U E O T
H L L O A O Z P L O R S R T N
S I F O R C F A O M E L F I T
H W Y R Z Z I W P R M S A A Z
O O C B N N A E T E K T L R O
G L R J R E V I R J N O L T Q
F P Z E E E M Y A U G I Q S G
E P P E T S E R O F S Y V H N
K A S H S R A M J U J S R A X
C N C W R W J Q V B A S I N R
S F G J W Y P U L M D V Q F N
```

BASIN	MOUNTAIN
CANAL	OASIS
CANYON	PLAIN
CAPE	RAPIDS
DESERT	RAVINE
FISSURE	RIVER
FOREST	STEPPE
GLACIER	STRAIT
HILL	SWAMP
LAKE	WATERFALL
MARSH	WOODLAND

No 14
Clouds

```
V P C W O N S U E L I P M M Z
O H L M H O R S E T A I L S M
Z I N O C K Q L I V N A U S A
T C O N T R A I L S L L U G R
U S U T A M M A M T U T R F A
T Q H M J M U N O M A I E A K
C C S Y U E Q S U R V Y D L C
Y U R A D L T C T R A I N L H
C M C I R R O S T R A T U S F
L U J A A T O N T I O J H T X
O L S T L B U L I R Y G T R I
N U U A M I H E O M E S V E V
I S C I R R U S S G B A J A S
C O N V E C T I O N I U M K U
V E O R O G R A P H I C S S G
```

ALTOCUMULUS	HORSE TAILS
ALTOSTRATUS	HYDROLOGIC
ANVIL	JETSTREAM
CIRROSTRATUS	MAMMATUS
CIRRUS	NIMBOSTRATUS
CONTRAILS	OROGRAPHIC
CONVECTION	PILEUS
CUMULONIMBUS	RAIN
CUMULUS	SNOW
CYCLONIC	THUNDER
FALL STREAKS	VIRGA

M Words

```
S K M L C L C P O U M W F J Q
M L F L E S Y M D A J K D D C
N U A E T A R E C A M N E K X
M M D E J Q R A C O U E L U O
J K F D M M W S V B S E Z A M
A T K F Y S D U I K N C Z M E
J G Y X O E S R M E Q B U A E
E L O H P G O E F D L G M R N
O M M P I M A M R E T T U M Y
M H O I C N A E P T P T I R S
C M L N N D I N L B S D C R W
P W E E D U C T M I N I M U M
S B S V Q A S P O X M H M X P
V S T K U A Y M M I L L E R G
S R T L E S R O M N Y I J G Y
```

MACAW	MOISTURE
MACERATE	MOLEST
MAZE	MONDAY
MEALS	MOPPED
MEANNESS	MORIBUND
MEASUREMENT	MORSEL
MILLER	MUDDY
MIMICRY	MUTTER
MINIMUM	MUZZLED
MINUS	MYOPIC
MISTRESS	MYSELF

American States

```
M O Y O A I N R O F I L A C H
T I P O J A R I Z O N A S R X
P A S Q Y F G O S N D R Y D O
P Z D S H G S I O N I L L I K
P K K I O D A R O L O C R Z H
X W I B R U K E N T U C K Y S
S N E W Y O R K V B T A S A M
N W N B M S L I Y E A M W I X
V A I O A X R F N R H O C G W
G K M S G G P I A F H H S R G
I S N L I E A E S G I A W O N
T A T N O M R E V G X L U E Y
K L I X O H I O A E Y K H G F
Y A H F O E S N T S I O W A Q
L B U N A H Y N S J M R W O Z
```

ALASKA	MICHIGAN
ARIZONA	MISSOURI
CALIFORNIA	NEW YORK
COLORADO	OHIO
FLORIDA	OKLAHOMA
GEORGIA	OREGON
ILLINOIS	TEXAS
IOWA	UTAH
KANSAS	VERMONT
KENTUCKY	VIRGINIA
MAINE	WISCONSIN

UP Words

```
G F Z E Q C M U P V T Z G D Z
E W Z T U X L O G K Y F E M I
F E T N R O E G N J K I I R H
D L P A O Y N B I H D R X D Q
S L M K V I T O M H Q A E S N
G I I I G R R O O T E D T H J
A N R N C T U L C J N A D E S
G G I I O D D S C E G X S D D
I R S D U I E Y H E T T U A F
B L I Z N T W N D T A Y A R M
K H N G T A I E R I E E O G M
V G G I R A T G R U B N T L S
V Q N D Y F E S H B T N D X E
E G X S I Z X G W T B I P P G
N Q O L X V S P Q X N S W K W
```

BEAT	RISING
BRINGING	ROOTED
COMING	RUSH
COUNTRY	SETTING
DATED	STAGED
ENDED	STAIRS
FRONT	STANDING
GRADE	TIGHT
HOLDING	TURNED
LIFTED	WARD
LOOKING	WELLING

Weapons

```
X D W P T E N O Y A B R D L N
S Y C R D R F M Z J E K F U X
T A Y I A A E I T D D V G P N
Y E B O G E L L N S A E I Q F
S Q I R G J P I F K N K H A C
X J A B E D W S E I E P G A R
O O G S R E L L H S R I L K O
N D E C D O I C T E G S W O S
Z E S I T S A A A Z D T Z O S
Y P S M S M F D Y T N O X Z B
T R A I Q F D Z S V A L J A O
X O M T A E I E D W H P H B W
J T E A R G A S A S O L U E D
T D O R R E V L O V E R E L R
R Q U U I R W C S W O R D Q T
```

ASSEGAI

BAYONET

BAZOOKA

BOWIE KNIFE

BROADSWORD

CATAPULT

CROSSBOW

DAGGER

HAND GRENADE

MACHINEGUN

MISSILE

PIKESTAFF

PISTOL

REVOLVER

RIFLE

SABRE

SCIMITAR

SIDEWINDER

SPEAR

SWORD

TEAR GAS

TORPEDO

Palindromes

```
Q Y I S H S S X V O E N X I D
K A K M U A U N Q A S T L I F
F I I R A D A R E P A P E R R
C X O K A Y A K U Z G X V R S
J O O B U C I L O T A B E S I
S G X P E Z L V N T S F L O U
T H M C R U B I J B E L K L F
A P A T P B D I R R P N O O N
T R D H P N E E R E S R E S X
S T A N S F V C E W E X L T Z
S M M Y F I I P N D E O N W K
P D B U V V W K D Z S X Y Z V
B Y D E I F I E D M O G F U A
J N R C K V R O T O R N S C W
L N W B S Y V S F Q K J I J J
```

CIVIC	REDDER
DEED	REFER
DEIFIED	REPAPER
KAYAK	REVIVER
LEVEL	ROTOR
MADAM	SAGAS
NOON	SEES
PEEP	SHAHS
PULL UP	SOLOS
RACECAR	STATS
RADAR	TENET

Astrology

```
N O O A F Q T G E A W I I C D
V D N W L X P P L E O N I F M
P F R O W I O N E F I T E C S
E R O Z I C D A M M K T Z O O
G R C I S T C E E A L A I N W
M T I O H D C G N N K U R J J
A E R F S A G I T T A R I U S
C O P J Q W Q C D Z S U E N E
H H A L B C F U U E Y S Y C I
A F C L A A A S A T R A B T R
R Q T I E N W P L R B P S I A
T P D G M C E I C V I R G O P
G O J O V E B T Z T D U J N X
Z T O I P R O C S S E C S I P
L N I U A T Z T R C D S R W Y
```

AQUARIUS	LEO
ARIES	LIBRA
CANCER	MOON
CAPRICORN	PISCES
CHART	PLANETS
CONJUNCTION	PREDICTION
CUSP	SAGITTARIUS
ELEMENT	SCORPIO
FIRE	TAURUS
GEMINI	VIRGO
HOROSCOPE	ZODIAC

No 21

Breakfast

```
W N R M M B B I L S E U M K O
K S E O T A M O T C G N B K O
D S M O K E D F I S H A M I B
G S S Q K S I U Z L S E U N S
T R Y Z S E J G V W E O P L B
P O A C H E D E G G A D V R Y
X M A P G M K G L E U F E S J
A X A N E T U A E P D A F G W
E D A R W F E F L R D E W L G
T R S N M R R K F F E B I M E
O G X M E A C U T I N E X R E
A B A C O N L U I X N R G Z F
S C R O I S S A N T Q W O H F
T Z M U E N F G D A M J B C O
H O U Z G R H O N E Y H O I C
```

BACON	KEDGEREE
BOILED EGG	MARMALADE
BREAD	MUESLI
CEREAL	MUFFIN
COFFEE	ORANGE JUICE
CORNFLAKES	POACHED EGG
CROISSANT	SMOKED FISH
FRIED EGG	TEA
GRAPEFRUIT	TOAST
HAM	TOMATOES
HONEY	WAFFLE

No 22
BIG Words

```
V D V C Z P L R K F L S B H C
E N B I G A M I S T T I W R U
U A B F E X N U C O G Y E Z M
B B I D O D G J H B E H K A K
I G G Y B U S S A N T Y B C T
G I H E B I G N O O Z R I W O
B B A U S I G M R Z N T G Q O
E I N G B T G B I Z S O S B F
N G D A H I G D U G E G P I G
O E T E B I C S I S Z I E G I
S A O L B E M B N P I B N W B
M R L G V U Y H Q I P N D I B
Y E B I G B O N E D C E E G Y
R D E B I G T I M E P J R S G
R E M A G G I B I G B U C K S
```

BIGAMIST	BIGFOOT
BIG BAND	BIG GAME
BIG BANG THEORY	BIG HAND
BIG BEN	BIG LEAGUE
BIG-BONED	BIG MONEY
BIG BROTHER	BIGOTRY
BIG BUCKS	BIG SHOTS
BIG BUSINESS	BIG SPENDER
BIG DEAL	BIG STICK
BIG DIPPER	BIG TIME
BIG-EARED	BIGWIGS

No 23
Active Words

```
R E T B T A C T I V E Q T R S
T T L N V B L N J N R X P B V
T N E I C I F F E L O L M Q R
G X B M G N Y R O T N I O V V
F J B B D A G L D X R V R B G
G F A L I E V I T A R E P O G
Y N F E T L M F E H Z L L V E
L Q I I T J S P F I G Y P A L
I U C R T U U P L N X I J B P
V I G O R O U S I O W N R J P
I C B T E I G L S R Y N U P U
N K K R O W T A H J I E A W S
G X U I I S P S I M I T D S O
J T W B U S Y A F E R V E N T
U Z L B X X K R G Y R R G D V
```

ACTIVE	LIVELY
AGILE	LIVING
ALERT	NIMBLE
AT WORK	OPERATIVE
BRISK	PROMPT
BUSTLING	QUICK
BUSY	SPIRITED
EFFICIENT	SPRIGHTLY
EMPLOYED	STIRRING
ENERGETIC	SUPPLE
FERVENT	VIGOROUS

No 24

Just Desserts

```
Z W J A V O L V A P Z S E O E
A T I R A M I S U I E S Y A A
B A Q B W G L M M L S B K L D
A P S Q A I P E O U A B Y C N
G P P A N K R R O K S R O T U
L L V R I I E M E F T O V E S
I E U N N T A D F S K W K N T
O P P G I E R U A I G N B A R
N I U F R I P P E L W I M P U
E E O C C M M S L X A E L I D
Z R E E A A N T O Z A S J G E
P C H E E S E C A K E D K N L
I O R R B D O O F L E G N A Y
W C C A R A M E L W X J T R F
D Y C E U E C L A I R S M F T
```

ANGELFOOD	FRANGIPANE
APPLE PIE	ICE CREAM
BAKED ALASKA	MERINGUE
BAKED RICE	MOUSSE
BROWNIES	PAVLOVA
CARAMEL	PROFITEROLES
CHEESECAKE	PUMPKIN PIE
COOKIES	STRUDEL
CREAM PASTRY	SUNDAE
CREAM PUFF	TIRAMISU
ECLAIRS	ZABAGLIONE

No 25
ABLE Words

```
B K B D T U C S A P W S Z B T
D E H A M A I P A R A B L E V
F Q B Z P Z M F Q N I G T A T
E L G A E Y P A S S A B L E F
E L B A D A E R Q N M O L E C
Y L B V W V R E L I A B L E E
E L E A F O R M I D A B L E L
E C L L N Q X X B N A S L A B
L E B U B E D D O L B B U K A
B S A A J A M I I K A G E I R
A G D B L E T A S R H L N G O
K H N L V S V I E A B X A I M
R N E E E A F S B A B B B B Z E
O T B U B I I L N A L L L A M
W I Q F H M E U P E H D E W H
```

AMENABLE	MISERABLE
AVAILABLE	PARABLE
BENDABLE	PASSABLE
CAPABLE	QUESTIONABLE
DISABLE	READABLE
ENABLE	RELIABLE
FORMIDABLE	SIZEABLE
GABLE	TABLE
HABITABLE	UNABLE
LAUGHABLE	VALUABLE
MEMORABLE	WORKABLE

Colors

```
N X B V V V P Y V B N L B M F
C N L T P Q H Z D X N O H N N
O G E G O B Y I E L P R U P J
Y W M Z U D C N D M O M I N B
B W O L L E Y D Y B E G O A J
O W N Y T V T I S S L R Q F N
S T T T R Y I G I C P U A L D
M Y C I A L O O A Q A W E L F
P U B Y M R U M L M N R S N D
L E T U A Q E M A E B P L E D
N E O N R N R R A G T E W E L
X X G U I O I U H U E Q R R T
R E T Z N N S H D C W N S G V
B E I G E C L E B C O X T O V
K D H E D K T A G B T F M A C
```

AMBER	MACENTA
AQUAMARINE	OCHRE
BEIGE	ORANGE
BLUE	PURPLE
CYAN	ROSE
EMERALD	RUBY
FAWN	SCARLET
GOLD	TURQUOISE
GREEN	ULTRAMARINE
INDIGO	VIOLET
LEMON	YELLOW

No 27

Monster Mash

```
A Q A P K C S U K J E L F N K
R I R V S C Y H Y F C J D U I
U N C K A H G B E K R A K E N
S M A U G R O N E L I Z Q O G
N H M Z D O D G I R O C W R K
M C P B G A Z Y G H S B F E O
W U I A H U I A H O T A Z Y N
C H Z L R N L C S Q T E U O G
C I X R I U L D I U Q H H R R
J U S O N F A G G E D O R T E
D Q W G P B O T T V E E L S T
M Q G Y I C N E O Z N O M E T
C U X R E N F A F N S P D D I
D C Y C L O P S P A I U E A R
T U M F S E C R F I I M R C D
```

AGGEDOR	KING KONG
BALROG	KRAKEN
CYBERSAUR	MACRA
CYCLOPS	MEDUSA
DESTROYER	MINOTAUR
FAFNER	NAZGUL
FASOLT	SHELOB
FENDAHL	SHOGGOTH
GODZILLA	SLEIPNIR
GRETTIR	SMAUG
HYDRA	THE THING

No 28

Presidents

```
Y H F H B U S J K R G C H R B
Y L R V O M X U K X W T O E E
E I H P A K E N N E D Y O A X
L N A D Y W I L S O N D V G G
N C A R T E R M B U S H E A X
I O R V A N B U R E N N R N E
K L T E T C A O U N G F H O B
C N Y G U R O N C L I N T O N
M V G Y N S U O A E P X D L J
D Z E B E I T M L H W I O J A
D G K V R R I D A I C L G N V
S J E F F E R S O N D U K J H
B L C L E V E L A N D G B W D
T K E I S E N H O W E R E J Q
L H A J H K W N Q P U R O J J
```

ADAMS	JOHNSON
BUCHANAN	KENNEDY
BUSH	LINCOLN
CARTER	MCKINLEY
CLEVELAND	NIXON
CLINTON	REAGAN
COOLIDGE	ROOSEVELT
EISENHOWER	TRUMAN
GARFIELD	VAN BUREN
HOOVER	WASHINGTON
JEFFERSON	WILSON

Fungi

```
B J R E T S Y O N I C R O P A
J B E T O A D S T O O L T Y J
Q G N L D D N F Q S G D R C P
P E T I F T O F E H I I U N C
M B L F P F T R Q I N C M H U
V R C L U T U C J I K F P K P
A O D B E S O R L T C K E N F
L W I I S R M L T A A U T L U
L N R U H H E O X K P X Y A N
A C L A A B D T R E C A I R G
B A R C A M D F N E G A F O I
F P S T I P E W E A L S L C K
F C R T F S I Z R Q H L C B O
U O V O L O P I N G V C E Q N
P M A H P A C T A L F I P P E
```

BLACK TRUFFLE	OVOLO
BROWN CAP	OYSTER
CEP	PIED DE MOUTON
CHANTERELLE	PORCINO
CORAL	PORTABELLINI
CUP FUNGI	PUFFBALL
ENOKI	ROSE RUSSULA
FLAT CAP	SHIITAKE
FLY AGARIC	STIPE
INK-CAP	TOADSTOOL
MOREL	TRUMPET

Physics

```
S H B T P N C E A B S Z B H U
N Q Q P S A L V L K R A U Q N
U E I I W E R G E Y L D C O E
K Y W E C W P T F L Y I R Z G
H P D T V V M U I N O T U L P
E R R S O I Z S A C S C C C E
C O L A Y N T M Y Y L A I I H
N T E N X I I C L P T E N T T
E O E G C C Q K A A O S I E Y
I N O S S C Y C L O T R O N N
C U O T Z X Z Y E E I G T U P
S O I R F I S S I O N D C N K
G N V O J T A N C G R L A A E
A T O M S V O L T M E T E R J
E L N I J D B D Q I N A H W S
```

ANGSTROM	KLYSTRON
ATOMS	NEWTON
BALLISTICS	NUCLEI
CATALYST	PARTICLE
CYCLOTRON	PLUTONIUM
DYNAMICS	PROTON
EINSTEIN	QUARK
ELECTRON	RADIOACTIVE
ENTROPY	SCIENCE
FISSION	VELOCITY
IONS	VOLTMETER

Words Containing IF or BUT

```
G L M C V P G P U L F N U O K
B U T T E R N K A G T I A N Q
U B H M R R I T B C F V Z Z C
T M D P O B T H T F I R D A O
T H I N B U T I E I R F N P T
O C S U B D U Q F W H A I F U
N E T E E R B F I I T D I C B
Y Z R S A I I E W U E L X X I
U F E W T F F E B T R D Y S L
Q H H P I T I M U I R F W T A
L Q C M F E A B A J I I E U H
I P T Z Y R I G M L F F O B I
R E U N N R Q N P T I S J E N
J G B J T D A M L N E O Q D B
I Y M Z P E A Y K S D T K O A
```

ADRIFT	HALIBUT
AIRLIFT	KIBBUTZ
AMPLIFY	KNIFE
BEATIFY	PACIFIC
BUTCHER	RAMBUTAN
BUTTER	REBUTTAL
BUTTING	SWIFTLY
BUTTON	TERRIFIED
CERTIFIED	THRIFT
DEBUTS	TRIBUTE
DRIFTER	WIFE

Water

```
P J M K S L Y J L X L B U O R
P G E I I N I A T N U O F Z B
G U S H I N G T N E R R O T W
H A T P Q L W P H I N E L J U
O H U C I L U A R D Y H L P I
T G A S A R O R T G S O A V S
W Z R R J R R O N E B L F N L
B X Y I X S A I P G R E N H M
D H X V A V W T G L N F I Q H
J N A E C O E N A A R I A B C
L G C R L L I G S C T I R L I
Y A P F P H O T U I R E H P L
T T N O T Y S I Z L T U M W S
B T R A K Y I S T R E A M E W
H D B I C S E S P U D D L E V
```

BATHING	IRRIGATE
BOREHOLE	OASIS
CANAL	OCEAN
CATARACT	PUDDLE
DELUGE	RAINFALL
DROPLET	RIVER
ESTUARY	SPRING
FLOWING	STREAM
FOUNTAIN	TORRENT
GUSHING	WATERFALL
HYDRAULIC	WHIRLPOOL

No 33

Musical Instruments

```
O O R Q S P S C G Z Z N B H T
F E O H S N U C Z U Q N P X I
I O C L A R I N E T I E S M K
V B A S S O O N H L T T Z B X
E O R T O X O A O R Q E A E F
N G I Q A H R I O T A P Z R X
O I N D P M V M F C I M M Y C
H H A O O B B H C A E U R L F
P U L N X O J O N T I R E R F
O Y I O N H R O U N L T D E E
X C G E P D O L O R H O R N A
A J U A I Z F H K Z I K O R J
S N V O A A P R A H E N C K O
G I N F M U R D E L T T E K Q
W V U K E L E L E P Z H R O B
```

ACCORDION

BASSOON

CLARINET

EUPHONIUM

FLUTE

GUITAR

HARMONICA

HARP

HORN

KETTLEDRUM

LYRE

OBOE

OCARINA

PIANO

RECORDER

SAXOPHONE

TAMBOURINE

TROMBONE

TRUMPET

UKELELE

VIOLIN

XYLOPHONE

No 34
Bible Characters

```
C M L G N I L L T R O R J P V
B R R H A J I L E I N A D H R
L D C D W B W P X H B U I V L
I C A Q Q I R B A R A B B A S
Q M T W M Q A I A T J H Z B M
M F J E B O R H E I S A A C Z
H A M P G A A P N L R O C K U
C G O I H M G D Z U D N Y O M
O L S T I S A M S O N T M D B
V I E Q C V Q C R B J D A M Q
S S S U I N U E P E T E R Z S
O Y C D M I H S S P V R Y Q G
N R H L U A P U H O Z E O B L
D D E X H C S Z K S A J K I Z
Q D V I H A I R A H C A Z G C
```

ABRAHAM	JACOB
ADAM	JESUS
BARABBAS	LAZARUS
CAIN	MARY
DANIEL	MOSES
DAVID	NOAH
ELIJAH	PAUL
EVE	PETER
GABRIEL	SAMSON
HEROD	SAMUEL
ISAAC	ZACHARIAH

K Words

```
W M N N Q Y C W B B X N Y O W
K O N I L J C T E Y A N P B T
E D T O T O Y K K T K P G N C
Y G Z W T A U E F L R X Y E P
H N D C O O R A G N A K D T N
O I D E D K K E O J C E Q E N
L K Z L L N A C K U P T T X D
E V I B I W K S T P K T S I E
K K T B E E O N A I I L O T K
A V Q O D J E N T K M E Y I C
N X F N E K D C K G K D G A O
S K O K A I H I B T I R I W N
A K L Y K E T C H U P U T U K
S I A W N W Q T A U Q M U K L
I K I S S C Z M A Q K F R M F
```

KAFTAN	KISS
KANGAROO	KITCHEN
KANSAS	KITE
KAYAK	KITTEN
KENTUCKY	KNOBBLE
KERATIN	KNOCKED
KETCHUP	KNOWLEDGE
KETTLEDRUM	KOWTOW
KEYHOLE	KUMQUAT
KIDNAPPED	KUWAIT
KINGDOM	KYOTO

No 36
Art Terms

```
H S T R W X P Z Z W I X L T G
Z C Y J S A V N A C U B I S M
M Q T M L O I L S E D P E U F
U G P E B T A R N F A F Y I S
I H T X K O N I R S I T O O E
D T H T C S L E T L N F O R A
E B P R V T S I L A E R R U S
M P A J U C C L S N T T H A C
J H A O O H I T F M S X W R A
C G L C E T E C H N I Q U E P
I G D S S X I J N I T H V P E
A L F A T D U H S L R B I M F
Q A V U W J N I L S A H Z E T
U Z R V G T I A R T R O P T F
K E G D O V E R L A Y B L P Z
```

ARTIST	PALETTE
CANVAS	PASTICHE
CHARCOAL	PORTRAIT
CUBISM	SEASCAPE
FRESCO	SKETCH
GLAZE	STILL LIFE
LANDSCAPE	SURREALIST
MEDIUM	SYMBOLISM
OILS	TECHNIQUE
OUTLINE	TEMPERA
OVERLAY	TEXTURE

No 37
Absolutely!

```
R W A J S R E T U L O S B A G
Q O X R A D L A U T C A G M E
O D X O B G B N U S J F Q U N
N E K H H I A W A Q T P R S G
E C P N C I T A R C O T U A Q
Q I O F S D I R C L N O D N E
J D S M U E R U A E I E H C R
T E I G P A E A D R S T D E T
E D T X R L V N E P Y R A R C
M A I G E S E P O R J L K T E
A D V C M P M T S E H T R A F
G W E S E I I R E A L L Y I R
D P V D M C Y B G E N U I N E
N U N L I M I T E D Y I P C P
J I S Z P L J F K O N M K S O
```

ABSOLUTE

ACTUAL

ARBITRARY

AUTOCRATIC

CERTAIN

COMPLETE

DECIDED

DESPOTIC

END

FARTHEST

GENUINE

IDEAL

IMPERIOUS

INDEPENDENT

PERFECT

POSITIVE

REAL

REALLY

SUPREME

TRUE

UNLIMITED

VERITABLE

Animal Heroes and Heroines

```
W E M P M A R T S O I K N E O
K K W S K I P P Y B T G R Y I
C N R C D X C U M X Y E R U P
T W I S H B O N E B W U Y T A
S L N L R E P P I L F Y H Q O
F N T B T N E V O H T E E B B
M X I E H O Y T S U D I R Z G
I J N E B J L I A A E S C O B
N B T M G A L E L H R S U P A
J O I U H V B Z C E M A L T B
Z L N R E K S R G N S L E G B
H A G R C H P G Q E A P S X R
J C H A M P I O N M E L A S L
I L L Y Z R L J E U R X D J N
R B M N T E M O C K E Q G H H
```

BADE	LANCELOT LINK
BEETHOVEN	LASSIE
BENJI	MR ED
BLACK BEAUTY	MURRAY
CHAMPION	RIN TIN TIN
CHEETAH	SALEM
COMET	SILVER
FLICKA	SKIPPY
FLIPPER	TRAMP
FURY	TRIGGER
HERCULES	WISHBONE

No 39

X Words

```
M P K N Z L E N O H P O L Y X
K E Y N R T T X Y L O P I A C
Q R L N A L Y X S I Y X N D A
U U A Y G S H S K N Y T G X M
N U I N X Q P K X L H Y E Y S
B Q N C O U O E E I S R H I O
H I E T A N R N U A O P S P L
T Z X K O O E M G G A O E G Y
I I E W P X X X R R H B X N X
L N N H P X H A G T Z T R I K
O C I B O H P O N E X Q E Y L
N L C S D H L A S A W K X A Q
E X U N I Y X E N A R T H R A
X N S C X Y L O C O P A Z X O
Y A G V S C N X I V B N Z G L
```

XANTHIUM

XANTHOSIS

XENARTHRA

XENIAL

XENICUS

XENOLITH

XENON

XENOPHOBIC

XEROGRAPHIC

XEROPHILE

XEROPHYTE

XERXES

XHOSA

X-RAYING

XYLAN

XYLEM

XYLENE

XYLOCOPA

XYLOGRAPHY

XYLOPHONE

XYLOPIA

XYLOSMA

No 40
Knots

```
B F T O N K K C A S M N X R T
O T K Z A D O G S H A N K G N
W H C T I H E V O L C N T R G
K T D H L G Z O A L A O I A G
N H R C K J Z R A H N N D N D
O U A T N R I A S K G N I N E
T M W I O A U P G H E L E Y H
M B K H T A E A I B S B E K A
H K N L E E B T H R R S V N L
X N O E H C C S A O P A J O F
B O T S C H I J H L G E I T H
P T T S I M H C I J J Y D D I
W M B O E G N C B O A K N O T
W V F L L A E P E G K N O T C
G D F E N I L W O B K O O N H
```

ANCHOR BEND

BAG KNOT

BOA KNOT

BOW KNOT

BOWLINE

CLOVE HITCH

DOGSHANK

DRAW KNOT

EYE SPLICE

FLEMISH BEND

GRANNY KNOT

HALF HITCH

JAR SLING

LARIAT LOOP

NAIL KNOT

OSSEL HITCH

PEG KNOT

RING HITCH

SACK KNOT

SHEEPSHANK

THUMB KNOT

ZIGZAG BRAID

Puzzled?

O	W	J	G	D	S	G	N	I	V	L	O	S	R	Q
R	G	I	C	G	Y	O	X	O	S	F	I	E	G	C
Q	L	G	E	M	N	S	S	O	A	C	S	N	K	M
N	U	W	U	O	Q	E	L	I	M	A	Z	E	K	U
X	G	O	G	L	D	I	F	F	E	R	E	N	C	E
T	K	R	T	O	Y	G	L	T	S	A	W	E	R	R
T	A	D	C	E	N	P	N	O	R	C	K	S	O	U
M	W	W	A	C	S	I	S	I	Q	R	N	Z	S	G
L	G	H	C	R	A	E	S	D	R	O	W	C	S	I
K	C	E	V	R	L	Q	J	O	I	S	I	S	W	F
C	M	E	B	Z	S	J	G	T	N	T	G	V	O	M
E	L	L	Z	A	E	C	U	G	P	I	N	C	R	U
Q	I	U	F	M	X	L	Z	Y	R	C	M	L	D	R
L	P	O	E	M	O	K	R	W	C	I	G	O	L	W
S	H	U	Y	S	B	C	U	S	C	A	D	Q	D	D

ACROSTIC	JIGWORD
BOXES	LINK
BRAINTEASER	LOGIC
CLUE	MAZE
CODES	NONOGRAM
CROSSWORD	PUZZLE
CRYPTIC	QUOTES
DIFFERENCE	SOLUTIONS
DOMINO	SOLVING
FIGURE	WORDSEARCH
GRID	WORDWHEEL

No 42
Finance

```
G N S S G S G N I V A S O N S
S Y N U K C K Q U N T O A W M
M E R L D C R E D I T O R S Z
U S C E T I O F I A L O P T B
I N N N G I S T C K S E E A Z
M E A D A R R C S T C G L D T
E P N E N V O I O U D A Y N R
R X W R G U D F L U N T T L A
P E A S N D T A B C N F A A N
F Q R T T B T N E M E T A T S
V Q D C Z I N T E R E S T I F
M T R A N S A C T I O N S P E
O D E G T C O V P T E S S A R
E E V R E S E R N N T P W C K
B F O L K N K I H N G X A L T
```

ACCOUNT	LENDERS
ADVANCES	LOAN
ASSET	OVERDRAWN
BALANCE	PREMIUMS
BUDGET	RESERVE
CAPITAL	SAVINGS
CREDITORS	SPECULATING
DISCOUNT	STATEMENT
EXPENSE	STOCKS
FORGERY	TRANSACTIONS
INTEREST	TRANSFER

No 43

Fairy Stories and Rhymes

```
O U W M A R G E R Y D A W P X
R A P U N Z E L O C G N I K A
M I S S M U F F E T Z R L Z Q
O L S I N B A D A B E E L S N
I U P Y M L T C Z K A L Y K E
H C U E I P Y D C L I L W C E
C Y B Z T S L U L J L I I O U
C L C O S E T E D L V M N L Q
O O E U P Y R N S H Y Y K I W
N C P O M E A P V I S L I D O
I K K M D K E J I R M L E L N
P E O N C V R P J P D O V O S
U T I A B A B I L A E J N G X
U C J A C K H O R N E R U G B
J A C K S P R A T N E H D E R
```

ALI BABA

BO PEEP

CINDERELLA

GOLDILOCKS

JACK AND JILL

JACK HORNER

JACK SPRAT

JOLLY MILLER

KING COLE

LUCY LOCKET

MARGERY DAW

MISS MUFFET

PETER PIPER

PINOCCHIO

PUSSY CAT

RAPUNZEL

RED HEN

SIMPLE SIMON

SINBAD

SNOW QUEEN

TOMMY TUCKER

WILLY WINKIE

No 44
P Words

```
M A Z K C B C Q E E N P I W N
Y R P L K I I J L L V R B O J
R K O T F R N U D D V E H Y E
P E S F V P A C C D P T I P P
L H T O R R P A I A Y T H E A
A L U N U E E D C P F Y P I T
C J R A I V P I C B S A R X T
E I E P U A F I I I S E E I E
B W M R Z I P M C T L P A P R
O M S E C L B I U B L R C I K
J S I S D I A R A A T E H X H
V A Z S T N E R N R B T E W Y
G C U U T G A E O I L Z R C I
Y W O R K P N P Q N S E A K S
J S G E X Z O T E P Y L O N P
```

PACIFIC	PIXIE
PADDLE	PLACEBO
PAINTER	PORTRAIT
PANDEMIC	POSTURE
PANIC	PREACHER
PARABLE	PRESSURE
PASTURE	PRETTY
PATTER	PRETZEL
PERFORM	PREVAILING
PHYSICIAN	PYLON
PICNIC	PYTHON

No 45

In the Kitchen

```
E A C L W O B R A G U S B C U
P P B O S P T C U T I D A E X
U A C N F U P I E D I S H R A
C R E L N F G F V N S L F E O
A I T A N S E A N E L W I A T
E N A D E S S E R T B O W L E
T G L L C Z R O C T L B S B A
E K P E D P L O L U O G P O P
A N A A L E F W A T P N H W O
S I E A D F O L H K V I G L T
P F T I E B U K F T S X H S M
O E S E P T N A P G N I Y R F
O H P U A D J O W R J M H W B
N O O P S P U O S K D X M W U
T S S Q E E Y E V E Y S O E X
```

CASSEROLE DISH

CEREAL BOWL

COFFEE CUP

COFFEE POT

DESSERT BOWL

DINNER PLATE

FRYING PAN

LADLE

MIXING BOWL

PARING KNIFE

PIE DISH

SOUP BOWL

SOUP SPOON

SPATULA

SUGAR BOWL

SUGAR TONGS

TEA PLATE

TEACUP

TEAPOT

TEASPOON

WHISK

No 46

Pokemon Characters

```
G G M T E S Z X D J V H Y X F
F N O M M W E R U A S Y V I B
F C U L A P A L H U Q D W P S
T W D T E Z G V B B W P M L Y
E D O B I M A L E A X R I U H
N L D R H K A K R D F Z Z V X
T S A D V S C C A I U E P Z K
A H P K T H A I Z L N D L R I
C I R O A N G L L G A C O C E
R X I A I B E N S N A K E E X
U S S N U Q U S O D A R A Y G
E X E G G C U T E G N R B V U
L Q E G F R Y K O E W A B O F
U S L U H C A K I P U E S A K
V A A W G P G D W F S N D G D
```

ADRA	GEODUDE
ALAKAZAM	GOLEM
ARBOK	GYARADOS
ARCANINE	IVYSAUR
BLASTOISE	KABUTOPS
CHARIZARD	LICKITUNG
CLEFABLE	PIKACHU
DEWGONG	SANDSLASH
DODUO	SEEL
EKANS	TENTACRUEL
EXEGGCUTE	VULPIX

Under Arrest

```
D P J N H M O M F D O C T K C
E V P J M N L F E X T C K N F
I A J R O U U T T V N W H Z C
S P E S B C A P T U R E G H C
T P I G D I U C I S N A E X F
O R E N N R R I Q C J C L C C
P E A W R Z E B M Y K F C A H
F H W E R H S H M D D U R T S
I E T C U R T S B O A R P C M
L N R R Q N R T G T E Z A H O
I D S U A O A A B S N U N O F
A E T R C Q I Y T U G E J L J
J L R V K E N L S C A E F D N
B A Y U E J S D I J G W A T A
W Y L E B B X E Z I E S B D M
```

APPREHEND	INTERRUPT
ARREST	JAIL
CAPTURE	OBSTRUCT
CATCH	PICK UP
CHECK	PRISON
CUSTODY	RESTRAIN
DELAY	SECURE
DETAIN	SEIZE
ENGAGE	STAY
HANDCUFF	STOP
HOLD	WARRANT

Famous Artists

```
J C R Y Y C L E H G E U R B T
L O I G G A V A R A C K I D O
A N G E T N A M F I F L N T Z
C O N S T A B L E N H A T U E
B N I E B L O H Z S R E E R U
L O M M T E E L K B R U N N Q
L D T A H T T X M O E P N E S
A B T T M T P E T R N I A R A
G P Z I I O R N L O O G Z F L
A R Q S Q C I T W U I E E C E
H N H S A T E E L G R E C O V
C O L E G N A L E H C I M R P
F F N B J R O L L E T A N O D
Z D M D A V I N C I J Y R Y N
A B M G Q X V A N D Y C K X I
```

BOTTICELLI	HOLBEIN
BRUEGHEL	KLEE
CANALETTO	MANTEGNA
CARAVAGGIO	MATISSE
CEZANNE	MICHELANGELO
CHAGALL	REMBRANDT
CONSTABLE	RENOIR
DA VINCI	TINTORETTO
DONATELLO	TURNER
EL GRECO	VAN DYCK
GAINSBOROUGH	VELASQUEZ

No 49
Dickensian Characters

```
J D H A A D B Z E O T N E Y X
J N M C Y D G U H Q W N L M A
S T R Y V E R I L G H C F Y L
G A S N Q L N Y E L R A M A J
Q S B I L L S Y K E S I I J I
M X Q P W Y E I G M T E T L J
G N C M Q T F O R M O I Y G L
I I I I T Y R K A A O W N E K
S F T K L C E E C G T N I Z W
B F O S V N D K V W F I T D V
Y U T E W A T I P I P L F N J
D V M I D N R M D T L D P I Q
P T G B Q D E S S C R O O G E
U S C Z L W N I O H B C T A X
R Y A G R E T L A W G O T F I
```

BILL SYKES

BULL'S-EYE

BUMBLE

CODLIN

FAGIN

FRED TRENT

MAGWITCH

MARLEY

MR KENWIGS

NANCY

OLIVER TWIST

PIP

POTT

ROGER CLY

SCROOGE

SKIMPIN

SMIKE

STRYVER

TINY TIM

TOOTS

VUFFIN

WALTER GAY

No 50

Big Adventure

```
Z H Z U V U W V J M B S O W O
M S L L I R H T T P U G L S B
L A I R T S M O W O E V T N U
V R E S I R P R E T N E H V W
Q S B L I E I G J I X L F T L
B U O K R R A W A C B O T T E
T O S I L R C T I U R J N P C
F I L R U T R T S T M R E F N
R F L O M E E R U T N E V D A
R E C L C M Z I V D A C E O H
U P G N E K T B Z R G K N Q C
T U U N P Y B M V A J L E Y D
I I T D A R I N G Z B E S X I
H L B O L D U E G A S S A P I
N H J X K T O X Q H K S J V R
```

ADVENTURE	FORTUITY
BOLD	HAZARD
CHANCE	PASSAGE
COURAGEOUS	PERIL
CRISIS	RASH
DANGER	RECKLESS
DARING	RISK
ENTERPRISE	STAKE
EVENT	THRILLS
EXCITEMENT	TRIAL
FOOLISH	UNCERTAIN

No 51

Aim

```
W G K K Y E T N V W M H Q P X
G F K R O C L J R W S U T H K
P M I N T E N D W W E H C Y F
I J A E O B J E C T I V E D R
Y B T R A I N M D N L X R K C
K U Z J K G P W T N P X I M U
A V E G I M R E W D E P D I L
R F T S Z B N A N X L T D A K
E W E A T T E M P T P E O R Q
M D N S I O K A D U P G V W H
E F F O R T N D R O P R U E D
H S N C T U M P I I B A T I L
C V G G D H O N F M N T Q V L
S P B U N S T C T T H G I S P
D H I R E A S O N Q H E C B A
```

AIM	LEVEL
ATTEMPT	MARK
BEARING	OBJECTIVE
COURSE	PLIES
DESIGN	POINT
DIRECT	PURPOSE
DRIFT	REASON
EFFORT	SCHEME
END	SIGHT
GOAL	TARGET
INTEND	TENDENCY
INTENTION	TRAIN
	VIEW

Q Words

```
Q M V P M N D V H E E Y M Z J
P Q Q U A N T I T Y C V X T U
V E Q U E L L I N G V N R R A
Y L F G I Y Q G X A P J I A U
N B E E K C S U D E T S E U Q
E B Q R L U K A A W F R I Q Q
E I I Q D N A S K C I U Q X Z
U U Q U P I P J I M K J S B Q
Q Q U A D R A N G L E U W S Y
L U E F H V G A F L V A R T N
Q A S F D I U B N E T E I U Q
F I T I K Q E I J Q Q L R D J
K N I N E S R E T R A U Q F Z
X T O G N I Z Z I U Q I Y Y T
L Z N X T L I U Q U I N T E T
```

QUACK	QUESTED
QUADRANGLE	QUESTION
QUAFFING	QUIBBLE
QUAGMIRE	QUICKSAND
QUAINT	QUICKSILVER
QUALITY	QUIETEN
QUANTITY	QUILT
QUARTER	QUINCE
QUARTZ	QUINTET
QUEEN	QUIRKY
QUELLING	QUIZZING

135

B Words

```
W D T S H T S V I L I Z A R B
W L N N H T M R G P I H S P O
P E O R I N A N C A M G S X M
V I L E U R I E T E K N A L B
J F Y T V Z P R R T I I P B A
Y E B T Z U F E O B L B Y O R
D L A U Q D H W U W C B B T D
R T B B J P K E A L E O R A K
O T E Z S C L R W P B B B W N X
C A W O Q R B B I G O T R Y N
I B I O G R A P H Y J N G Y D
Y B L I J W W N T A T N P I H
A Y D R M O S S O L B R I E F
N D E B L V P K W H D X K Z D
T I R B E A U T Y R C A Z D Q
```

BABYLON

BATTLEFIELD

BEAUTY

BEWILDER

BIGOTRY

BIOGRAPHY

BIOSPHERE

BLANKET

BLOSSOM

BLOWPIPE

BLUEPRINT

BOBBING

BOMBARD

BOTANY

BRAWL

BRAZIL

BREATH

BREWER

BRIEF

BUTTER

BUZZING

BYPASS

No 54

Capitals of the Americas

```
R T D O G A I T N A S A C F J
J J X C A Y E N N E X B A H N
Q F A W A T T O R D B S R S Z
C D N O T G N I H S A W A L K
L O N L A P A Z C N D N C A A
O P E W H S H N S O J Y A I U
A B A D O B A A A O C L S B G
Y L I N I T L N S V T I J N A
X I E R A V E E J U A I X D N
L U F N A M E G N U N H U E A
B I S D I M A T R H A C P Q M
L B O G O T A C N O I N I P I
P R M J T L I R I O E H W O L
I B R A S I L I A T M G M V N
Z L F Y H B X A K P Y N K P P
```

ASUNCION

BOGOTA

BRASILIA

BUENOS AIRES

CARACAS

CAYENNE

GEORGETOWN

HAVANA

LA PAZ

LIMA

MANAGUA

MEXICO CITY

MONTEVIDEO

OTTAWA

PANAMA CITY

PARAMARIBO

QUITO

SAN JOSE

SAN JUAN

SAN SALVADOR

SANTIAGO

WASHINGTON DC

No 55

Boys' Names

```
I W Q Z E L U J E K W J B S E
O R W Q R R N P S E W E E U U
I R C O N R A D H P L A R Z N
C G T Z E A I T S I Z J X X D
L H T W I L T M E J L N E I X
T Z I B W A S A R Y K I J Y Y
T V L B M N I I R L F A P F D
K K A N X Q R L U Z M L N E A
I M U D L N H L S E S O A O E
R V F R A N C I S T T S I G K
K E I H L M X W E D W A R D U
M C T N Z O I P L L P O B A L
D A X E C W H X L H E N R Y K
N T F V P E J X U G K K W A M
G Z L W N N U R S F Z G B U Q
```

ADAM

ALAN

BRIAN

CHRISTIAN

CONRAD

EDWARD

FRANCIS

GEORGE

HENRY

JAMES

KIRK

LUKE

MATTHEW

NATHAN

OWEN

PETER

PHILIP

RALPH

RUSSELL

STEPHEN

VINCE

WILLIAM

Hard Words

```
H D N O M A I D M V F W T G I
B E L J G N I D L E I Y N U D
T L U C I F F I D F K I A U D
P F U Z B D P G Y C S M T Z E
U W I F G O E I O I V P S L R
S G F R I Z S R M K P E I H O
L N L Y M C T O R Y Y N S K M
A I I P X N R N R O T E E C R
B L N P I P E E R Y M T R G A
O E T R M K N S M O M R B R Y
R E Y O E V U H S N B A A A L
I F C D I L O S Y E U B N N E
O N E T A R U D B O P L U I E
U U W Y O N S E V E R E H T T
S S E N D R A H Z V D I A E S
```

ARMORED	RIGID
DIAMOND	ROCKY
DIFFICULT	SEVERE
FIRMNESS	SOLID
FLINTY	STEELY
GRANITE	STRENUOUS
HARDNESS	STUBBORN
IMPENETRABLE	UNCOMPROMISING
LABORIOUS	UNFEELING
OBDURATE	UNMERCIFUL
RESISTANT	UNYIELDING

No 57

Languages

```
C X V I N B T D V X B J J H W
Q N A M R E G E K I B O D S B
O Q F I N N I S H U H C H I F
H H V C M G T E R W R I B D R
S J T N W A Y M J Q P D T E E
I Y U Y A L S A L O G N I W N
K D Q B I I P N R C R A M S C
R U S S I A N T A H E L A L H
U T D R N O U E S A E E N O S
T C J E O G E I M P K C D F I
D H S L U K L V Z R A I A U N
X E L E A G L Q K J A N R R A
U A S K N M N A I L A T I F D
W E W E W E W F C H V A N S A
C Y F D O V G T H A F G M E H
```

AFRIKAANS

ARMENIAN

BENGALI

DANISH

DUTCH

ENGLISH

FINNISH

FRENCH

GERMAN

GREEK

ICELANDIC

ITALIAN

JAPANESE

KURDISH

MANDARIN

PORTUGUESE

RUSSIAN

SPANISH

SWEDISH

TURKISH

VIETNAMESE

WALLOON

Snakes

```
G U Y L V U R U T U M A M B A
P B O O M S L A N G D W K L K
B B B E H P I W L N E E G R K
L S E L G P O G O P K N A P S
A I I C A R D C E A R I R K B
U D K N B C A P N O T A T C T
E E D G E N K S C P I I E O H
C W N E A G E T S R U V R P X
J I Z F R L S S I S B G S P C
K N Y N T O G E V G N O N E U
T D Q T H A K E M I E A A R W
E E A G H I N B A S P R K H I
Z R T B N O H T Y P S E E E D
Q Q Q G M W U D B C O B R A E
Y P F X Q K U C R M H I S D K
```

ADDER

ANACONDA

ASP

BLACK TIGER

BOA

BOOMSLANG

COBRA

COPPERHEAD

GARTER SNAKE

GHOST CORN

GRASS SNAKE

KING BROWN

KRAIT

MAMBA

PRAIRIE KING

PYTHON

RATTLESNAKE

SIDEWINDER

TAIPAN

URUTU

VENOM

VIPER

No 59

Tea Time

```
G F I M T J N M K N V U W L N
R F U A N A H A P U T A L E O
E U T S I R A T N A P U R A L
E M V S M A V C H D Z I B W Y
N O S A R Q T H O Q X E H O E
T U K B E K Q A E E M N U H C
R S R E P S G U R O G I N C A
X S E T P N P J T U K M A G M
D A R J E E L I N G T S N N O
E A L S P L G P D H S A N I M
Q N N L N I O N F E D J M N I
O I M N U W I L A D R E O G L
G H V T D D A Y E R G L R A E
W C C E L H A T C L O T E B F
B S R C C C I B I J Y V X G Q
```

ASSAM	HAPUTALE
BADULLA	HUNAN
CAMOMILE	JASMINE
CEYLON	MATCHA UJI
CHINA	MATURATA
CHUN MEE	NINGCHOW
DARJEELING	ORANGE PEKOE
EARL GREY	PEPPERMINT
GINSENG	RATNAPURA
GREEN	RUSSIAN
GUNPOWDER	SPIDERLEG

Mythical Goddesses

```
G  I  T  I  E  T  A  C  E  H  H  F  M  L  A
F  G  B  A  R  T  E  M  I  S  A  Q  V  T  D
K  Y  N  A  K  N  I  D  E  M  E  T  E  R  Y
A  W  R  O  E  A  A  D  W  N  K  S  S  I  W
Q  I  R  H  I  A  N  N  O  N  B  H  Q  E  F
P  W  T  R  S  Z  S  H  Q  R  K  Q  N  F  V
M  A  O  S  V  R  P  T  I  M  H  S  K  A  L
I  O  A  T  E  E  D  A  A  R  L  P  G  Z  S
N  N  R  Y  S  H  N  R  N  R  A  P  A  I  A
E  M  R  R  E  I  O  U  J  D  T  T  S  I  L
R  D  E  M  I  R  L  U  S  R  O  E  H  L  A
V  P  I  V  U  G  F  L  H  P  M  R  L  S  C
A  W  S  A  I  V  A  U  A  E  L  J  A  T  I
U  C  T  H  N  L  H  N  N  C  Y  O  H  P  A
H  Z  C  W  F  A  S  D  K  R  B  H  B  Y  W
```

APHRODITE	ISHTAR
ARTEMIS	LAKSHMI
ASTARTE	MINERVA
ATHENE	MORRIGAN
AURORA	NEMESIS
CALLISTO	PANDORA
DEMETER	PERSEPHONE
DIANA	RHIANNON
FREYA	SALACIA
HECATE	VENUS
HESTIA	VESTA

No 61
On the Farm

```
M A N R D C M W H F W C D A R
D T W X E M S O R L S P A O Z
B L C O K Z F U R L I S I S Y
V N A E N O I T A G I R R I S
D I T C H T F L H S B V Y L F
N V T J T D D A I R H L S O M
W X L R L P Z S R T Y P H Z Z
F N E E E S U O H M R A F J G
L E I P M A N U R E H E H L Q
S F Y P O N D E A M R A F W Q
H D E O Q V X C K W X A N O N
P E E H S F E N K C R R D D U
P O S H Q H A E Q M I Z P A B
L T D N S D A F E U Q H I E J
H Y I C Y B A R N M B E C M H
```

BARN	FRUIT TREES
CATTLE	HAY
CHICKENS	HOPPER
DAIRY	IRRIGATION
DITCH	MANURE
FARMER	MEADOW
FARMHAND	PIG
FARMHOUSE	POND
FENCE	SHED
FERTILIZER	SHEEP
FIELD	SILO

No 62
Abrupt

```
H H V L P N D R X N K G Q S A
Z S C C O R B E S G N W J J K
T U R R G D E L P J E Z J C E
X N H A P E E C U M T M U D E
N C A G H M F T I N A R U B U
T O S G A I S H C P T R Z R O
L V T E E T T I S E I U C K I
B D Y D R L E J Q T P T Y D E
I U Q I O L E T K K I X O D U
N J B I T I P N P M C F E U Q
I N Z R R R Y L I U E X F N S
F I N C O N S I D E R A T E U
F I Y U H K K A X I P B M A R
R L G M S K E A D E G G A J B
L H S U D D E N O O E D R V F
```

ABRUPT	INELEGANT
BLUNT	JAGGED
BROKEN	PRECIPITATE
BRUSQUE	PRECIPITOUS
CRAGGED	ROUGH
CRAMPED	RUDE
CURT	SHORT
HARSH	STEEP
HASTY	STIFF
ILL-TIMED	SUDDEN
INCONSIDERATE	UNEXPECTED

TEN at the End

```
Z X J W U R O T T E N N J C Y
W T X H B Y J J Y N E T S A F L
Q N N E T T I M T Q F N N L G
W E E A V X K A S O X E N I R
N T T T Y P E W R I T T E N A
E S R E A R E E L A N H T E I
T I A N H E S C E E E G S T D
T R M T T H H B A N T I I H V
I H S E O N W T E G A A L G L
R C N R L O E T O U E R G I K
W Q T L R N E T G M B T I L Q
D E K B R I G H T E N S J N D
N S F S U P P J E A U Z Q E C
A G L Q U N E T T I B T P F Q
H C S K V X G X T I O H R P M
```

BATTEN	MOTHEATEN
BITTEN	NEATEN
BRIGHTEN	QUIETEN
BROWBEATEN	ROTTEN
CHRISTEN	SMARTEN
ENLIGHTEN	STRAIGHTEN
FASTEN	SWEETEN
FORESHORTEN	THREATEN
GLISTEN	TYPEWRITTEN
HANDWRITTEN	UNBEATEN
MITTEN	WHEATEN

No 64

O Words

```
E W X V P A A K A H P L M L M
O B L I Q U E R U T R E V O O
P O Y U K Q J Z E L C A R O P
T S S E R G O D R D G T Z E P
I S G U V G T O R C H I D T O
M W O R O M N I V O R O U S R
U N D A C R K A D H O U C A T
M O D D C E E O M F H I C C U
L I M K A G N N F S L S Z T N
S T E U S T K E O L R X V U E
B A N L I O R N A T E A H O H
N V T C O I E T A R E P O M C
H O S H N F O R C H E S T R A
P C I G W R E K R O W T U O T
Q O E J R X X W K N V P O N T
```

OARSMAN	OPTIMUM
OBLIQUE	ORACLE
OCCASION	ORCHESTRA
ODDMENTS	ORCHID
OFFERING	ORNATE
OGRESS	ORTHODONTICS
OHIO	OSCILLATOR
OMNIVOROUS	OUTCAST
ONEROUS	OUTWORKER
OPERATE	OVATION
OPPORTUNE	OVERTURE

No 65
Shades of Yellow

```
C O W V W B G Y I J C O R N S
H P R I M R O S E Z E D E U A
R G E P N C E Y P C R R B N B
O A M A I Z E Y G Q H P M R Y
M E X G A M B O G E C P A E R
E X C Z U Y E G G Y O L K W T
K Z A S Q A L N X L L E P O N
W D N L U Y N O T I K D O L J
V S A O F O Z H P D L R R F C
W E R E R Q H R G O A A G N H
A L Y F X B E T G F G T C U A
R P F W Y T R D N F V S Q S F
T A F E A N L N D A D U L G O
S N Y C N O M E L D X M Q Z Z
U G G N D C Z M G S N M T R P
```

AMBER	MAIZE
BRONZE	MUSTARD
CANARY	NAPLES
CATERPILLAR	OCHRE
CHROME	OLD GOLD
CORN	ORPIMENT
DAFFODIL	PRIMROSE
EGG YOLK	SAFFRON
FLAX	STRAW
GAMBOGE	SUNFLOWER
LEMON	XANTHOUS

World Wines

```
P S F L X A A Q D R P D W L V
Y I S W A N S I L B A H C N C
L D A J O I R H O C K O I F O
K I N L R S P R L M E R L O T
A O L U Y T D O J H I T S S E
V E J W G E Q T Y O Z I G L S
G X C H A R D O N N A Y N C D
R Z E U U S U T T L R Y I H U
E R X C N G O B O M I M L A R
N T B I A N I J C E H L S M H
A O Z J I S U E K D S Q E P O
C K G P C A L I F O R N I A N
H A W K E S B A Y C A W R G E
E Y G B A F W Z B D Q H S N P
C K T E R A L C A B E R N E T
```

ALOACE	GRENACHE
BEAUJOLAIS	HAWKE'S BAY
BORDEAUX	HOCK
BUROUNDY	MEDOC
CABERNET	MERLOT
CALIFORNIAN	PINOT NOIR
CHABLIS	RETSINA
CHAMPAGNE	RIESLING
CHARDONNAY	RIOJA
CLARET	SHIRAZ
COTES DU RHONE	TOKAY

Magic

```
Q C V S Y R V Z T T E H F P X
S Z X E E F A Y K D X W V E C
M O M W P A E B F S G N I R O
L V O A E A R P B K W W U F C
E P I J G D C Q U I A N P O N
I L E T O I N S Z T T O Q R J
Q K D Y O W C A E R S T R M A
J Q C I T N R R W V E S S Y X
M H Z I S D T F L O W E R S X
J L A B R A C A D A B R A T D
W B K Y N T P H A I L P O I E
E I E K A F D P A B R Y B F O
V R A Z P M X R E I G E O Y O
P D R O W S B R A A N H R L G
Z R M M A R E P A C R S L V Q
```

ABRACADABRA	MYSTIFY
BIRD	PERFORM
CAPE	POWER
CARD TRICK	RABBIT
CHAINS	RINGS
DISAPPEAR	STOOGE
ESCAPE	STUPEFY
FAKE	SWORD
FLOWERS	WAND
HEY PRESTO	WATER TANK
MAGIC	WIZARDRY

No 68

Religions

```
L P R I X A N N V H C X R M R
Y A R E K A U Q F H I O Z I H
I D N E T R S C R K M N U L O
I M W O S M S I O A T C D S L
M S Z A I B S P N N E O L U O
S I L H W T Y C A F L N U M N
I H N A I R A T I N U F T S F
A K I A M T S G E K E U H I H
D I N N H E K J E R Q C E N Z
U S P O T I W U U R I I R I M
J W L O N O M R O M G A A V K
S I R N A C I L G N A N N L F
C P J A I N I S M L B I O A B
Q B U D D H I S M X M S M C T
D R W T S I D O H T E M L M J
```

ANGLICAN	METHODIST
BUDDHISM	MORMON
CALVINISM	MUSLIM
CHRISTIAN	PRESBYTERIAN
CONFUCIANISM	PROTESTANT
CONGREGATIONAL	QUAKER
HINDU	ROMAN CATHOLIC
ISLAM	SHINTOISM
JAINISM	SIKHISM
JUDAISM	TAOISM
LUTHERAN	UNITARIAN

No 69
Prominent Stars

```
Q P T R R I X V E G A A F D Z
F H A I S P R R N Y V C O H L
R E G U L U S A M V L H I W M
O E D B X K P W Z P B Z F P E
L A L T A I R O Q I M O P F S
R J L N A K A T N I M L A R U
X L A D B R O T S A C R A I E
D F G E E Q N R L V C I F N G
M T N D C B I H O T P P L B L
S E R A T N A S U R O A O P E
D A R M F U Q R O L J A O J T
A O L A T X U C A P E L L A E
W Q R T K S Y R O N L C N Q B
G V U W A O I P S U I R I S J
F E F E N S B F X Q T M O F Z
```

ALDEBARAN	MERAK
ALTAIR	MINTAKA
ANTARES	MIZAR
ARCTURUS	POLARIS
ATLAS	POLLUX
BETELGEUSE	PROCYON
CANOPUS	REGULUS
CAPELLA	RIGEL
CASTOR	SIRIUS
DENEB	SPICA
FOMALHAUT	VEGA

No 70
Words Ending in FUL

```
O Z U R J J Y O A Q O N G E A
R T A C T F U L W D Z Y W W O
J E H Y W H D O F E A R F U L
T E S A G B N A E L E U E L U
J A O P N D E L I I L D T X F
O N L S E K Q A Z G G O R M D
Y B U R P C F L U H B Q U I E
F L F Z P H T U I T L U T N E
U U R F A T G F L F I O H D N
L F E V I U Q S U U S F F F I
F E E B N N M S J L S V U U G
Q T H D F E V E N T F U L L Z
D A C L U F M R A H U M Q J Y
U R V K L U S T F U L S R A I
M G J B T L A S K I L F U L E
```

AWFUL	MINDFUL
BEAUTIFUL	NEEDFUL
BLISSFUL	PAINFUL
CHEERFUL	RESPECTFUL
DELIGHTFUL	SKILFUL
EVENTFUL	STRESSFUL
FEARFUL	TACTFUL
GRATEFUL	THANKFUL
HARMFUL	TRUTHFUL
JOYFUL	TUNEFUL
LUSTFUL	WONDERFUL

No 71
Casino

```
R M G X O D L Y R E C L L C Y
T A C J H D N L B C E K B Y S
O G S H R E G U O R E K O P S
W I N N I N G V O R B W R D L
E N U I Q P W P L A Y E R O B
V K Z K T G S D N X A A I L D
I X A Y C T A K I D C Q O P K
S X G T C A E Z G C B C J Z O
J K N G S R J B Z D E A L E R
D B O Z H A O K E M C S U F D
K C X U U C T U C K D I U B V
T C B U F C Q R P A E N B J E
Z Z H B F A D O K I L O C N G
W H E E L B T G X A E B H U X
N N A D E T T E L U O R C S U
```

BACCARAT	PLAYER
BANKER	POKER
BETTING	ROLL
BLACKJACK	ROUGE
CARDS	ROULETTE
CASINO	SHOE
CHIPS	SHUFFLE
CROUPIER	SPREAD
DEALER	STAKE
DICE	WHEEL
JACKPOT	WINNING

Not on a Diet

```
Z R S F D C S T S E I R F U E
B J L V H O T D O G S V O D X
C B S G O E P D Z N R S T T U
N A G R K V O U C H E E S E P
B H N X E H T M A T G I L C U
J A I D F T A P A H R R F A R
S L D U Y F T L J U U T P R Y
A T D J E X O I A A B S I A S
X G U M M C E N R X M A U M E
E T P N O C S G L F A P R E K
O D O H A R I S L O H O C L A
A B C O S E L F F A W H H A C
U N E E V A P C O R I M H R P
T Y V E J M A T N A D N O F P
H R P J R A G U S H Q G A Z E
```

ALCOHOL	FUDGE
BEER	HAMBURGERS
CAKES	HOT DOGS
CANDY	JAM
CARAMEL	PASTRIES
CHEESE	PEANUTS
CREAM	POTATOES
DUMPLINGS	PUDDINGS
FONDANT	SUGAR
FRIES	SYRUP
FRITTERS	WAFFLES

Famous Paintings

```
C L F T S E P M E T E H T X M
A M S E C A R G E E R H T Y O
L A M E N T A T I O N H X R N
V E Q C T I S A P S E Z O E A
A R T R O S A E D R O A H L L
R C X S I E N W E E K C C G I
Y S W K T W W P Y Y L I T G S
S E E J I N U O C A E N A U A
C H T N K B I S T L H R W J L
T T D F L Z L A I P D E T E L
S O A I D U N E S D G U H H E
W P C S B A T H E R S G G T R
N A N D R O M E D A U L I A B
P A R A D I S E W C S O N K M
S U M S A R E E D D K V F N U
```

ANDROMEDA	NIGHT WATCH
BATHERS	OPEN WINDOW
CALVARY	PARADISE
CARD PLAYERS	THE HAY WAIN
DUNES	THE JUGGLER
ERASMUS	THE KISS
FOUR SAINTS	THE REPUBLIC
GUERNICA	THE SCREAM
LAMENTATION	THE TEMPEST
LEDA	THREE GRACES
MONA LISA	UMBRELLAS

No 74
Herb Garden

```
Q I J Z S N Y J T A T T O R L
C L L U I O J P N N H F H S B
O H L R G R I Z I Y C T J Q K
T K I N T F Z M M O R U Q Y A
R P D V X F R E R Y O O Y C I
K N C W E A M I E B X R I I C
V B W H E S A J P A E P S L J
O O A P G N R Y P L L Z E A B
C J S Y D R O S E M A R Y N L
L A V E L D J C P L V P E T I
E C R S C E R A N I S E E R V
N O G A R R A T L F Y R G O R
N E O J W S M F M L O V A G E
E U P G B A S I L C I D S P H
F B O W P T Y R O V A S P H C
```

ANISE	LOVAGE
BALM	MARJORAM
BASIL	PARSLEY
BAY LEAF	PEPPERMINT
CARAWAY	ROSEMARY
CELERY	SAFFRON
CHERVIL	SAGE
CHIVES	SAVORY
CILANTRO	SPEARMINT
DILL	TARRAGON
FENNEL	THYME

Jobs

```
C W R E T N E P R A C S W E V
U T C E T I H C R A O U T A D
B O V R S A L E S M A N L B E
A Q X E T S I G O L O E G L C
S C G G C T E R M B T K E S O
P J I A S E J R E I A C U U R
W L U N R Z P A D T T R M R A
K B U A A G O T N R S V B V T
R K L M Z H E O I I I E W E O
E G A P B A C C K O T A R Y R
L C W O C E I E N E N O H O N
C P Y H Q A R K M V E I R R F
K U E S N U R S E H I P S M I
S R R D W E I N K U C U E T R
M N Z W A I T R E S S M O R D
```

ARCHITECT	MECHANIC
BARBER	NURSE
CARPENTER	PLUMBER
CLERK	SALESMAN
DECORATOR	SCIENTIST
ELECTRICIAN	SHOP MANAGER
FORESTER	SURVEYOR
GEOLOGIST	TEACHER
HAIRDRESSER	VALET
JANITOR	WAITRESS
LAWYER	ZOOKEEPER

No 76

Shells on the Shore

```
S  R  E  T  S  Y  O  N  B  E  U  N  C  G  H
S  O  L  E  N  T  A  T  R  O  U  G  H  J  N
M  Z  O  L  Y  B  O  T  W  M  Q  N  C  B  J
Y  A  V  L  R  F  I  N  M  I  L  A  N  S  M
J  R  E  U  L  M  X  U  E  L  L  U  O  P  F
M  X  T  M  T  E  L  H  E  L  Q  T  C  G  X
D  X  I  U  B  I  H  H  E  E  I  I  K  W  P
V  Y  N  R  T  U  S  S  C  P  M  L  N  Y  W
O  P  I  E  Z  E  S  P  N  O  Q  U  Y  I  A
S  C  H  X  L  U  M  M  G  R  A  S  N  S  I
V  O  C  D  M  T  V  Y  O  I  O  K  E  Z  R
U  N  E  S  X  O  P  Q  H  T  L  H  A  B  W
X  E  T  I  N  O  M  M  A  E  N  C  T  S  H
N  A  R  Q  F  T  X  Y  U  H  V  E  F  U  R
R  F  Z  M  S  H  Z  N  Q  N  U  W  I  K  S
```

AMMONITE	NUMMULITE
CONCH	OYSTER
CONE	QUAHOG
ECHINITE	RAZOR
HORNSHELL	SOLEN
MILLEPORITE	STAR
MITRE	STONE LILY
MUREX	TOOTH
MUSSEL	TROUGH
NAUTILUS	TURBAN
NEEDLESHELL	WINKLE

Ancient Civilizations

```
K V Z U Y E I H K N S F O E O
G B Z I N A Y A M I N C A N Q
A X A H C H X I R A E B T L Z
P V L B F T N R C T P J G S X
P Q W C Y O W D Z H O U U T V
B E C H A L D A E A N M Y D V
H E R N M B O H V A E A S S I
B I T S J X N N E R G A M S Z
T Y T A I A N A I L B G H O H
S M D T M A M A I A L A D P R
I O Q O I A N S T R N E W N D
Y P T D R T T A L G Y J N Y G
R T Y A N A E A N I M S X I A
O L T P N A I T P Y G E S U C
P V S E N S S Y S A B A E A N
```

ARAMAEAN	MINAEAN
ASSYRIAN	MINOAN
AZTEC	OTTOMAN
BABYLONIAN	PERSIAN
CHALDAEAN	ROMAN
EGYPTIAN	SABAEAN
HELLENIC	SABATAEAN
HITTITE	SHANG
INCA	SUMERIAN
LYDIAN	XIA
MAYAN	ZHOU

No 1

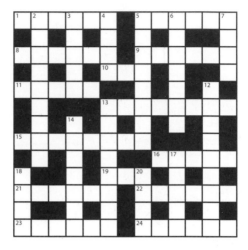

Across

1 Without much intelligence (6)
5 Expensive (6)
8 Fumbled (6)
9 Truly (6)
10 Lyric poem (3)
11 Might (5)
13 Looking gloomy (8)
15 Fireproof material considered carcinogenic (8)
16 Loose coverall reaching down to the ankles (5)
19 Spherical object (3)
21 Lacking in pigmentation (6)
22 Yearly (6)
23 Produces flowers (6)
24 Time of celebration in the Christian calendar (6)

Down

2 Calculated use of violence against civilians (9)
3 Aperture in the iris of the eye (5)
4 Extinct bird of Mauritius (4)
5 Slipshod (8)
6 Firm and dependable especially in loyalty (7)
7 Child's stringed toy (2-2)
12 Relate (9)
13 In the open air (8)
14 Hitchcock film of 1958 (7)
17 Subtraction sign (5)
18 Young sheep (4)
20 Cook in an oven (4)

No 2

Across

1 Marked by care and persistent effort (9)

8 Capacious (5)

9 Lightweight cord (5)

10 Theatrical entertainment (5)

11 Sugary (5)

12 One in pursuit (6)

13 Order of business (6)

17 Right-hand page of a book (5)

20 Conduit for carrying off waste products (5)

22 Obvious and dull (5)

23 Natives of Geneva, for example (5)

24 Non-deciduous (9)

Down

1 Throbbed dully (5)

2 Seedless raisin (7)

3 Say out loud for the purpose of recording (7)

4 Cause to be indebted (6)

5 Preserves (5)

6 Speedily (5)

7 Meeting for boat races (7)

12 Engage in boisterous, drunken merry-making (7)

14 Young goose (7)

15 Not in any place (7)

16 Bracelet (6)

18 Bedroom on a ship (5)

19 Corpulent (5)

21 Rule over (5)

No 3

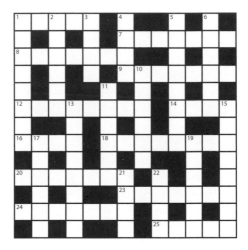

Across

1 Skin disease affecting domestic animals (5)

7 Insane person (7)

8 Group of people attractively arranged (7)

9 Core, meaning (7)

12 Consider as perfect (8)

14 Always (4)

16 Bait (4)

18 Short prayer of thanks before a meal (8)

20 Shrivels up (7)

23 Raise to a higher position (7)

24 Persistently thoughtful (7)

25 Mixture of rain and snow (5)

Down

1 Fabric (8)

2 Bite off very small pieces (6)

3 Fencing sword (4)

4 Sticky paste (4)

5 Unnatural lack of color (8)

6 Round shape (6)

10 Scandinavian kingdom (6)

11 Prepared wood (6)

13 Transparent gem (8)

15 Army unit smaller than a division (8)

17 Combined (6)

19 Glacial period (3,3)

21 Visionary (4)

22 Implores (4)

No 4

Across

- **1** Spider's snare (6)
- **4** Odors (6)
- **7** For one's entire existence (8)
- **8** Arduous (4)
- **9** Coil of knitting wool (5)
- **10** Practitioner of rigorous self-discipline (7)
- **12** Plain-woven cotton fabric (6)
- **13** Seller (6)
- **15** Closest (7)
- **18** Fragrant garden flowers (5)
- **20** Country once called Persia (4)
- **21** Outside (8)
- **22** Be undecided (6)
- **23** Far from the intended target (6)

Down

- **1** Small compartments (5)
- **2** Protects from impact (7)
- **3** Rose, sweet briar (9)
- **4** Utterances made by exhaling audibly (5)
- **5** Bent from a vertical position (5)
- **6** Cocktail of orange liqueur with lemon juice and brandy (7)
- **11** Depressing (9)
- **12** Human race (7)
- **14** Written account (7)
- **16** Make suitable for a new purpose (5)
- **17** Remove the fleece from (5)
- **19** Contrite (5)

No 5

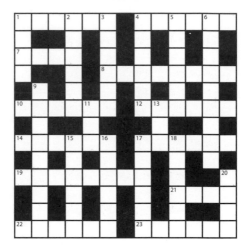

Across

- **1** Children's outdoor toy (6)
- **4** Softly bright or radiant (6)
- **7** Opposed to (4)
- **8** Sent word (8)
- **10** Alloy used when melted to join two metal surfaces (6)
- **12** Local church community (6)
- **14** Cloud bearing rain (6)
- **17** Unwrinkled (6)
- **19** Aromatic shrub (8)
- **21** High in stature (4)
- **22** Save from sin (6)
- **23** Shelled, aquatic reptile (6)

Down

- **1** Secure against leakage (4)
- **2** Hand-held piece of armor (6)
- **3** Victorious contestant (6)
- **4** Portable computer (6)
- **5** Discuss, talk about (6)
- **6** Condition of being indispensable (9)
- **9** Power or right to give orders or make decisions (9)
- **11** Large Australian bird (3)
- **13** Upper limb (3)
- **15** Farewell remark (3-3)
- **16** Metallic element, Na (6)
- **17** Actor's lines (6)
- **18** Shellfish which produces a pearl (6)
- **20** Flat mass of ice floating at sea (4)

No 6

Across

- **1** Implied (5)
- **4** Postal service for overseas (7)
- **8** Ballet position (9)
- **9** Inventories (5)
- **10** Come about (9)
- **13** Moved forward by leaps and bounds (6)
- **14** Formed or conceived by the imagination (4,2)
- **16** Trite or obvious remark (9)
- **19** Poised for action (5)
- **20** Make stronger (9)
- **22** Number in one century (7)
- **23** Layers (5)

Down

- **1** Pills (7)
- **2** Fear resulting from the awareness of danger (13)
- **3** Crisp bread (5)
- **4** Sleeveless outer garment worn by Arabs (3)
- **5** Tall perennial grasses (5)
- **6** Preference that comes from considerable experience (8,5)
- **7** Belgian city (5)
- **11** Correct (5)
- **12** Called (5)
- **15** Egyptian paper reed (7)
- **16** Cause to wither (5)
- **17** Conclude by reasoning (5)
- **18** Upright (5)
- **21** Disencumber (3)

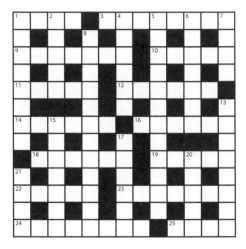

Across

1 Basic rhythmic unit in a piece of music (4)
3 Supports oneself, survives (8)
9 Line on a map connecting points of equal height (7)
10 Protective garment (5)
11 Dog-like nocturnal mammal (5)
12 Tolerance (6)
14 Located beneath something else (6)
16 Dried grape (6)
18 Journey by hunters (6)
19 Jargon (5)
22 Civilian clothing (5)
23 Relating to those 13 to 19 years old (7)
24 Soubriquet (8)
25 Musical finale (4)

Down

1 Shot played in tennis (8)
2 Musical which includes the song *Tomorrow* (5)
4 Boisterous and disobedient (6)
5 One who supervises the physical aspects in the production of a show (5,7)
6 Do something to a greater degree (7)
7 Grains on the beach (4)
8 Someone whose age is in the nineties (12)
13 Bête noire (8)
15 Vehicles in motion (7)
17 Person who is tricked or swindled (6)
20 Product of seabirds, used as a fertilizer (5)
21 Sign of the future (4)

No 8

Across

1 Wrestle (7)
5 Mix up or confuse (5)
8 Attempt to anticipate or predict (6-5)
9 Angry dispute (3-2)
11 *The* ___, tragi-comic play by Shakespeare (7)
13 Delete or remove (3,3)
14 Chronological records (6)
17 Money (7)
18 Run off to marry (5)
19 Not kept up-to-date with knowledge (3-8)
22 Rile (5)
23 Break into many pieces (7)

Down

1 Of the stomach (7)
2 Curve (3)
3 Large mass of land projecting into the sea (9)
4 Four score (6)
5 Reverential salutation (3)
6 Bold outlaw (9)
7 Spew forth lava and rocks (5)
10 Scientific study of food and drink (9)
12 US state, capital Saint Paul (9)
15 Slim (7)
16 Living, independent things (6)
17 Coconut meat (5)
20 Put in a horizontal position (3)
21 Encountered (3)

No 9

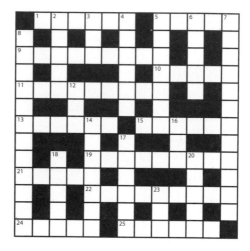

Across

1 Severe or trying experience (6)
5 Prickly desert plants (5)
9 Absence of the sense of pain without loss of consciousness (9)
10 Identifying appellation (5)
11 Profession of belief (9)
13 Subtle difference in meaning (6)
15 Sepulchres (6)
19 Mixture of sweet-scented materials (3-6)
21 Harnesses (5)
22 Occurring every third year (9)
24 Lucifer (5)
25 This or that (6)

Down

2 Thoroughfares (5)
3 Ovum (3)
4 Leaseholder (6)
5 Noisy talk (7)
6 Fabric (5)
7 Overpoweringly attractive (12)
8 Stubbornly obstructive, unwilling to cooperate (12)
12 Number of years in a decade (3)
14 Windlass used when weighing anchor (7)
16 Second person pronoun (3)
17 Endeavor (6)
18 Hungarian composer of classical music (5)
20 Lift up (5)
23 Egg of a louse (3)

No 10

Across

- **4** Russian tea urn (7)
- **7** Habitual, inveterate (7)
- **8** Adult male elephants (5)
- **9** Desert in Egypt (5)
- **10** Flightless extinct bird (3)
- **11** Desire persistently (5)
- **12** Moderately fast of musical tempo (9)
- **14** Mark (the scale of an instrument) in the desired units (9)
- **17** Control a vehicle (5)
- **18** Astern (3)
- **19** Move furtively (5)
- **21** Fire-raising (5)
- **22** Probe (7)
- **23** Dispenser that produces a vapor to relieve congestion (7)

Down

- **1** Decorates with frosting (4)
- **2** Trimmed back (6)
- **3** World's third largest body of salt water (6,5)
- **4** Large shrimp often coated in batter (6)
- **5** Crude, coarse (6)
- **6** Vibrate with sound (8)
- **8** Arm of the Atlantic Ocean to the west of France (3,2,6)
- **12** Capital of the United Arab Emirates (3,5)
- **13** Cherry brandy (6)
- **15** Rubbish (6)
- **16** Buzz ___, US astronaut who walked on the moon (6)
- **20** Stretched out (4)

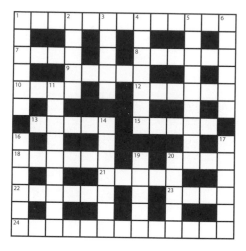

Across

1 Scapula (8,5)
7 The cards held in a game of whist (4)
8 Concurs (6)
9 Flip to a vertical position (5)
10 Stare at lustfully (4)
12 Official language of Hungary (6)
13 Scour vigorously (5)
15 Physical strength (5)
18 Relating to the stars (6)
20 Group noun for quails or larks (4)
21 Wide open (5)
22 Ruined (6)
23 Digit written as IV in Roman numerals (4)
24 Interpret in the wrong way (13)

Down

1 Place of learning (6)
2 Not justified (5)
3 Yield to another's wish or opinion (5)
4 Street plan (4,3)
5 Gas used chiefly in welding (9)
6 Make certain of (6)
11 Places, sites (9)
14 After the expected or usual time (7)
16 Two-wheeled horse-drawn covered carriage (6)
17 Cross-breed (6)
19 Thin biscuit (5)
20 Accord or comport with (5)

No 12

Across

1 Type of firework (5)
5 Red eruption of the skin (4)
7 Foolish (6)
8 Position of professor (5)
9 Celestial body orbiting another (9)
10 US general (3)
11 Convalesced (9)
15 Instrument for recording steps taken (9)
19 Tear apart (3)
20 Of very great significance (9)
21 Tea-time sweet bread roll (5)
22 Develop (6)
23 Wise Men (4)
24 Tie the limbs of a bird before cooking (5)

Down

1 Reaping hook (6)
2 Not affected by time (6)
3 Treasurer at a college or university (6)
4 Boring (8)
5 Gives an answer (7)
6 Fried quickly in a little fat (7)
12 Elementary particle with a negative charge (8)
13 Spanish classical guitarist, Andrés ___ (1893-1987) (7)
14 Siren of German legend (7)
16 Brown with a reddish tinge (6)
17 Brass, like gold, used to decorate furniture (6)
18 Rates of travel (6)

No 13

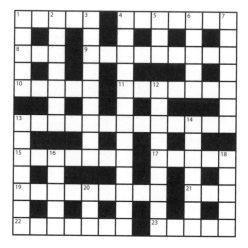

Across

- **1** Lads (5)
- **4** Socially awkward or tactless act (4,3)
- **8** Centre (3)
- **9** Distorted and unnatural, hideous (9)
- **10** French river (5)
- **11** Person who receives support and protection from an influential patron (7)
- **13** British colony in the Caribbean (6,7)
- **15** Hybrid between grapefruit and mandarin orange (7)
- **17** Type of pansy (5)
- **19** Disguised (9)
- **21** Hard durable wood (3)
- **22** Sound excluder (7)
- **23** Panache (5)

Down

- **1** Popular board game (5)
- **2** Convenient facility (7)
- **3** Isolate in a discriminatory way (9)
- **4** Gastrointestinal disorder (4,9)
- **5** Employ (3)
- **6** Cause to feel resentment (5)
- **7** Israeli coins (7)
- **12** Lacking conscious awareness of (9)
- **13** Semiprecious yellow quartz (7)
- **14** Newly invented word or phrase (7)
- **16** More courteous (5)
- **18** Leg joint (5)
- **20** Mousse applied to the hair (3)

No 14

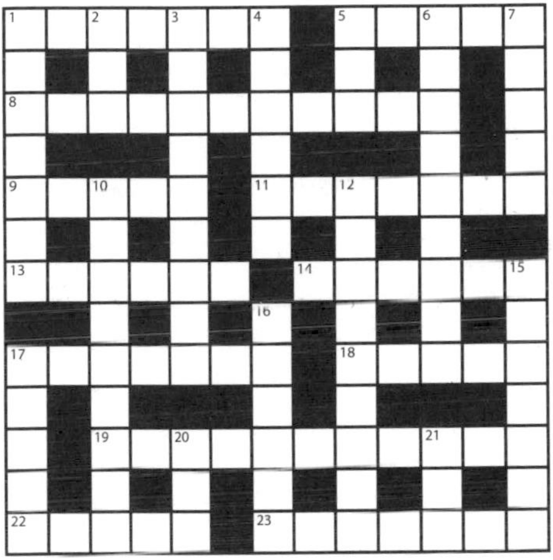

 is at bottom right.

Across

1 Ceased (7)
5 Liquid (5)
8 Happiness (11)
9 Relieved (5)
11 Smooth talker (7)
13 Heavenly (6)
14 Mailed (6)
17 Burnt sugar (7)
18 Greek letter (5)
19 Look into (11)
22 Tendon (5)
23 Corrected (7)

Down

1 Do well (7)
2 Possess (3)
3 False name (9)
4 Tear off (6)
5 Charge (3)
6 Final demand (9)
7 Discourage (5)
10 Monarch (9)
12 Next to (9)
15 Cul-de-sac (4,3)
16 Ionized gas (6)
17 Traverse (5)
20 Solemn pledge (3)
21 Append (3)

No 15

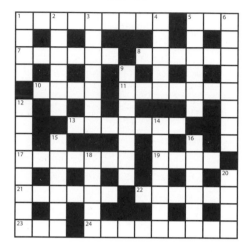

Across

1 Outset (9)
5 Males (3)
7 Decide (6)
8 Send for (6)
10 Successor (4)
11 Equilibrium (7)
13 Appease (7)
17 Indoor shoe (7)
19 Versifier (4)
21 Young swan (6)
22 Surgeon (6)
23 Untruth (3)
24 Forever (9)

Down

1 Dollar (4)
2 Mittens (6)
3 Nose opening (7)
4 Thin porridge (5)
5 Instant (6)
6 Rubbish (8)
9 Little-known (7)
12 Of the body (8)
14 Tropical storm (7)
15 Unmarried (6)
16 Edible seed of the pea family (6)
18 Fragment (5)
20 Quarry (4)

No 16

Across

1 Held legally responsible (6)
5 Booome different (6)
8 Terminate a life (4)
9 Absolute (8)
10 Skinflint (5)
11 Imposing in scale (7)
14 Sheep's coat (6)
15 Aplenty (6)
17 Whodunnit (7)
19 Sounding as if the nose were pinched (5)
21 Make by putting pieces together (8)
23 Frozen rain (4)
24 Orb, globe (6)
25 Pushed gently against (6)

Down

2 At the start (9)
3 Accept (7)
4 Apiece (4)
5 Race between candidates for elective office (8)
6 Book of maps (5)
7 Obtain (3)
12 Adaptable (9)
13 Extremely bad (8)
16 Found extremely repugnant (7)
10 Melodic subject of a musical composition (5)
20 Observed (4)
22 Plant fluid (3)

No 17

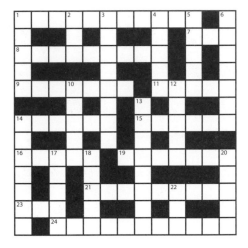

Across

1 Limit (11)
7 One of four playing cards in a deck (3)
8 Escapade (9)
9 The past (7)
11 Pale purple (5)
14 Emphasize (6)
15 Selected (6)
16 Hearty enjoyment (5)
19 Able to float (7)
21 Two-hulled boat (9)
23 Witness (3)
24 Viewpoint (11)

Down

1 Get to (5)
2 Fasten (3)
3 Concern (8)
4 Perfect (5)
5 Bellybutton (5)
6 Dictionary (7)
10 Robbery (5)
12 Tusk material (5)
13 Precise (8)
14 Propose (7)
17 Snooze (5)
18 Take place (5)
20 Nervous (5)
22 Suitable (3)

No 18

Across

1 Locate (4)
3 Amount (8)
7 Point to (8)
8 Egg-shaped (4)
9 Device that supplies warmth (6)
10 Hazard (6)
11 Lever operated with the foot (5)
12 More than enough (5)
15 Searched for (6)
18 High-pitched (6)
19 Fork prong (4)
20 Unmarried man (8)
21 Win approval or support for (8)
22 Confront with resistance (4)

Down

1 Shock (6)
2 Floated (7)
3 Dispute (7)
4 In front (5)
5 Sharp-pointed tip on a stem (5)
6 Swing used by circus acrobats (7)
11 Supply (7)
12 Newspaper piece (7)
13 Make believe (7)
14 Annually, every twelve months (6)
16 Estimate (5)
17 Shinbone (5)

Across

1 Engrave (4)

3 Runaway (8)

9 Apprentice (7)

10 Flavor (5)

11 Leg joint (5)

12 Retainer (7)

13 Make a journey (6)

15 Superior (6)

18 Into pieces (7)

19 Rough path (5)

21 Frequently (5)

22 Problem (7)

23 Surpassed (8)

24 Genuine (4)

Down

1 Take out (7)

2 Fissure (5)

4 Troubled (6)

5 Road junction (12)

6 Immediate (7)

7 Vote into office (5)

8 Freedom (12)

14 Water-dwelling (7)

16 Alleviate (7)

17 Twist, squirm (6)

18 Unaccompanied (5)

20 Yellow fossil resin (5)

No 20

Across

1 Shelter from danger (6)
7 Opposite (7)
8 Material (6)
9 Insect's feeler (7)
10 Appeared (6)
13 Instruction (5)
15 Equipment (4)
16 Epic tale (4)
17 System of principles or beliefs (5)
18 Roof of the mouth (6)
21 Windstorm characterized by a funnel-shaped cloud (7)
23 Vocalist (6)
24 Exclude (disturbing memories, for example) from the conscious mind (7)
25 Discuss (6)

Down

2 Rub out (5)
3 Cunning (5)
4 Line of ore between layers of rock (4)
5 Practice (9)
6 Take revenge for a perceived wrong (9)
10 Name written in one's own handwriting (9)
11 Hired soldier (9)
12 Short sleep (4)
14 Let go of (4)
19 Tolerate (5)
20 Something considered choice to eat (5)
22 Platter (4)

No 21

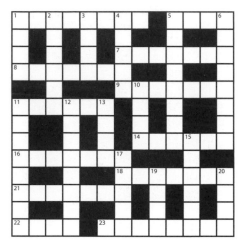

Across

1 Split up (8)
5 Former (4)
7 Shine wetly (7)
8 Victory (7)
9 Consistency (7)
11 Drawing (6)
14 Hypothesis (6)
16 Bed covering (7)
18 Connected (7)
21 Move forward (7)
22 Hill of sand (4)
23 Intensity (8)

Down

1 Notice (4)
2 Commend (6)
3 Chamber (4)
4 Close-fitting (5)
5 Convinced (8)
6 Inclination (8)
10 Revise, amend (4)
11 Sword sheath (8)
12 Shorten (8)
13 Keep secret (4)
15 Choosing (6)
17 Deal with (5)
19 Similar to (4)
20 Hyphen (4)

No 22

Across

1 Rarely (6)
7 Worker (8)
8 Features (3)
9 Mouth fluid (6)
10 Give up (4)
11 Related to, or of the moon (5)
13 Dependent (7)
15 Feeling (7)
17 Water lily (5)
21 Obnoxious child (4)
22 Mountain range (6)
23 Large container (3)
24 Courage (8)
25 Number in one dozen (6)

Down

1 Shoal of (6)
2 Reduce (6)
3 Deserve (5)
4 Clothing (7)
5 Biting fly (8)
6 Area, zone (6)
12 Height above sea level (8)
14 Gun holder (7)
16 Looking glass (6)
18 Tourism (6)
19 Understated (6)
20 Large meal (5)

No 23

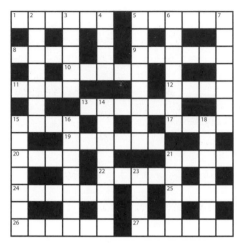

Across

1 Give in (6)
5 Crushed (6)
8 Symbol (4)
9 Lawsuit (6)
10 Proprietor (5)
11 Always (4)
12 Proficient (4)
13 Feeling of pleasure and enjoyment (6)
15 Reduction (4)
17 Take home (4)
19 Not in a specified place (6)
20 Swerve (4)
21 Inclined surface (4)
22 Insectivorous terrestrial lizard (5)
24 Slacken (6)
25 Shelf-like bed (4)
26 Spanish rice dish (6)
27 Improved (6)

Down

2 Expose (7)
3 Lesser (5)
4 Rotation (4)
5 Defender (8)
6 Feeling of righteous anger (7)
7 Dark cell (7)
14 Official emblem (8)
15 Evolve (7)
16 Sunshade (7)
18 Love affair (7)
21 Computer-controlled machine (5)
23 Association (4)

No 24

Across

1 Feeble (4)
3 Calling (8)
9 Teaching (7)
10 Subject (5)
11 Extricated (12)
14 Curved line (3)
16 Scowl, glare (5)
17 Observe (6)
18 Difficult to reach (12)
21 Once more (5)
22 Disturb (7)
23 Maternal (8)
24 Sacred (4)

Down

1 Pull back or move away (8)
2 Name that has been assumed temporarily (5)
4 Possess (3)
5 Hostile (12)
6 Make an impact on (7)
7 Pleasant (4)
8 Meaning (12)
12 Battery terminal (5)
13 Graveyard (8)
15 Get in touch with (7)
19 Well done (5)
20 Tranquil (4)
22 Everything (3)

Across

1 Lesson (5)
4 Remains (7)
8 Falsehood (3)
9 Crowd actor (5)
10 Stroll, saunter (5)
11 Commitment (10)
13 Set of steps (6)
15 Picture painted on a plaster wall (6)
18 Assessment (10)
22 Insect in the stage between egg and pupa (5)
23 Flat-topped hill (5)
24 In the past (3)
25 Article of clothing for cooler climates (7)
26 Golf club (5)

Down

1 Fissure (8)
2 Behaved (5)
3 Defamation (7)
4 Refuse to accept or acknowledge (6)
5 Commence (5)
6 Open to doubt or suspicion (7)
7 Constant (4)
12 Finished (8)
14 Unfavorable (7)
16 Arc in the sky (7)
17 Structure for storing aircraft (6)
19 Bounded (5)
20 Paid close attention to (5)
21 Added to (4)

No 26

Across

1 Cloth (6)
7 Friendly (8)
8 Similar (4)
10 Surgical knife (6)
11 Thoughtful (4)
12 Finger or toe (5)
13 Wanderer who has no established residence (7)
16 Items that can be cleaned by washing (7)
18 Quick, fast (5)
21 Ship's prison (4)
23 Volcano cavity (6)
25 Get rid of (4)
26 Without equal (8)
27 Specialist (6)

Down

1 Set up (6)
2 Simmer (4)
3 Capture (5)
4 On edge, jumpy (7)
5 Covering to disguise or conceal the face (4)
6 Woman with fair skin and hair (6)
9 Country (6)
14 Was apprehensive about (6)
15 Tube which conveys air in and out of the lungs (7)
17 Concurred (6)
19 Tyrant (6)
20 Artificial (5)
22 Female child (4)
24 Govern (4)

No 27

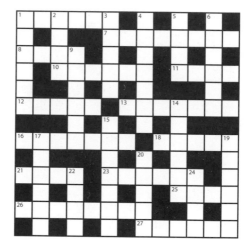

Across

1 Uneasy (12)
9 Assertion (5)
10 Primitive (5)
11 Petroleum (3)
12 Come into (5)
13 On the whole (7)
14 Thrilled (6)
16 Resolve (6)
20 Bowling pin (7)
22 Correctly (5)
24 Health resort (3)
25 Large grassy plain (5)
26 Mannerism (5)
27 Quarrel (12)

Down

2 Shrub (5)
3 Regret (7)
4 Sunken (6)
5 Honorable (5)
6 Immediate (7)
7 Do well (5)
8 Plot, plan (6)
15 Wildlife (7)
17 Printed mistake (7)
18 Plantation (6)
19 Next to (6)
20 Uninterrupted (5)
21 Light sandal (5)
23 Particle (5)

Across

1 Convert into cash (6)
4 Transferring possession of something (6)
7 Deposit of personal property as security for a debt (6)
9 Time limit (8)
11 Slightly wet (4)
14 Dirty (7)
15 Having little money (4)
16 Tiny amount (4)
17 Short, curved sword (7)
18 Sharp-tasting (4)
21 Almond-flavored biscuit (8)
22 Small hairpiece to cover partial baldness (6)
24 Of nerves (6)
25 Misleading falsehood (6)

Down

1 Swift, quick (5)
2 Fantasy (5)
3 Product of a hen (3)
4 Actors' make-up (11)
5 Fiddler (9)
6 Strong air current (4)
8 Instructive (11)
10 Sweet plant fluid (6)
12 Single-celled, water-living protozoon (6)
13 Buyer (9)
19 Cider fruit (5)
20 Make a weak, chirping sound (5)
21 Principal (4)
23 Poem with complex stanza forms (3)

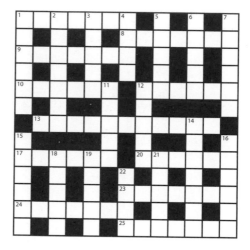

Across

1 Fame as a performer (7)
8 Study (7)
9 Bowl-shaped drinking vessel used in a religious service (7)
10 Attacker (6)
12 Origin (6)
13 Last but one (11)
17 Turn up (6)
20 Get away (6)
23 Original disciple (7)
24 Ice mass (7)
25 Wanted intensely (7)

Down

1 Safe (6)
2 Greed (7)
3 Ambition (5)
4 Converge (4)
5 Freight (5)
6 Venomous snake (5)
7 Defeated (6)
11 Instrument for drawing straight lines and measuring lengths (5)
12 Malice (5)
14 Betrayer of one's country (7)
15 Vicious (6)
16 Decapitate (6)
18 Of the pope (5)
19 Steer clear of (5)
21 Items of footwear (5)
22 Difficult (4)

Across

- **4** Exhibit (7)
- **8** In front (5)
- **9** Expanse of scenery (9)
- **10** In that place (5)
- **11** Fell back (9)
- **13** Required (6)
- **16** Level, floor (6)
- **20** Get even (9)
- **23** Peak of a cap (5)
- **24** Permission (9)
- **25** Sibling's daughter (5)
- **26** Look up to (7)

Down

- **1** Design (7)
- **2** Opposite (7)
- **3** Deadbeat (5)
- **4** Give to a charity (6)
- **5** Believe to be true (7)
- **6** Slightest (5)
- **7** Surrender (5)
- **12** The night before (3)
- **14** Organ of sight (3)
- **15** Magnify (7)
- **17** Adult male chicken (7)
- **18** Longed (7)
- **19** Device that attracts iron (6)
- **20** Come back (5)
- **21** Lock of hair (5)
- **22** Occurrence (5)

No 31

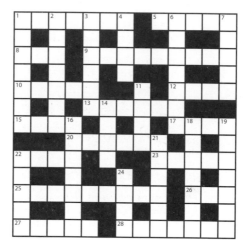

Across

1 Lucky (7)
5 Weary (5)
8 A single (3)
9 Practical (9)
10 Bone cavity (5)
12 Simple (4)
13 Poem part (6)
15 Soft or weak (4)
17 Dull, dreary (4)
20 Talisman (6)
22 Commotion (4)
23 Painting stand (5)
25 Unaware (9)
26 Large vase (3)
27 Condescend (5)
28 Promote (7)

Down

1 Flower (7)
2 Undying (7)
3 Emphasis (6)
4 Pull, haul (4)
6 As an alternative (7)
7 Decline (5)
11 Leg joint (4)
14 Like this (4)
16 Smart and stylish (7)
18 Savior (7)
19 Equilibrium (7)
21 Made fun of (6)
22 Torrent (5)
24 Additional (4)

No 32

Across

1 Characterized by insincerity, evasive (6)
3 Consortium of companies (6)
7 Arousal of the mind to special creativity (11)
10 Clergyman ministering to an institution (8)
11 Molding, in the form of the letter S (4)
13 Capital of Switzerland (5)
14 Mediterranean island (5)
18 Turn or place at an angle (4)
19 Pipe made of gourd (8)
21 Female to whom one is related by marriage (6-2-3)
22 Fertilized egg (6)
23 Completely lacking (6)

Down

1 Sew together (6)
2 Not worth considering (8)
4 Waterless (4)
5 Food store (6)
6 Abandoned child who roams the streets (5)
8 Having no definite form (9)
9 Onset of darkness (9)
12 Animal or plant that lives in or on a host (8)
15 On land (6)
16 Gateaux (5)
17 Melted (6)
20 Catch sight of (4)

No 33

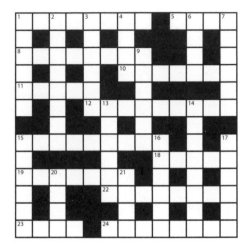

Across

1 Deduct, take away from (8)
5 Close to (4)
8 Pertinent (8)
10 Serious (7)
11 Loop in a rope (5)
12 Clever joke (9)
15 Discount (9)
18 Nimble, spry (5)
19 Flightless African bird (7)
22 Object serving as a model (8)
23 At any time (4)
24 Affection (8)

Down

1 Potent (6)
2 Shouted (8)
3 Appraisal (6)
4 Walking-stick (4)
6 Border (4)
7 Pattern in music (6)
9 Design marked on skin (6)
13 In one piece (6)
14 Point to (8)
15 Raw recruit (6)
16 Slept (6)
17 Niche or alcove (6)
20 Melody (4)
21 Leading man (4)

Across

1 Moment (7)
7 Material (6)
0 Lion-like (7)
10 Accepted (5)
11 After that (4)
12 Evidence (5)
16 Strongroom (5)
17 Heavy book (4)
21 Overhead (5)
22 Hair cleanser (7)
23 Well-mannered (6)
24 Devoid of (7)

Down

1 Blow up (7)
2 Rubbed (7)
3 Steer clear of (5)
4 Animated film (7)
5 Male duck (5)
6 Perfume (5)
8 Callous (9)
13 Purplish-red (7)
14 Underwater missile (7)
15 Down payment (7)
18 Contented (5)
19 Globe, planet (5)
20 Pass out (5)

No 35

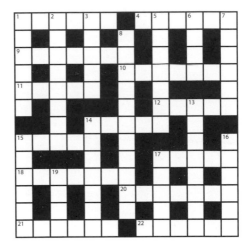

Across

1 Next to (6)

4 Conformed to some shape or size (6)

9 Treeless grassy plain (7)

10 Contaminate (7)

11 Gleaming (5)

12 Lukewarm (5)

14 Careless speed (5)

15 Ravioli, for example (5)

17 Hidden supply (5)

18 Endeavor (7)

20 Keep out (7)

21 Hang freely (6)

22 Defective (6)

Down

1 Get around, circumvent (6)

2 Roomy (8)

3 Soiled (5)

5 Set apart (7)

6 Ballet dancer's skirt (4)

7 Act against an attack (6)

8 Stood for (11)

13 On time (8)

14 Damaging, likely to cause injury (7)

15 Even-tempered (6)

16 Only, just (6)

17 Chocolate beverage, popular bedtime drink (5)

19 Rotation (4)

No 36

Across

- **1** Lose consciousness (5)
- **4** Run away (7)
- **8** Indistinct (7)
- **9** Tirades (5)
- **10** Material for jeans (5)
- **11** Protection (7)
- **12** For the most part (6)
- **13** Covering (usually of cloth) that shelters an area from the weather (6)
- **16** Value highly (7)
- **18** Traverse (5)
- **20** Rowdy fight (5)
- **21** Germ-free (7)
- **22** Thrown out (7)
- **23** Complete (5)

Down

- **1** Located (5)
- **2** Lacking regard for the rights or feelings of others (13)
- **3** Heat-related (7)
- **4** Apprehend (6)
- **5** Tennis stroke that puts the ball into play (5)
- **6** Bird-watcher (13)
- **7** Obliterate (7)
- **12** Gruesome (7)
- **14** Extremely old (7)
- **15** Pursued (6)
- **17** Arm off of a larger body of water (5)
- **19** Incantation (5)

No 37

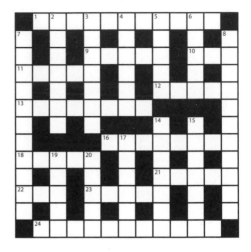

Across

1 Outcome of an event (11)
9 Monster (5)
10 Be in debt (3)
11 Wear away (5)
12 Thespian (5)
13 Unequalled (8)
16 Inhabitant (8)
18 Rope used to restrain an animal (5)
21 Pound, pulse (5)
22 Organ of hearing (3)
23 Insect grub (5)
24 Slowed down (11)

Down

2 Fought back (7)
3 Gravely (7)
4 Misgivings (6)
5 Additional (5)
6 Hit hard (5)
7 Somnambulist (11)
8 Unfortunate (11)
14 Dried grape (7)
15 Impulse, whim (7)
17 Accusation (6)
19 Concur (5)
20 Divide by two (5)

No 38

Across

1 Put on clothes (7)

6 Foreshorten (3)

8 Wrong action attributable to bad judgment (5)

9 Military unit (7)

10 Building for carrying on industrial labor (5)

11 Well-known (8)

13 Third sign of the zodiac (6)

15 Upper part of a nose (6)

18 Spectator (8)

19 Preliminary sketch (5)

21 Dissimilar (7)

22 Adhere, stick (5)

23 Fire residue (3)

24 Striking (7)

Down

2 Set free (7)

3 Ruining (8)

4 Refusal to admit something (6)

5 Enfold (4)

6 Brought into existence (7)

7 Producing a sensation of touch (7)

12 Conceited (8)

13 Boat seen on the canals of Venice (7)

14 King or queen (7)

16 Small cucumber pickled whole (7)

17 As much as necessary (6)

20 Miss a step and fall (4)

No 39

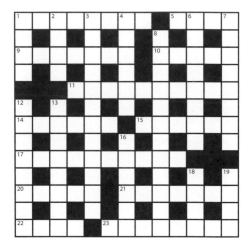

Across

1 Retract (8)
5 Trundle (4)
9 Deadlock (7)
10 Purpose (5)
11 Desire to travel (10)
14 Treachery (6)
15 Frightened (6)
17 Synthetic (10)
20 Unlawful act (5)
21 Lifting (7)
22 Excavations (4)
23 Of late (8)

Down

1 Delay (4)
2 Variety (4)
3 Unhappy (12)
4 List of items for discussion (6)
6 Death notice (8)
7 Leeway, scope (8)
8 Grateful (12)
12 High-tech (8)
13 Very critical (8)
16 In short supply (6)
18 Clenched hand (4)
19 Unattractive (4)

Across

1 Ousted (7)
5 Sanctify (5)
7 Play for time (5)
8 Spectacles (7)
9 Entourage (7)
10 Mannerism (5)
11 One who cuts down on food intake (6)
13 Suitable for use as food (6)
18 Something with value (5)
20 Unfavorable (7)
21 Tooth doctor (7)
22 Jeweled headdress (5)
23 Plant stem (5)
24 Introduce (7)

Down

1 Wanted intensely (7)
2 Childish talk (7)
3 Peace and quiet (7)
4 Stabbing weapon (6)
5 Explosion (5)
6 Out of the ordinary (7)
12 Look over carefully (7)
14 Keen enthusiast (7)
15 Heavy fire of artillery (7)
16 Stylish and graceful (7)
17 Portable computer (6)
19 Believe (5)

No 41

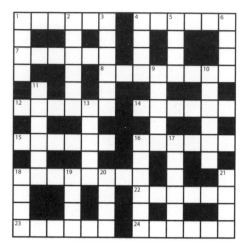

Across

1 Nothing (6)
4 Polish off (6)
7 Heavenly (6)
8 News broadcast (8)
12 Walk wearily (6)
14 Alternative name for the voice-box (6)
15 Bird enclosure (6)
16 Recollection of past events (6)
18 Single man (8)
22 Chauffeur (6)
23 Posted, sent (6)
24 Take away (6)

Down

1 Connecting point at which several lines come together (4)
2 Acquired (6)
3 High-pitched (6)
4 Young horse (4)
5 Appellation by which one is known (4)
6 Religious song (4)
9 Rental contract (5)
10 Disregard (6)
11 Unimportant things (6)
13 Deep ravine (5)
16 Unlawful premeditated killing (6)
17 Spiritualist (6)
18 Soothing oil (4)
19 Body of a ship (4)
20 Dry ground (4)
21 Genuine (4)

No 42

Across

1 Deluge (5)
4 Prisoner (7)
7 Brief stop (5)
8 Showing very poor skill in handling difficult situations (8)
9 Distance across (5)
11 Calmness (8)
15 Story below ground (8)
17 Christmas song (5)
19 Time-related (8)
20 Amusement (5)
21 Concentrated extract (7)
22 Shabby (5)

Down

1 Extravagantly fanciful and unrealistic (9)
2 Little-known (7)
3 Gradual falling off from a better state (7)
4 Wardrobe (6)
5 Deeply sad (6)
6 Pay a call on (5)
10 Unfriendliness (9)
12 Admiration (7)
13 Place of seclusion (7)
14 Pointed beard (6)
16 Wide street (6)
18 Sign of the zodiac (5)

No 43

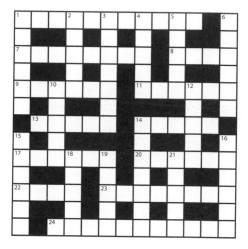

Across

- **1** Likelihood (11)
- **7** Great in quantity (8)
- **8** Adhesive paste (4)
- **9** Strappy shoe (6)
- **11** Set of clothes (6)
- **13** Force out of one's property (5)
- **14** Simple seat without a back or arms (5)
- **17** Protective head covering (6)
- **20** Young swan (6)
- **22** In addition (4)
- **23** Discretion in practical affairs (8)
- **24** Vengeance (11)

Down

- **1** Impose a penalty (6)
- **2** Produce offspring (5)
- **3** Brochure (7)
- **4** Noosed rope (5)
- **5** Close-fitting (5)
- **6** Detective (6)
- **10** Scar where the umbilical cord was once attached (5)
- **12** Angry look (5)
- **14** Give in, yield (7)
- **15** Beat soundly (6)
- **16** Spread by scattering (6)
- **18** Large deer (5)
- **19** Thin candle (5)
- **21** Welcome (5)

No 44

Across

- **1** Symbol (4)
- **3** Disparage (8)
- **9** Go before (7)
- **10** Graph (5)
- **11** Offspring (5)
- **12** Cure-all (7)
- **13** Red-skinned fruit (6)
- **15** Shooting star (6)
- **17** Nunnery (7)
- **18** Spiny plants (5)
- **20** Commerce (5)
- **21** Memory loss (7)
- **22** Salad sauce (8)
- **23** Extremely (4)

Down

- **1** Cultured, appealing to those having worldly knowledge and refinement (13)
- **2** Estimate (5)
- **4** Free from an obligation (6)
- **5** Emitting light as a result of being heated (12)
- **6** Large packet of shares (7)
- **7** Remarkable (13)
- **8** All the same (12)
- **14** Composite image (7)
- **16** Over-exert (6)
- **19** Hindu social class (5)

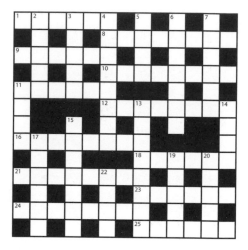

Across

1 Fix together (6)
8 Sufficient (8)
9 Chess piece (6)
10 Location (8)
11 Go hungry (6)
12 Recent arrival (8)
16 Light purple (8)
18 Make a low noise, like thunder (6)
21 Spineless (8)
23 Fabricate, make up (6)
24 Conjuror (8)
25 Avaricious (6)

Down

2 Rotate rapidly (5)
3 Detest (5)
4 Occurred (8)
5 Not so much of (4)
6 Public sale of lots to the highest bidder (7)
7 Swimming style (6)
11 Loose earth (4)
13 Disturbing (8)
14 Uncommon (4)
15 Earthenware (7)
17 Hooded waterproof jacket (6)
19 Motion picture (5)
20 Wrinkled (5)
22 Platform (4)

No 46

Across

1 Exceptionally bad (8)
5 Lengthy (4)
8 Brilliant (5)
9 Large smooth mass of rock (7)
10 Mediocre (7)
12 The act of passing money in return for goods or services (7)
14 Inquisitive (7)
16 Slim or small (7)
18 Bedecked (7)
19 Condition (5)
20 Looked at (4)
21 Unnecessary (8)

Down

1 Plate (4)
2 Vigor (6)
3 Dropped off (9)
4 Pleasantly optimistic (6)
6 Trying experience (6)
7 Dazzlingly beautiful (8)
11 Wholly absorbed, as in thought (9)
12 Win approval or support for (8)
13 Turn into (6)
14 Baby's bed (6)
15 Elaborately decorated (6)
17 Information (4)

No 47

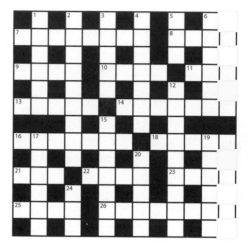

Across

7 Keep in a certain state (8)
8 Dressed (4)
9 Overdue (4)
10 Broad smile (4)
11 Illuminated (3)
13 Curt, brusque (5)
14 Study of animals (7)
16 Wrench (7)
18 Light meal (5)
21 Apple seed (3)
22 DNA unit (4)
23 Look good on (4)
25 Brave man (4)
26 Plentiful (8)

Down

1 Violent (6)
2 Endless (9)
3 Freight (5)
4 Sharp-edged tooth (7)
5 Do something (3)
6 Proverb (6)
12 Next to (9)
15 A number of (7)
17 Levered, forced (6)
19 Customer (6)
20 Thighbone (5)
24 Monopolize (3)

Across

1 Compel (5)
7 Desert, leave (7)
8 Decompose (3)
9 Highly offensive, arousing aversion or disgust (9)
11 Spooky (5)
12 Wedding (8)
16 Informal photograph (8)
20 Unskillful (5)
21 Incorrect (9)
23 Nocturnal bird of prey (3)
24 Someone who travels for pleasure (7)
25 Admission (5)

Down

1 Penalty (7)
2 Go back (6)
3 Special design or symbol (6)
4 Epic tale (4)
5 Strange, out of the ordinary (7)
6 Beneath, below (5)
10 Upper body (5)
13 Long, narrow passageway (5)
14 Stonework (7)
15 Entirely (7)
17 Paper handkerchief (6)
18 Organized opposition to authority (6)
19 Fatality (5)
22 Swearword (4)

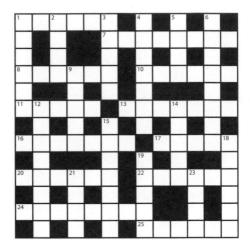

Across

1 Flowery (6)
7 Seemed, gave a certain impression (8)
8 Express astonishment or surprise (6)
10 Hair curler (6)
11 Sizeable (5)
13 Cowboy film (7)
16 Against the law (7)
17 Female fox (5)
20 Evaluate (6)
22 Strongly opposed, loath (6)
24 Game played with rectangular tiles (8)
25 Assert with a view to subsequent proof (6)

Down

1 Official (6)
2 Terminated, past (4)
3 Serving spoon (5)
4 Rejected with contempt (7)
5 Frozen rain (4)
6 Practice (8)
9 Indistinct (5)
12 Passing reference or indirect mention (8)
14 Two times (5)
15 Large and imposing residence (7)
18 Sewing tool (6)
19 Spicy sauce to accompany Mexican food (5)
21 Way out (4)
23 Impolite (4)

No 50

Across

- **1** Floated (7)
- **7** Visualize (7)
- **8** Spoken (5)
- **10** Implement, tool (7)
- **11** Cloth woven from flax (5)
- **12** Vigorous (9)
- **16** Waterproofed canvas (9)
- **18** Very angry (5)
- **20** Fictional character who rubs a magic lantern (7)
- **23** Narrow ravine (5)
- **24** Three pronged spear (7)
- **25** Vacation (7)

Down

- **1** Reside (5)
- **2** Creator (8)
- **3** Water down (6)
- **4** Donated (4)
- **5** Overlook (4)
- **6** Turn aside (7)
- **9** Movie theatre (6)
- **13** Friendly (6)
- **14** Soundly beaten (8)
- **15** Furtiveness (7)
- **17** Duration (6)
- **19** Hard blackish wood (5)
- **21** Opera song (4)
- **22** Sketched (4)

No 51

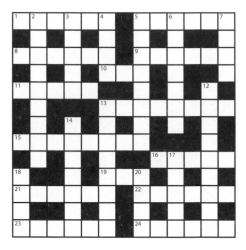

Across

1 Combatant who is able to defeat rivals (6)
5 Method (6)
8 Pay close attention to what is being said (6)
9 Light wind (6)
10 Acquire (3)
11 Long firearm (5)
13 Aromatic (8)
15 Enjoyable (8)
16 Molten rock in the Earth's crust (5)
19 Disorderly crowd of people (3)
21 Impenetrable equatorial forest (6)
22 Assumes (6)
23 Feel remorse for (6)
24 Result (6)

Down

2 At first (9)
3 Complete (5)
4 One step of a ladder (4)
5 Take away (8)
6 Attendant on an airplane (7)
7 Encounter (4)
12 Mysterious (9)
13 Broken piece (8)
14 Tiredness (7)
17 Remote in manner (5)
18 Slightly open (4)
20 Uncovered (4)

No 52

Across

- **1** Practical method applied to some particular task (9)
- **8** Commit to memory (5)
- **9** For each (3)
- **10** Upper body (5)
- **11** Dispel gloom (5)
- **12** Compose a letter (5)
- **14** Armed fight (6)
- **16** Food basket (6)
- **20** Small porch (5)
- **23** Perspiration (5)
- **25** Pay increase (5)
- **26** Mature (3)
- **27** Dirt-free (5)
- **28** Very good (9)

Down

- **1** Subject (5)
- **2** Flow of electricity through a conductor (7)
- **3** Not supporting or favoring either side (7)
- **4** Surface excavation for extracting stone or slate (6)
- **5** Arm joint (5)
- **6** Spiny succulent plants (5)
- **7** Ambiguous (7)
- **13** Outer part of a wheel (3)
- **14** Request earnestly (7)
- **15** Number in a brace (3)
- **17** Weapon store (7)
- **18** Get ready (7)
- **19** Medical center (6)
- **21** Frequently (5)
- **22** Dried plum (5)
- **24** Act of stealing (5)

Across

- **1** Terrible (5)
- **7** Insect's 'feeler' (7)
- **8** Changed (7)
- **9** Came out (7)
- **12** Confrontation (8)
- **14** Computer memory unit (4)
- **16** Ostracize (4)
- **18** Duration (8)
- **20** Kneecap (7)
- **23** Augur (7)
- **24** Church tower (7)
- **25** Irrigate (5)

Down

- **1** Testing (8)
- **2** Debacle (6)
- **3** Delayed (4)
- **4** Lose brightness (4)
- **5** Undressed (8)
- **6** Make up (6)
- **10** Handbook (6)
- **11** Small piece of food (6)
- **13** Marveled (8)
- **15** Give rise to (8)
- **17** Wellbeing (6)
- **19** Creepy-crawly (6)
- **21** Highest point (4)
- **22** Increase (4)

No 54

Across

1 High-pitched noise resembling a human cry (6)

4 Nothing (6)

7 Climbed (8)

8 Tolerate (4)

9 Room used for reading and writing (5)

10 Penned, put in words (7)

12 Having a strong effect (6)

13 Excessive pride (6)

15 Sated, full (7)

18 Roman god of love (5)

20 Component (4)

21 Obstinate (8)

22 Formal pact (6)

23 Move away (6)

Down

1 Items of furniture designed for resting on (5)

2 Recently enlisted soldier (7)

3 Irritation (9)

4 Point directly opposite the zenith (5)

5 Welcome (5)

6 Oppression (7)

11 Quickly aroused to anger (9)

12 Low wall (7)

14 Get better (7)

16 Money container (5)

17 Appetizing (5)

19 Closely crowded together (5)

No 55

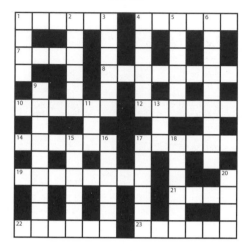

Across

1 Band of fabric worn around the neck as a tie (6)
4 Portray (6)
7 Aristocrat (4)
8 Stick out (8)
10 Brought up (6)
12 In accord with the latest fad (6)
14 Entertained (6)
17 Pulchritude (6)
19 Blameless (8)
21 Older than (4)
22 For the most part (6)
23 Intrude in other people's affairs (6)

Down

1 Replica (4)
2 Against (6)
3 Three-legged stand (6)
4 Very religious (6)
5 Penetrate with a sharp implement (6)
6 Applicant (9)
9 Instrument played by blowing into the desired holes (9)
11 Female sheep (3)
13 Wheat-like cereal plant (3)
15 Purloined (6)
16 Profoundly (6)
17 Lowest part of anything (6)
18 Out of the country (6)
20 Gratis (4)

Across

1 Rubbed (5)

4 Talk about (7)

8 Word or phrase used to fill out a sentence or a line of verse without adding to the sense (9)

9 Swift, quick (5)

10 Onlooker (9)

13 Verbal puzzle (6)

14 Tree limb (6)

16 Followed (9)

19 Gas which acts as a screen for ultraviolet radiation (5)

20 Give knowledge to (9)

22 Rushing stream (7)

23 Pass on (5)

Down

1 Fighter (7)

2 Upright (13)

3 Actions (5)

4 Brief swim (3)

5 Exhausted (5)

6 Inadvertent (13)

7 Absolute (5)

11 Part, bit (5)

12 Telegram (5)

15 Frankness (7)

16 Slumbered (5)

17 Bird of prey (5)

18 Contributor (5)

21 Young child (3)

No 57

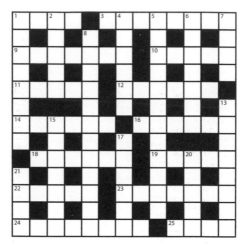

Across

1 Curse (4)
3 Mishap (8)
9 Radical (7)
10 Inexpensive (5)
11 Light narrow boat (5)
12 Small river (6)
14 Protection (6)
16 Pointer (6)
18 Rich and elaborate cake (6)
19 Greek letter (5)
22 Limits within which something can be effective (5)
23 Sanctified (7)
24 Sugar cane syrup (8)
25 Property (4)

Down

1 State of the sky when covered by clouds (8)
2 Mythological giant (5)
4 Fold line (6)
5 Confined, as in a jail (12)
6 Green gem (7)
7 Subdivision of a particular kind of thing (4)
8 Even so (12)
13 Looked at attentively (8)
15 Washcloth (7)
17 Speak indistinctly (6)
20 Tagliatelle or ravioli, for example (5)
21 Native to (4)

No 58

Across

1 Location of a building (7)

5 Stand watch over (5)

8 Trained (11)

9 Set of recordings, especially musical (5)

11 Bad-tempered (7)

13 Very powerful (8)

14 Animal-drawn sledge (6)

17 Governing body (7)

18 Poison of snakes, etc (5)

19 Plant-eating insect with hind legs adapted for leaping (11)

22 Narrow shelf (5)

23 Cravings (7)

Down

1 Enthusiastic approval (7)

2 Spanish nobleman's title (3)

3 Inscrutable (9)

4 Selfishly unwilling to share with others (6)

5 Weapon that discharges a missile (3)

6 Kidnapping (9)

7 God or goddess (5)

10 Resented (9)

12 Unaware (9)

15 Upper-arm bone (7)

16 Concluded (6)

17 Christmas song (5)

20 Imitate (3)

21 For every (3)

No 59

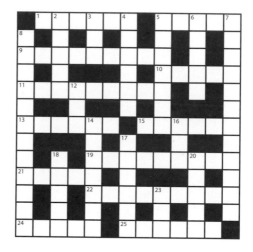

Across

1 Tenant (6)
5 Fragrance (5)
9 Meeting (9)
10 Inuit dwelling (5)
11 Annoyed (9)
13 Put out (6)
15 Remember (6)
19 Outer layer of the skin (9)
21 Backbone (5)
22 Trite remark (9)
24 Cheap restaurant (5)
25 One who reduces food intake in an effort to lose weight (6)

Down

2 Happen (5)
3 Wildebeest (3)
4 Revolve (6)
5 Shorten (7)
6 Strangely (5)
7 Achieved (12)
8 Gave up (12)
12 Small hotel (3)
14 Climbing plant (7)
16 Automobile (3)
17 Sorcerer (6)
18 Female fox (5)
20 Pale purple (5)
23 Frozen water (3)

No 60

Across

- **4** Linked (7)
- **7** Expand (7)
- **8** Reward (5)
- **9** Minutes (5)
- **10** Epoch, age (3)
- **11** Historical object (5)
- **12** Bequest (9)
- **14** Derided (9)
- **17** Ward off (5)
- **18** Chapeau (3)
- **19** Elf or fairy (5)
- **21** Magnificence (5)
- **22** Food provider (7)
- **23** Hideaway (7)

Down

- **1** Eager (4)
- **2** Scheduled (8)
- **3** Reliable (11)
- **4** Venerate (6)
- **5** Trivial thing (6)
- **6** Soaked (8)
- **0** Get involved (11)
- **12** Jeopardize (8)
- **13** News item (6)
- **15** Perceive, notice (6)
- **16** Great comfort (6)
- **20** Nobleman (4)

No 61

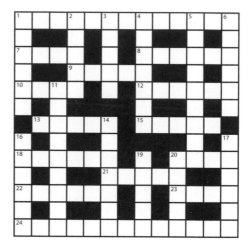

Across

1 Rude (13)
7 Piece of fabric used as a signalling device (4)
8 Covert (6)
9 Japanese poem (5)
10 Informal talk (4)
12 Turn down (6)
13 Thing of value (5)
15 Great fear (5)
18 Live, dwell (6)
20 In this place (4)
21 Deep blue (5)
22 Tolerated (6)
23 As well (4)
24 Quarrelsome (13)

Down

1 Imperfection in a bodily system (6)
2 Correct (5)
3 Undress (5)
4 Made certain (7)
5 Privileged (9)
6 Written message addressed to a person or organization (6)
11 Helping, lending a hand (9)
14 Foot lever (7)
16 Fleet of warships (6)
17 Undergo a change or development (6)
19 Constructed (5)
20 Vital organ of the body (5)

No 62

Across

1 Indefinite quantity of something having a specified value (5)
5 Region (4)
7 Lay bare for all to see (6)
8 Region of South Africa (5)
9 Delayed (9)
10 Be mistaken or incorrect (3)
11 Strengthen and support with rewards (9)
15 Kept an eye on (9)
19 That girl's (3)
20 Not widely liked (9)
21 Fatuous (5)
22 Substance found in tea (6)
23 Large and scholarly book (4)
24 Visitor (5)

Down

1 Desired (6)
2 Take back (6)
3 Assistant (6)
4 Carry on (8)
5 Spray can (7)
6 Concentrated extract (7)
12 Fluent, smooth-spoken (8)
13 Windstorm (7)
14 Quick-witted retort (7)
16 Audacious (6)
17 Idiomatic expression (6)
18 Clergyman (6)

No 63

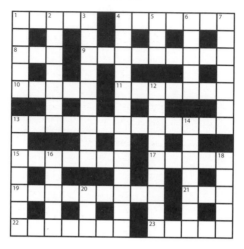

Across

1 Pointed (5)
4 Officer in command of a ship (7)
8 Flightless Australian bird (3)
9 Deepest (9)
10 Mushrooms, etc (5)
11 Diplomatic (7)
13 Consisting of a haphazard assortment of different kinds (13)
15 Shiny silk-like fabric (7)
17 Of comparatively little physical weight (5)
19 Appalled (9)
21 Extremely cold (3)
22 Detect with the senses (7)
23 Numeral (5)

Down

1 Ledge (5)
2 Male graduate (7)
3 Special advantage or benefit not enjoyed by all (9)
4 Configuration of stars as seen from Earth (13)
5 State of equality (3)
6 Detached (5)
7 Stinging plants (7)
12 Finished (9)
13 Provided with a worthy adversary or competitor (7)
14 Currently happening (7)
16 Companies (5)
18 Lovers' secret rendezvous (5)
20 Strong anger (3)

Across

1 Unrestrained and violent (7)
5 Yawns wide (5)
8 For good (11)
9 Accolade (5)
11 Existing as an essential characteristic (7)
13 Degree, magnitude (6)
14 Relating to the mountains (6)
17 Defraud (7)
18 One sixteenth of a pound (5)
19 Commotion (11)
22 Large truck (5)
23 Ballroom dance (7)

Down

1 Substitute (7)
2 Impair (3)
3 Deserted (9)
4 Dissertation (6)
5 Intestine (3)
6 Licensed medical practitioner (9)
7 Holy man (5)
10 Cancellation of civil rights (9)
12 Repository for voting slips (6,3)
15 World's highest mountain (7)
16 Snub (6)
17 Ability (5)
20 Engage in espionage (3)
21 Neither (3)

No 65

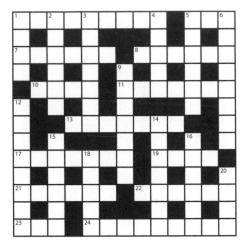

Across

1 Open to more than one interpretation (9)
5 Prosecute (3)
7 Detesting (6)
8 Treated with excessive indulgence (6)
10 Allows (4)
11 Person who takes long walks in the country (7)
13 Devoid of practical purpose (7)
17 Shake with fear (7)
19 Slightly open (4)
21 Spiritually converted (6)
22 Set a match to (6)
23 Playing-card (3)
24 Characterized by toilsome effort (9)

Down

1 Throb dully (4)
2 Annoy (6)
3 First book of the Old Testament (7)
4 Group of many insects (5)
5 Muffle, suppress (6)
6 Imaginary place of great wealth and opportunity (2,6)
9 Basket on wheels (7)
12 Frenzy (8)
14 Walk with a lofty proud gait (7)
15 Decrepit (6)
16 Coarse cloth (6)
18 Colored transparent gemstone (5)
20 Honey-producers (4)

Across

1 Pressure line on a weather map (6)
5 Enveloping bandage (6)
8 Military signal at lights out time (4)
9 Long-legged bird (8)
10 Bottle that holds oil or vinegar for the table (5)
11 Portion (7)
14 Elongated cluster of flowers (6)
15 Domesticated llama (6)
17 Regular payment to a retired person (7)
19 Wood nymph (5)
21 Wanderer who has no established residence (8)
23 Den (4)
24 Parts of the year (6)
25 Group of six (6)

Down

2 Series of steps (9)
3 Put under a military blockade (7)
4 Overabundant (4)
5 The longest typewriter key (5,3)
6 Saying that is widely accepted on its own merits (5)
7 Ugly, evil-looking old woman (3)
12 Variety of peach (9)
13 Extremely poisonous (8)
16 Bewilder (7)
18 Vertical passage into a mine (5)
20 Chances (4)
22 In the past (3)

No 67

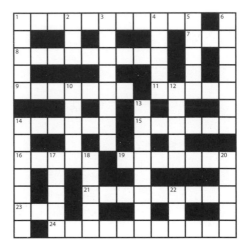

Across

1 Orange or lemon, for example (6,5)
7 Gradation of a color (3)
8 Muttering discontentedly (9)
9 Habitual method of procedure (7)
11 Murdered (5)
14 Charge falsely or with malicious intent (6)
15 Counterpane (6)
16 Moves back and forth, pitches (5)
19 Accommodating (7)
21 Honesty, moral integrity (9)
23 Prepare leather (3)
24 Money paid out (11)

Down

1 Roll of tobacco (5)
2 Male sheep (3)
3 Sliver (8)
4 Impulses (5)
5 Eighth letter of the Greek alphabet (5)
6 Acquired knowledge (7)
10 Sycophant (5)
12 Behaves in a sneaky and secretive manner (5)
13 Mixed haphazardly (8)
14 Difference of opinion (7)
17 Unaccompanied (5)
18 Implement used to sharpen razors (5)
20 Domestic birds (5)
22 Add up (3)

No 68

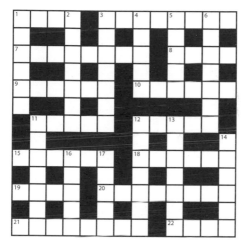

Across

1 Lacking hair (4)
3 Good-looking (8)
7 Recently married person (8)
8 Curved gateway (4)
9 ___ Mahler, composer, 1860-1911 (6)
10 Automatic response (6)
11 Alcoholic apple drink (5)
12 Fruit or vegetable pulp (5)
15 Lays out in a line (6)
18 Small wave on the surface of a liquid (6)
19 Assist in doing wrong (4)
20 Thin unleavened pancake (8)
21 Metal or paper medium of exchange (8)
22 Corrosive compound (4)

Down

1 Not dangerous to health (6)
2 Watered down (7)
3 Notwithstanding (7)
4 Lowest point (5)
5 Muffler (5)
6 Large heavy knife used for cutting vegetation (7)
11 Arctic deer with large antlers (7)
12 Assume or act the character of (7)
13 Reproduction (7)
14 Put behind bars (6)
16 Modify (5)
17 Glossy fabric (5)

No 69

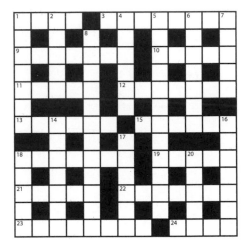

Across

- **1** Section of glass (4)
- **3** Pasta made of crushed and steamed semolina (8)
- **9** Disbeliever (7)
- **10** Endure (5)
- **11** Fit out (5)
- **12** Experienced person (3,4)
- **13** Gas found in the atmosphere (6)
- **15** Making an attempt (6)
- **18** Experiencing motion nausea (7)
- **19** Leg bone (5)
- **21** Secreting organ in animals (5)
- **22** Large hemispherical percussion instrument (7)
- **23** Take too much medication (8)
- **24** Inlet (4)

Down

- **1** Inert medication (7)
- **2** Prime Minister of India from 1947 to 1964 (5)
- **4** Alternative (6)
- **5** Official clock setting in a local region (8,4)
- **6** Japanese paper-folding art (7)
- **7** Warhorse (5)
- **8** Lacking subtlety and insight (6-6)
- **14** Distance measured in three-foot units (7)
- **16** Coarse-grained rock, often pink or gray (7)
- **17** Shoes with wheels attached (6)
- **18** Prefix denoting a partly British connection (5)
- **20** Well done! (5)

No 70

Across

1 Express disapproval (6)
7 Radio or television signal receiver (7)
8 Scratched (6)
9 Reconstruct (7)
10 Towards the tail of a ship (6)
13 Type of heron (5)
15 Fleshy red crest on the head of a bird (4)
16 Small area of land (4)
17 Often the last movement of a sonata (5)
18 Item of hosiery (6)
21 Highly seasoned meat stuffed in a casing (7)
23 Ask for earnestly (6)
24 Partly coincide (7)
25 Song of mourning (6)

Down

2 Washtubs (5)
3 Shout of approval (5)
4 Joint protected in front by the patella (4)
5 Highly offensive (9)
6 Immaculate, impeccable (9)
10 A movement upward (9)
11 Porthole through which a weapon is fired (9)
12 Gas used in lighting (4)
14 Embedded part (4)
19 Republic in southern Asia (5)
20 Italian city on the river Po (5)
22 Snatch (4)

No 71

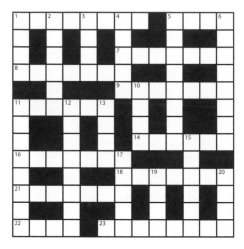

Across

1 Motorcar manufacturer (8)
5 In one's sleeping place (4)
7 Drink credited with magical power (7)
8 Take air in and out (7)
9 Wash clothes (7)
11 Short sleep (6)
14 Arboreal marsupial (6)
16 Equestrian footrest (7)
18 Remove the fastenings from (7)
21 Full of longing or unfulfilled desire (7)
22 Period of time (4)
23 Resent (8)

Down

1 Inhibit (4)
2 Go back to a previous state (6)
3 Table condiment (4)
4 Kick out (5)
5 Fabled island swallowed by an earthquake (8)
6 Place in which photographs are developed (8)
10 At the summit of (4)
11 Road that is raised above water or marshland (8)
12 Storyteller (8)
13 Country, capital Lima (4)
15 Marked by practical hard-headed intelligence (6)
17 Heartbeat (5)
19 Mix (4)
20 Heap (4)

No 72

Across

- **1** Kidnap (6)
- **7** Cosmos (8)
- **8** Dashed (3)
- **9** Earnings (6)
- **10** Twofold (4)
- **11** Put a stop to (5)
- **13** Cattle thief (7)
- **15** Person apparently sensitive to things beyond the range of perception (7)
- **17** Squander (5)
- **21** At liberty (4)
- **22** Intelligent (6)
- **23** By means of (3)
- **24** Turnaround (8)
- **25** Interfere (6)

Down

- **1** Turn up (6)
- **2** Refused (6)
- **3** Teacher (5)
- **4** So ugly as to be terrifying (7)
- **5** Long-running feud (8)
- **6** Got away (6)
- **12** Went beyond (8)
- **14** Talk about (7)
- **16** Wide road (6)
- **18** Dished up (6)
- **19** Infuriate (6)
- **20** Kingdom (5)

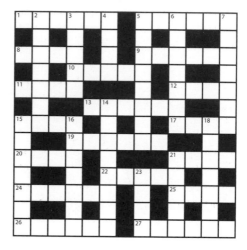

Across

1 Praised (6)
5 Lessen (6)
8 Monster (4)
9 Fortress (6)
10 Make up for past sins (5)
11 Company (4)
12 Encourage (4)
13 Tremble with fear (6)
15 Grew older (4)
17 Most fitting (4)
19 Solution or cure (6)
20 Sort, kind (4)
21 Regretted (4)
22 Relative magnitudes of two quantities (5)
24 Recording room (6)
25 Second letter of the Greek alphabet (4)
26 Mass departure (6)
27 Take off (6)

Down

2 Fishing (7)
3 Aspiration (5)
4 Extinct bird (4)
5 Was given (8)
6 Interrupt (7)
7 An abstract part of something (7)
14 Amusing (8)
15 Professional entertainer (7)
16 Looked forward to with fear and dismay (7)
18 Someone who doubts accepted beliefs (7)
21 Android (5)
23 Stepped (4)

No 74

Across

1 Squad (4)

3 Put ashore and abandoned on a desolate island (8)

9 Annoyed (7)

10 Prickle, barb (5)

11 Dubious (12)

14 Water frozen in the solid state (3)

16 Doomed (5)

17 Body of salt water (3)

18 Topping up (12)

21 Dwelling (5)

22 Depending on another for support (7)

23 Enjoyable (8)

24 Sweet, juicy, gritty-textured fruit (4)

Down

1 Serene (8)

2 Take part in a row (5)

4 Assistance (3)

5 Bizarrely (12)

6 Thin strips of pasta (7)

7 Completed (4)

8 Honesty (12)

12 Frequently (5)

13 Female child (8)

15 Ugly sight (7)

19 Mental picture (5)

20 Slightly wet (4)

22 Manage (3)

No 75

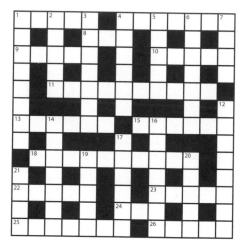

Across

1 Deadly (5)
4 Take to be true (7)
8 Consumed (3)
9 Extraterrestrial (5)
10 Distance downwards (5)
11 Given to excess in consumption of especially food or drink (10)
13 Personify (6)
15 Light wind (6)
18 Authorized (10)
22 Thespian (5)
23 Depart, go (5)
24 Billiards stick (3)
25 Give out (7)
26 Commercial exchange (5)

Down

1 Starred (8)
2 Binding (5)
3 Unhurried (7)
4 Loveliness (6)
5 Filled with a great quantity (5)
6 Adopt or support (7)
7 Reply that repeats what has just been said (4)
12 Stay of execution (8)
14 Bragged (7)
16 Curled lock of hair (7)
17 Puncture (6)
19 Latin for 'about' (5)
20 Excitement (5)
21 Set of two (4)

No 76

Across

1 Tyrant (6)
7 Prelude (8)
8 Present (4)
10 Sampled (6)
11 Choose (4)
12 Sincerely (5)
13 One more (7)
16 Unbiased (7)
18 Short-lived (5)
21 Immense (4)
23 Supporting beam, often made of steel or iron (6)
25 Uninteresting (4)
26 Confirmed (8)
27 Lengthen (6)

Down

1 Periodical that summarizes the news (6)
2 Having little impact (4)
3 Projection on a comb (5)
4 Lush, green (7)
5 Prevent (4)
6 Authoritative person who divines the future (6)
9 Medicinal pill (6)
14 Became (6)
15 Cheap purchase (7)
17 Rubbed out (6)
19 Deceived (6)
20 Coarse (5)
22 Small branch (4)
24 Principle (4)

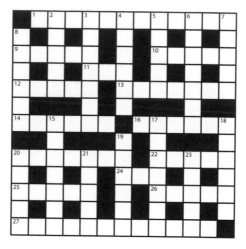

Across

1 Lacking social graces (12)
9 Astound (5)
10 Penalty (5)
11 Yes (3)
12 Luster (5)
13 Worked up, stimulated (7)
14 Choose (6)
16 Central part (6)
20 Largest anthropoid ape (7)
22 Piece of cloth used to mend a hole (5)
24 Foot digit (3)
25 Honest, blunt (5)
26 Court case (5)
27 Put out (as with a fire) (12)

Down

2 Angry (5)
3 Rinsed (7)
4 Maintenance (6)
5 Subject (5)
6 Failed to include (7)
7 Swiftness (5)
8 Overtook, went by (6)
15 Small seedless raisin (7)
17 Force that moves something along (7)
18 Breathe out (6)
19 Rich cream-cake (6)
20 Socially awkward or tactless act (5)
21 Describe as similar (5)
23 Strong string (5)

No 78

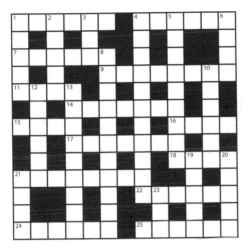

Across

1 Satisfy (6)
4 Mystery (6)
7 Catch fire (6)
9 Dearth, lack (0)
11 Large-scale (4)
14 Opposed to (7)
15 Farm building for housing poultry (4)
16 Division of quantity accepted as a standard of measurement (4)
17 Highest in stature (7)
18 Relieve (4)
21 Deep fissure (8)
22 Jeopardy (6)
24 Myth, fable (6)
25 Declared as a fact (6)

Down

1 Feeling of self-respect (5)
2 Boredom (5)
3 Division of a tennis match (3)
4 Ran into (11)
5 Association organized to promote art, science or education (9)
6 Stake in poker (4)
8 Set up (11)
10 Exceptional creative ability (6)
12 Correct (6)
13 Enchant, cause to be enamored (9)
19 Acute but unspecific feeling of anxiety (5)
20 Made a mistake (5)
21 Monk's hood (4)
23 Fitting (3)

239

No 79

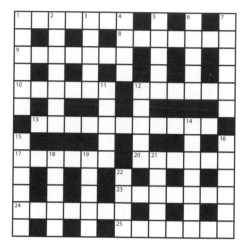

Across

1 Far-off (7)

8 Make better (7)

9 Knotted (7)

10 Nap in the early afternoon (6)

12 Confidential (6)

13 Similarity in appearance or superficial details (11)

17 Upward movement (6)

20 Resembling a horse (6)

23 Enduring (7)

24 Old Spanish ship (7)

25 Pleasure (7)

Down

1 Loathe (6)

2 Honest (7)

3 Assign (5)

4 Put things in order (4)

5 Backbone (5)

6 Pugilist (5)

7 Prosperity (6)

11 Confess (5)

12 Soothing ointment (5)

14 Scolding (7)

15 Make do (6)

16 Heaviness (6)

18 Young person, offspring (5)

19 More pleasant (5)

21 Large feather (5)

22 Set down (4)

Mind Puzzles

No 1
Dice-Section

Printed onto every one of the six numbered dice are six letters (one per side), which can be rearranged to form the answer to each clue; however, some sides are invisible to you. Use the clues and write every answer into the grid. When correctly filled, the letters in the shaded squares, reading in the order 1 to 6, will spell out the name of an animal.

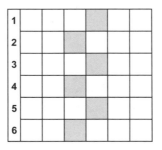

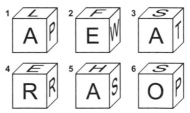

1 Package

2 Bloom

3 Month of the year

4 Feel remorse for

5 World's largest desert

6 Human being

No 2
Domino Fit

A standard set of twenty-eight dominoes has been laid out as shown. Can you draw in the edges of them all? The check-box is provided as an aid and the dominoes already placed may help.

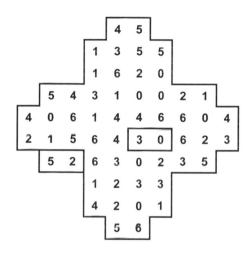

0-0	0-1	0-2	0-3	0-4	0-5	0-6	1-1	1-2
			✓					

1-3	1-4	1-5	1-6	2-2	2-3	2-4	2-5	2-6	3-3
							✓		

3-4	3-5	3-6	4-4	4-5	4-6	5-5	5-6	6-6

No 3
Latin Square

The grid below should be filled with the numbers from 1 to 6, so that each number appears exactly once in every row and every column. The clues refer to the sum of the numbers in the squares mentioned: for example, B C D 1 = 14 would mean that the numbers in squares B1, C1 and D1 add up to 14.

1 A 2 3 4 = 12

2 A B 5 = 4

3 B 1 2 = 9

4 B 4 5 = 3

5 B C D 1 = 14

6 C 2 3 4 = 6

7 C D 2 = 5

8 C D E 6 = 13

9 D 3 4 5 = 8

10 E 1 2 3 = 7

11 E F 4 = 10

12 F 2 3 = 8

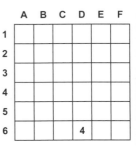

	A	B	C	D	E	F
1						
2						
3						
4						
5						
6				4		

No 4
Shape Spotter

Which is the only shape to appear twice in the picture below? Some shapes overlap others.

244

Ring-Words

From the 32 segments below, find 16 eight-letter words by pairing one set of four letters with another. All of the segments must be used once only.

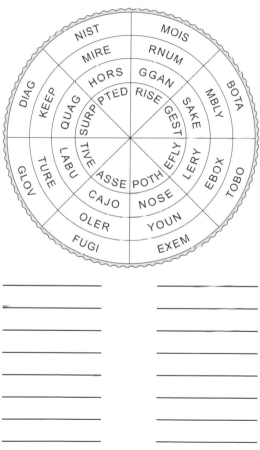

_____ _____

_____ _____

_____ _____

_____ _____

_____ _____

_____ _____

_____ _____

_____ _____

No 6
Around the Block

You won't need a starting block to get you under way, because it isn't a race! Just arrange the six-letter solutions to the clues into the six blocks around each clue number. Write the answers in a clockwise or anticlockwise direction and you'll find that the last answer fits into the first; the problem is to decide in which square to put the first letter of each word...

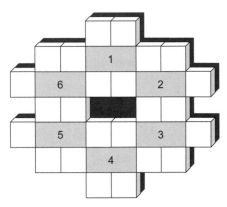

1 Beaded counting frame

2 Estimate the value of

3 Britain's longest river

4 Dried grape

5 Passageways between seats in a cinema

6 Dish on which a cup is placed

No 7
Around the Clock

Travel around the clock, one hour at a time, making 12 words all ending with the central letter. The letters to be placed in the empty squares are listed in the segment clockwise of the number to be filled. We've completed one already, in order to get you off to a timely start...

Now take the central letter of every even-numbered word and rearrange these to form another, meaning: traveling by plane.

___ ___ ___ ___ ___ ___

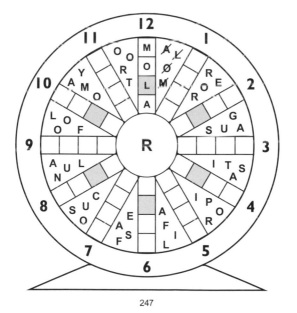

No 8
Numberfit

Can you fit all the listed numbers into the grid? One digit is already in place.

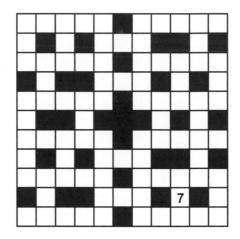

3 digits		5 digits	
188	562	11183	36150
192	563	12231	40351
233	572	17968	40745
281	636	21338	53270
285	671	24281	56225
330	775	24542	58106
356	791	27103	58235
449		30042	83064
484		35411	92679

A Matching Pair

Only two of these flower vases are identical in every way. Can you spot the matching pair?

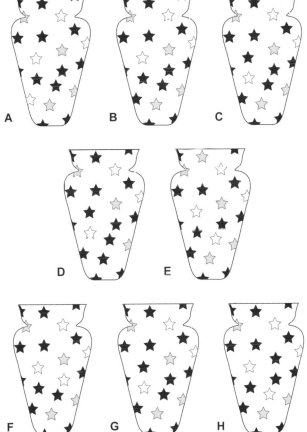

No 10

Roundacross

Beginning with clue No 1, track your way through the crossword, following the trail of clues. The last letter of one word becomes the first letter of the next.

1 Color, a mix of blue and green

2 Amuse

3 Usual, customary

4 African republic, capital Monrovia

5 Say sorry

6 South American country

7 Reproduction, copy

8 Air surrounding the Earth

9 Teaching

10 Slowly moving mass of ice

11 Plant with a thick, bulbous, edible yellow root

12 Deserted

13 Putting on clothes

14 Grotesque carving, on a church, eg

Magic Squares

Use the letters to the side of each grid to fill the crossword completely, in such a way that the words reading across are exactly the same as those reading downwards. For both crosswords, three letters have been given as a starter.

A~~A~~ A ~~B~~ ~~B~~ B

B E E E E

I I N N N

O O O O S

T T T Z Z

A	B			
B				

S	M			
M				

A A A A A

A A C C C

G I I K K

K ~~M~~ ~~M~~ N N

R R ~~S~~ Y Y

No 12

Sidewords

Start from either the top left square and follow a path downwards or from the bottom left square and follow a path upwards; a letter in a square is the same, no matter at which position you begin. Can you find the two sequences of words to match the clues?

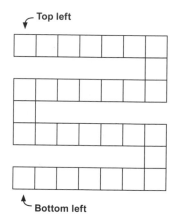

Top left

Bottom left

Clues from top left

1 Celebratory event (5)

2 Ms Fitzgerald, jazz singer (4)

3 Dwarf (5)

4 Prise (5)

5 Blemish (4)

6 Small drink (3)

7 Material used to make jeans (5)

Clues from bottom left

1 Squeeze (5)

2 Handgun (6)

3 U-shaped mark placed over a vowel (5)

4 Citrus fruit (5)

5 Ship's kitchen (6)

6 Extracted from the earth (4)

Summing up

Arrange each of the numbers 2, 4, 7 and 9, as well as one each of the symbols – (minus), x (times) and + (plus) once only in every row and column to arrive at the answer at the end of the row or column.

4	x	7	–	9	+	2	=	21
	■		■				■	
		■					=	27
	■		■				■	
							=	15
	■		■		■		■	
							=	17
=	■	=	■	=	■	=		
13		49		12		37		

No 14

Total Concentration

The numbers in each horizontal row add up to the totals to the right and those in each vertical column add up to the totals along the bottom.

The two longest diagonal lines also add up to the totals at the bottom. Your task is to fill in the missing numbers, which are all between 1 and 15 inclusive, and any number may be used more than once.

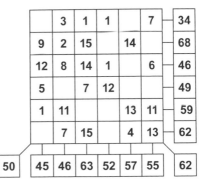

						Total
	3	1	1		7	34
9	2	15		14		68
12	8	14	1		6	46
5		7	12			49
1	11			13	11	59
	7	15		4	13	62

Diagonal total (left): 50

| 45 | 46 | 63 | 52 | 57 | 55 | 62 |

X Marks the Spot

Can you fit all the listed words into the grid? One is already in place.

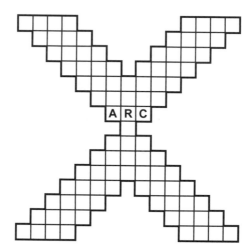

2 letters	4 letters	LAVA	STEM
ME	AWAY	LIST	STEP
NO	CANT	NEAR	STOP
ON	CLAM	NEWS	ZINC
WE	DATA	NUTS	ZONE
	EVER	OILS	
3 letters	FOAM	PAID	5 letters
ARC	FOND	PAIR	FINAL
ATE	GAME	RATS	STUNG
BUS	HAWK	SIDE	
LEG	HIDE	SLAP	7 letters
SEA	JOBS	SLID	CURRENT
YET	KING	SOLO	PLACING
	KITE	SONG	POSTMAN

No 16
Logi-5

The letters P, E, A, C and H should appear once in each row, as well as once in each column. Every heavily outlined shape of five smaller squares should also contain each of the letters P, E, A, C and H. Can you complete the grid?

		A		
		C		
				E
H				P

No 17
Wordwheel

How many words of three or more letters can you make from those in the wheel, without using plurals, abbreviations or proper nouns? The central letter must appear once in every word and no letter in a section of the wheel may be used more than once. There is at least one nine-letter word in the wheel.

No 18
Balancing the Scales

Given that scales A and B balance perfectly, how many sandcastles should be placed into the right-hand pan of scale C to make it balance?

Word Ladders

Change one letter at a time (but don't change the position of any letter) to make a new word – and move from the word at the top of the ladder to the word at the bottom using the exact number of rungs provided in each case.

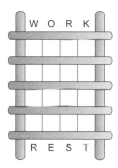

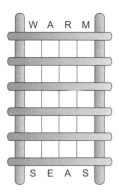

No 20

Link Words

Fit eight different words into the grid, so that each one links up with the words on either side, eg table - lamp - shade. When finished, read down the letters in the shaded squares to reveal another word, solving the clue.

PLASTER					OFF
FOOT					LADDER
PENCIL					PIPE
GRAND					OPERATOR
LEAP					MARCH
EXTRA					PIECE
TAIL					DRIER
BUBBLE					TOWEL

Clue: Marine creature _____

No 21

Word Power

Can you decide which of the four alternatives is the correct definition of the word

RETUSE

a To disqualify on the grounds of personal involvement

b Having the end rounded and slightly indented

c A type of sugar contained in fruits such as blackcurrants

d A puzzle in the form of a picture

258

No 22
Coded Quote

Decipher the code to reveal two lines from John Masefield's poem
Sea-Fever. Any letter which isn't used in the code has already been
placed into the grid.

Code =	A	B	C	D	E	F	G	H	I	J	K	L	M
Letter =										C			V

Code =	N	O	P	Q	R	S	T	U	V	W	X	Y	Z
Letter =		X	J	F	Z				Q				

W Y L X F A I G I D T F I

F U H X H S X S A S W T ,

F I F U H K I T H K E

X H S S T G F U H X B E ,

S T G S K K W S X B

W X S F S K K X U W Z

S T G S X F S C F I

X F H H C U H C N E ...

259

No 23
Whatever Next?

What time should appear on the final clock in the sequence below?

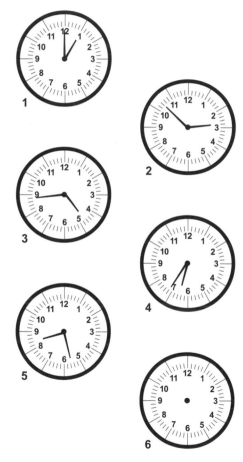

No 24
Pyramid Plus

Every brick in this pyramid contains a number which is the sum of the two numbers below it, so that F=A+B, etc. Just work out the missing numbers!

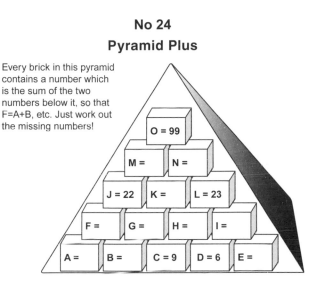

O = 99

M =   N =

J = 22   K =   L = 23

F =   G =   H =   I =

A =   B =   C = 9   D = 6   E =

No 25
The Value of Something

Each of the nine different letters in the word SOMETHING has been given a different value from 1 to 9, so S + O + M + E + T + H + I + N + G = 45. Your challenge is to find the value of each letter, given the clues below:

1 T + H + O + S + E = 27

2 S + T + O + N + E = 28

3 S + E + E + T + H + E = 26

4 G + H + O + S + T = 24

5 G + N + O + M + E = 23

6 T + H + E + S + E = 22

7 S + H + O + E = 22

8 M + I + S + T = 18

Letter =	S	O	M	E	T	H	I	N	G
Value =									

No 26
What's It Worth?

Each of the four symbols stands for a different number. In order to reach the total at the end of each row and column, what is the value of the heart, club, diamond, and spade?

♦	♣	♥	♠	= 22
♣	♥	♦	♣	= 29
	♣	♠	♠	= 10
♠		♦	♦	= 21
=	=	=	=	
19	19	24	20	

No 27
Mental Blocks

Solve this multiplication problem and write the numerical answer into the top set of boxes below the line. Then use the decoder to the left of the sum, writing the letters into the boxes beneath the numbers in order to find two words.

0	O
1	R
2	T
3	E
4	Y

5	H
6	I
7	D
8	P
9	S

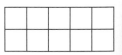

262

No 28
Hexafit

Can you place these six words into the hexagons? To fit them all in, some will have to be entered clockwise and others anticlockwise around the numbers. Two letters have already been put into position.

ARDENT

ENTIRE

GRATER

PARADE

REARED

URGENT

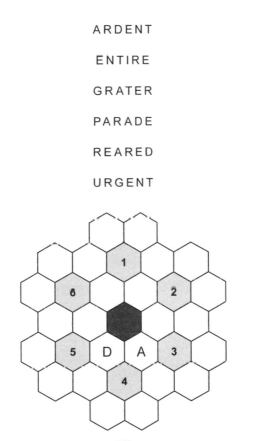

Do It Yourself!

In this crossword puzzle, the clues are listed in alphabetical order and there are no black squares in the grid. Your task is to black out the unwanted squares, so that the clues can be matched to the words in the finished puzzle.

S	T	I	T	C	H	E	S	A	N	E
P	A	C	K	H	O	P	I	L	O	T
E	L	E	V	A	T	O	R	E	I	C
E	N	C	I	L	E	S	F	U	S	E
C	A	R	E	L	E	S	S	L	Y	D
H	N	E	W	E	R	E	C	T	E	A
S	T	A	R	N	I	S	H	I	N	G
G	E	M	A	G	E	S	E	M	I	R
O	R	E	D	E	L	I	C	A	T	E
A	S	K	E	D	W	O	K	T	E	E
D	E	A	N	S	I	N	T	E	N	D

Abrupt	Hideout
Aviator	Lift
Consented	Loud
Consume	Mean to convey
Defiling, staining	Ownership
Disputed	Popular frozen dessert
Enquired	Precious stone
Final	Sew together
Form of address to a man	Verbal address
Fragile	Without caution

Box Clever

When the shape below is folded to form a cube, just one of the lettered alternatives can be produced. Which?

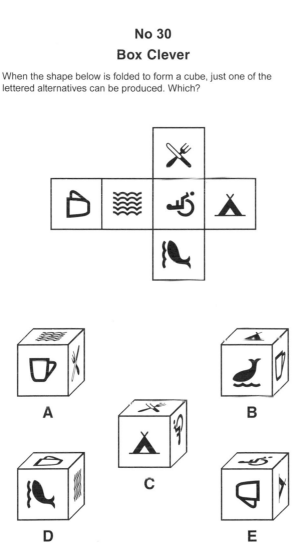

No 31
Latin Square

The grid should be filled with numbers from 1 to 6, so that each appears just once in every row and column. The clues refer to the digit totals in the squares, eg C D E 3 = 15 means that the numbers in squares C3, D3 and E3 add up to 15.

1 A 3 4 5 = 6   **7** C 3 4 5 = 15

2 A B 5 = 9   **8** C D E 3 = 15

3 A B 6 = 5   **9** D 2 3 = 7

4 B 1 2 3 = 11   **10** D E 5 = 6

5 B C 4 = 7   **11** D E F 2 = 7

6 B C D 6 = 9

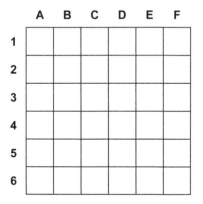

No 32
Egg Timer

Can you complete this puzzle in the time it takes to hard-boil an egg?
The answers to the clues are anagrams of the words immediately
above and below, plus or minus one letter.

1 Ancient way of measuring the hours

2 Ground surrounded by water

3 Garden pest

4 Metal fastening pin

5 Concluding

6 Ornament on top of a gable

7 Breaking down

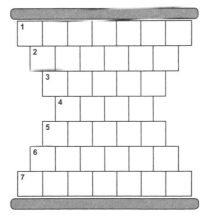

No 33

At Home

Three married couples have homes in the small block of apartments shown in the picture below. Given just four clues which contain all of the information you will need, can you solve this logic puzzle, discovering the first names and joint surname of each couple, together with the floor on which they live?

Third Floor

Second Floor

First Floor

1 Mr and Mrs Taylor's apartment is not on the first floor.

2 Judy's surname is Brown.

3 The apartment belonging to Mr and Mrs Jones is on a higher floor than Steven's apartment.

4 Rose is Colin's wife, but Ann isn't married to John.

Husband	Wife	Surname	Floor

No 34
Fallen Idols

The letters in the vertical columns belong in the squares immediately beneath them, but not necessarily in the given order. When entered correctly, they reveal the names of four well-known film stars.

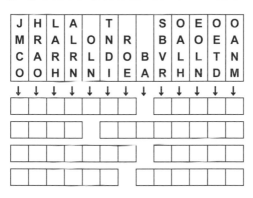

No 35
Writing Letters

Starting with the letter A, add a letter to make first a two-letter word, then add another letter to these two to make a three-letter word, then add another letter to these three to make a four-letter word, etc, rearranging the letters if necessary every time, until you have an eight-letter word for which the clue is: Systematic plan of action.

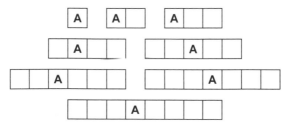

No 36

Couplets

The picture is of a central circle surrounded by shapes, linked to form six sets of three shapes apiece. Can you complete the puzzle by placing each of the two-letter groups below, one per shape, so that every set of three (the central circle, plus the two matching shapes diagonally opposite one another) forms a six-letter word? Whichever pair of letters you place in the central circle will appear in the middle of every word.

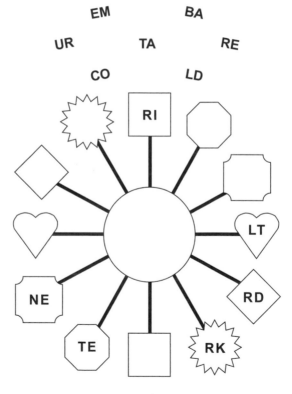

EM BA

UR TA RE

CO LD

RI

LT

RD

NE

TE RK

No 37

Character Assignation

Fill in the Across clues in this crossword in the normal way. Then read down the diagonal line of eight squares, to reveal: A character from Shakespeare's *Romeo and Juliet*.

1 Wired message

2 Pop the question

3 Shed for an aircraft

4 White in French

5 Ballerina's skirt

6 Decompose, decay

7 Word of greeting

8 Common blood type

Character: ___ ___ ___ ___ ___ ___ ___ ___

No 38

Alphabet Soup

Ladle the letters from the soup tureen and fit one into each of the 26 empty squares in the grid below, so that the finished result is a complete crossword containing words. All of the letters in the tureen must be used – thus no letter is used more than once.

ABCDEFGHIJK
LMNOPQRS
TUVWXYZ

No 39

It Doesn't Add Up

In the grid, leave 42 of the 49 numbers exactly where they are, but change the positions of the remaining seven in such a way that in every row, column, and long diagonal line of seven squares, the seven numbers total exactly 105.

15	22	8	11	17	2	27
2	26	14	23	7	12	20
10	19	4	27	14	22	8
23	7	11	20	3	27	15
28	14	22	7	12	20	4
20	4	28	15	22	6	10
9	12	17	3	29	14	23

No 40

Leftovers

Cross off words in the box as indicated by the instructions. The remaining words will form a common saying when read from left to right and line by line.

Cross off all alcoholic drinks.

Cross off all anagrams of TESLA.

Cross off all words with consecutive double letters.

Cross off all capital cities.

Cross off all words with the same first and last letter.

Cross off all zodiacal constellations.

Cross off all words containing two Ls.

Cross off all words that make another word when read backwards.

Cross off all precious stones.

RUBY	SLATE	GULP	ENTICE
SORRY	GREAT	METTLE	ARIES
RUM	GLADLY	PARIS	WINE
TALES	NYLON	MINDS	EMERALD
COLDLY	HAPPY	STALE	DENIM
THINK	REWARD	OPAL	WASHINGTON DC
VODKA	ATHENS	RAZOR	LEAST
LONDON	STEAL	REVEL	FLAIL
PISCES	TRUST	ALIKE	DIAPER
TARRED	GOING	BRANDY	LIBRA

No 41

Roundword

Write the answer to each clue in a clockwise direction. Every answer overlaps the next by two letters and starts in its numbered section. The solution to the final clue ends with the letter in the first section.

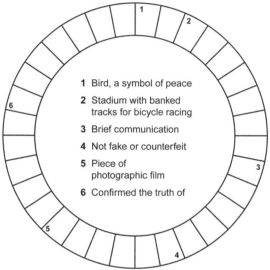

1 Bird, a symbol of peace

2 Stadium with banked tracks for bicycle racing

3 Brief communication

4 Not fake or counterfeit

5 Piece of photographic film

6 Confirmed the truth of

No 42

Word Power

Can you decide which of the four alternatives is the correct definition of the word

RAMULOSE

a   Coarse-grained, like sand or sugar

b   Having many mounds or small hills

c   Having numerous small branches

d   Covered with tiny scales or thorns

Deletions

There are 11 animals and a quote from Jonathan Swift hidden in this grid. Taking one letter from each box, cross off the six-letter words in the Across rows. Do the same for the five-letter words in the Down columns. When you have finished, the letters remaining will reveal a quote reading from left to right and row by row.

	1	2	3	4	5	6
1	K N B	A T O	W O D	G C I	S H E	M R E
2	W M O	A E I	T A N	E S A	Y E V	L E O
3	C R A	W G O	T U I	M S G	H A E	O R E
4	D L P	E O T	O E S	S B E	N U E	Y S M
5	R O A	A R U	R N B	G B L	I A F	E R T

Across

1 _____

2 _____

3 _____

4 _____

5 _____

Down

1 _____

2 _____

3 _____

4 _____

5 _____

6 _____

No 44

L Shapes

Twelve L-shapes like the ones below have been inserted in the grid: each L has a hole in it. There are three pieces of each of the four kinds shown below and any piece might be turned or flipped over before being put in the grid. No two pieces of the same kind touch, even at a corner. The pieces fit together so well that you can't see the spaces: only the holes show. Can you tell where the Ls are?

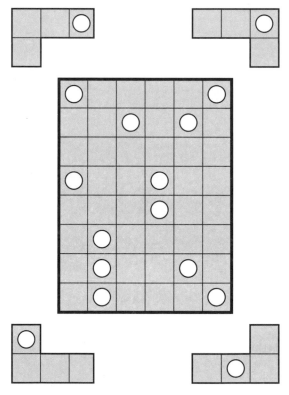

No 45
The Bottom Line

The bottom line of this grid is waiting to be filled. Every square in the solution contains only one letter from rows 1 to 5 above, although two or more squares in the solution may contain the same letter. At the end of every numbered row is a score, which shows:

1. the number of letters placed in the correct finishing position on the bottom line, as indicated by a tick; and

2. the number of letters which appear on the bottom line, but in a different position, as indicated by a cross.

Can you fill each of the four squares with the correct letter?

					Score
1	G	S	W	A	X
2	B	W	M	G	X
3	A	A	G	S	X
4	T	F	F	M	X
5	S	T	A	F	X X
					✓✓✓✓

No 46
Digital Detection

Given just five equations, can you find the value of the letters S-Q U A-R-E? Every letter should be replaced by a different digit. Use the grid to eliminate impossibilities, eg in clue 1, the square of the two-digit number SQ equals the four-digit number UARE, and since no number lower than 32 has a four-digit square, S is greater than 2; and no square ends in 2, 3, 7 or 8, so E cannot be 2, 3, 7 or 8.

1 $SQ^2 = UARE$

2 $S + Q = A$

3 $S - Q = R$

4 $S + R = E$

5 $Q - U = U$

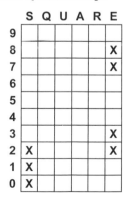

	S	Q	U	A	R	E
9						
8						X
7						X
6						
5						
4						
3					X	X
2	X					X
1	X					
0	X					

No 47
Simple as ABC?

Each of the small squares in the table below contains either A, B or C. Every row, every column, and each of the two long diagonals contains exactly two of each letter. The information in the clues refers only to the squares in that row or column. Only those clues necessary to solve the puzzle are given below. Can you tell the letter in each square?

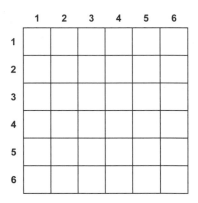

Across

2 Any three adjacent squares contain three different letters

3 The Cs are further left than the Bs

4 The Cs are between the Bs

5 The Cs are between the As

6 The As are between the Bs

Down

1 The As are between the Bs

2 The Cs are between the As

3 The Cs are between the As

4 The As are between the Cs

5 The As are higher than the Cs

6 The As are between the Cs

No 48
Dice-Section

Printed onto every one of the six numbered dice are six letters (one per side), which can be rearranged to form the answer to each clue; however, some sides are invisible to you. Use the clues and write every answer into the grid. When correctly filled, the letters in the shaded squares, reading in the order 1 to 6, will spell out the name of an animal.

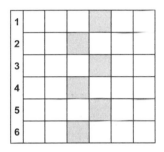

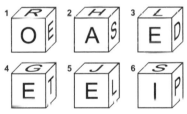

1 Thief

2 Look for

3 Oar used to propel a boat

4 Young swan

5 Precious stones, gems

6 Former name of Iran

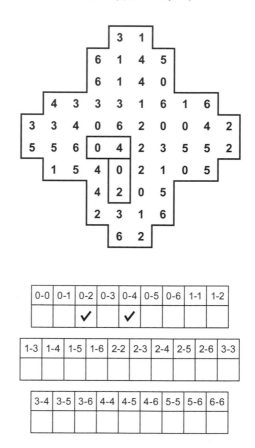

No 49

Domino Fit

A standard set of twenty-eight dominoes has been laid out as shown. Can you draw in the edges of them all? The check-box is provided as an aid and the dominoes already placed may help.

		3	1				
	6	1	4	5			
	6	1	4	0			
4	3	3	3	1	6	1	6
3	3	4	0	6	2	0	0	4	2
5	5	6	0	4	2	3	5	5	2
	1	5	4	0	2	1	0	5
		4	2	0	5
		2	3	1	6
		6	2

0-0	0-1	0-2	0-3	0-4	0-5	0-6	1-1	1-2
		✓		✓				

1-3	1-4	1-5	1-6	2-2	2-3	2-4	2-5	2-6	3-3

3-4	3-5	3-6	4-4	4-5	4-6	5-5	5-6	6-6

No 50
Latin Square

The grid below should be filled with the numbers from 1 to 6, so that each number appears exactly once in every row and every column. The clues refer to the sum of the numbers in the squares mentioned: for example, B C D 1 = 14 would mean that the numbers in squares B1, C1 and D1 add up to 14.

1 A 4 5 = 8

2 A B C 1 = 8

3 B C 2 = 5

4 B C 3 = 8

5 C 1 2 3 = 10

6 C D E 6 = 6

7 D E F 4 = 7

8 D 3 4 = 8

9 E 2 3 = 8

10 E 4 5 6 = 10

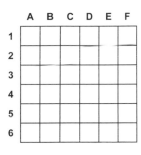

No 51
Shape Spotter

Which is the only shape to appear twice in the picture below? Some shapes overlap others.

No 52
Around the Block

You won't need a starting block to get you under way, because it isn't a race! Just arrange the six-letter solutions to the clues into the six blocks around each clue number. Write the answers in a clockwise or anticlockwise direction and you'll find that the last answer fits into the first; the problem is to decide in which square to put the first letter of each word…

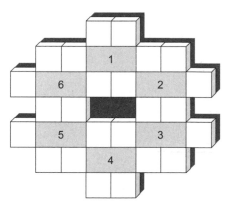

1 Plant commonly used in hedging

2 Try very hard

3 Reddish-brown color

4 Nocturnal marsupial

5 Easy, not complicated

6 Place of incarceration

No 53

Around the Clock

Travel around the clock, one hour at a time, making 12 words all ending with the central letter. The letters to be placed in the empty squares are listed in the segment clockwise of the number to be filled. We've completed one already, in order to get you off to a timely start…

Now take the central letter of every even-numbered word and rearrange these to form another, meaning: a moment in time.

____ ____ ____ ____ ____ ____

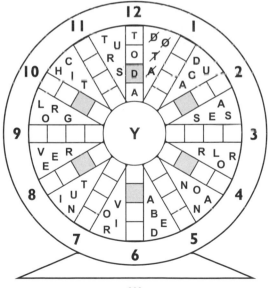

Numberfit

Can you fit all the listed numbers into the grid? One number is already in place.

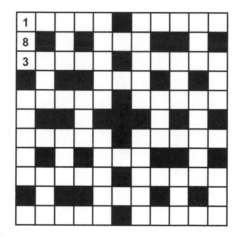

3 digits		5 digits	
104	496	10732	41310
182	498	13144	51690
183 ✓	541	14744	54312
195	666	21565	54986
290	715	24740	55435
323	794	28222	67805
402	939	34179	85647
461		35162	86544
464		35467	96492

No 55
Ring-Words

From the 32 segments below, find 16 eight-letter words by pairing one set of four letters with another. All of the segments must be used once only.

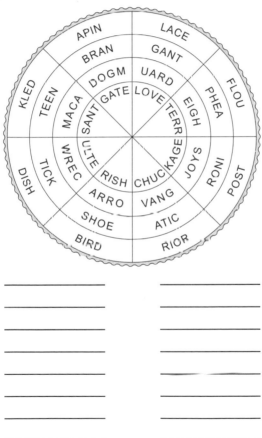

_____   _____

_____   _____

_____   _____

_____   _____

_____   _____

_____   _____

_____   _____

_____   _____

A Matching Pair

Only two of these snapshots of a tiger are identical in every way. Can you spot the matching pair?

No 57

Geography Spiral

Solve the clues in the normal way and enter them into the grid in a clockwise spiral. The last letter of each word is the first letter of the next. When finished, the letters in the shaded squares can be rearranged to form the name of a US state.

1 Country which shares a border with Chile (9)

2 Group of islands to the west of Portugal (6)

3 Flat grassland in tropical or subtropical regions (8)

4 Large bay in northern Canada (6)

5 World's longest river (4)

6 Capital city of Alberta, Canada (8)

7 European kingdom (6)

8 Californian national park (0)

9 River which flows through Iraq (9)

10 World's largest desert (6)

11 Seaport and capital of South Australia (8)

12 Extensive marshes of Florida (10)

13 Country of which Damascus is the capital city (5)

No 58

Magic Squares

Use the letters to the side of each grid to fill the crossword completely, in such a way that the words reading across are exactly the same as those reading downwards. For both crosswords, three letters have been given as a starter.

A A ~~D~~ D D | D | E | | | |
~~E~~ ~~E~~ E E E | E | | | | |
H I I I I
L L L L L
O S S V V

| M | A | | | |
| A | | | | |

~~A~~ ~~A~~ A A C
C E E F H
H I I L L
L L ~~M~~ O R
R R R V W

Sidewords

Start from either the top left square and follow a path downwards or from the bottom left square and follow a path upwards; a letter in a square is the same, no matter at which position you begin. Can you find the two sequences of words to match the clues?

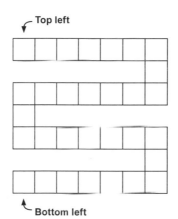

Clues from top left

1 Showy garden flower (6)

2 Low-fat Greek cheese (4)

3 Fly which transmits sleeping sickness (6)

4 Woman in charge of a hospital (6)

5 Sicilian volcano (4)

6 Light two-wheeled carriages (5)

Clues from bottom left

1 Austere (7)

2 High male singing voice (5)

3 Most docile (6)

4 Entire assets (6)

5 Give out or break down (4)

6 Possessed (3)

No 60
Summing up

Arrange each of the numbers 4, 6, 7 and 9, as well as one each of the symbols – (minus), x (times) and + (plus) once only in every row and column to arrive at the answer at the end of the row or column.

6	x	4	–	7	+	9	=	26
							=	16
							=	22
							=	58
=		=		=		=		
77		25		13		85		

No 61
Total Concentration

The numbers in each horizontal row add up to the totals to the right and those in each vertical column add up to the totals along the bottom.

The two longest diagonal lines also add up to the totals at the bottom. Your task is to fill in the missing numbers, which are all between 1 and 15 inclusive, and any number may be used more than once.

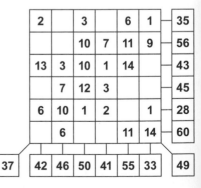

290

No 62
Wordwheel

How many words of three or more letters can you make from those in the wheel, without using plurals, abbreviations or proper nouns? The central letter must appear once in every word and no letter in a section of the wheel may be used more than once. There is at least one nine-letter word in the wheel.

No 63
Logi-5

The letters C, A, N, D and Y should appear once in each row, as well as once in each column. Every heavily outlined shape of five smaller squares should also contain each of the letters C, A, N, D and Y. Can you complete the grid?

A				
			C	
Y				
	D			N

No 64
Balancing the Scales

Given that scales A and B balance perfectly, how many buckets should be placed into the right-hand pan of scale C to make it balance?

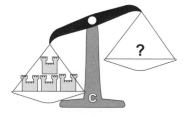

No 65
X Marks the Spot

Can you fit all the listed words into the grid? One is already in place.

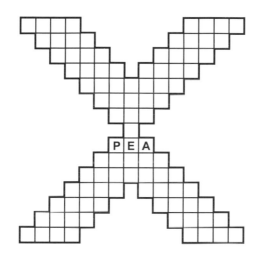

2 letters	4 letters	KNEW	SWIM
BE	ACID	KNIT	TEAM
IF	AREA	LAID	TRAY
NO	ASIA	LIES	WALK
TO	BEAM	LOAF	WASH
	BEST	OARS	
3 letters	BRAY	ONES	5 letters
ERA	BUSY	ORAL	ASHES
KIT	DEBT	PLAY	BLACK
PEA	DEEP	PLUS	
TEN	EAST	RUIN	7 letters
TUB	GEAR	SORT	SEAWEED
WAS	HERE	STEW	TEASING
	KEEN	STOP	WHEREAS

Word Ladders

Change one letter at a time (but don't change the position of any letter) to make a new word – and move from the word at the top of the ladder to the word at the bottom using the exact number of rungs provided in each case.

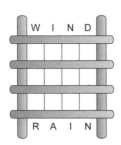

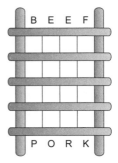

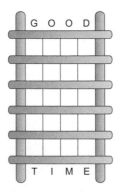

Chain Letters

Each of the groups of letters below consists of an eight-letter word reading either clockwise or anticlockwise. Can you identify them all?

1

```
R  R  A
E     N
B  A  T
```

2

```
A  I  R
B     E
A  C  T
```

3

```
H  Y  T
R     H
C  I  M
```

4

```
Y  C  L
C     A
L  I  C
```

5

```
T  N  I
M     O
E  N  T
```

6

```
R  L  I
A     E
N  G  R
```

7

```
V  I  L
A     A
T  E  S
```

8

```
A  C  T
N     I
I  N  O
```

No 68

Word Power

Can you decide which of the four alternatives is the correct definition of the word

MOREEN

a   A heavy type of fabric used especially in upholstery

b   Unlawfully distilled Irish whisky

c   A type of edible fungus, much prized for its nut-like flavor

d   A cultivated type of sour cherry, used in the making of jam

No 69
Coded Quote

Decipher the code to reveal quotation attributed to James Dent. Any letter which isn't used in the code has already been placed into the grid.

Code =	A	B	C	D	E	F	G	H	I	J	K	L	M
Letter =											V		

Code =	N	O	P	Q	R	S	T	U	V	W	X	Y	Z
Letter =					X				J		Q		

B   Q F S G F D U   T V N N F S

E B Z   J T   X I F O   U I F

T V O   J T   T I J O J O H ,

U I F   C S F F A F   J T

C M P X J O H ,   U I F

C J S E T   B S F   T J O H J O H ,

B O E   U I F   M B X O

N P X F S   J T   C S P L F O .

296

Whatever Next?

What number should appear in place of the question mark in the sequence below?

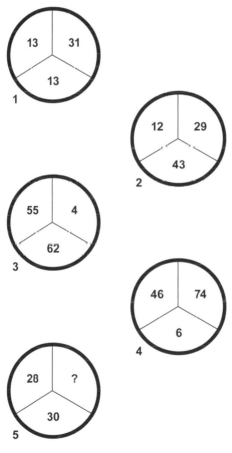

Pyramid Plus

Every brick in this pyramid contains a number which is the sum of the two numbers below it, so that F=A+B, etc. Just work out the missing numbers!

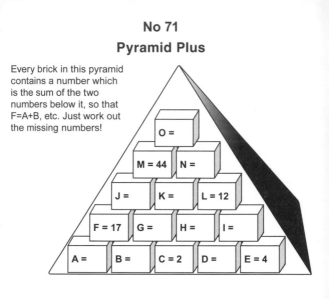

No 72
Critical Thinking Values

Each of the ten different letters in the phrase CRITICAL THINKING has been given a different value from 0 to 9, so C + R + I + T + A + L + H + N + K + G = 45. Your challenge is to find the value of each letter, given the clues below:

1 N + I + A + G + A + R + A = 39

2 T + R + A + C + K = 21

3 C + H + A + L + K = 16

4 K + I + N + G = 19

5 G + R + I + N = 27

6 C + H + A + I + N = 26

7 C + A + R + T = 20

8 G + R + A + N + T = 30

9 H + A + L + T = 12

Letter =	C	R	I	T	A	L	H	N	K	G
Value =										

No 73
What's It Worth?

Each of the four symbols stands for a different number. In order to reach the total at the end of each row, what is the value of the heart, club, diamond, and spade?

♦	♥	♣	♠	= 21
	♠	♦		= 12
	♦	♣	♦	= 14
♦	♠		♠	= 20

No 74
Mental Blocks

Solve this multiplication problem and write the numerical answer into the top set of boxes below the line. Then use the decoder to the left of the sum, writing the letters into the boxes beneath the numbers in order to find two words.

0	T
1	X
2	A
3	M
4	S

5	C
6	O
7	E
8	H
9	B

3	2	0	5	8

x | 3 |
|---|
| M |

Hexafit

Can you place these six words into the hexagons? To fit them all in, some will have to be entered clockwise and others anticlockwise around the numbers. Two letters have already been put into position.

BANANA

BEFALL

DANCED

JABBED

KILLER

LADDER

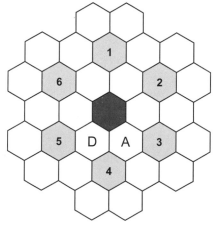

No 76
Do It Yourself!

In this crossword puzzle, the clues are listed in alphabetical order and there are no black squares in the grid. Your task is to black out the unwanted squares, so that the clues can be matched to the words in the finished puzzle.

T	A	X	I	S	A	R	O	U	N	D
A	M	P	N	O	T	E	D	S	A	Y
K	I	N	D	S	E	N	D	U	R	E
E	D	O	I	A	K	A	Y	A	K	I
N	O	R	A	L	E	N	Y	L	O	N
D	O	E	S	I	N	N	S	L	O	G
O	F	T	E	N	S	Y	O	Y	O	R
U	P	U	R	E	S	T	W	E	T	A
B	O	R	I	N	G	K	N	E	W	S
L	E	N	D	Γ	U	S	E	R	O	I
E	A	S	I	L	Y	Ⅽ	D	A	T	A

About
As a rule
Brings back
By word of mouth
Child's nurse
Child's stringed toy
Coloring by staining
Consumed
Consumption
Continent
Country, capital New Delhi
Fabric made from flax
Facts given
Frequently

Genial
Had possession
Increase twofold
Live on, persist
Man-made fiber
Minicab
Negative word
Remove
Rope used to brace a tent
Tavern
Tedious
Tidings
Without any trouble

Box Clever

When the shape below is folded to form a cube, just one of the lettered alternatives can be produced. Which one?

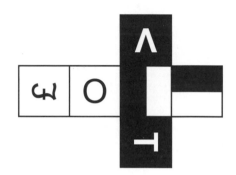

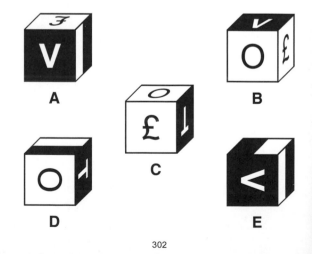

A

B

C

D

E

No 78

Sunbathing

Three women have laid out their towels as shown in the picture below, for a session of sunbathing. Given just four clues which contain all of the information you will need, can you solve this logic puzzle, discovering the name of the owner of each towel, together with the color of her bikini and towel?

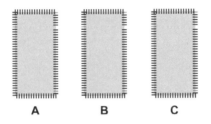

A   B   C

1 The three colors are lemon, pink and blue and no woman has a bikini of the same color as that of her towel.

2 Towel A (which is lemon in color) doesn't belong to Kate, whose bikini isn't lemon or pink.

3 The woman who owns towel B hasn't a blue bikini.

4 Towel A is furthest left. Charen's towel is further right than Pauline's.

	Name	Bikini color	Towel color
Towel A			
Towel B			
Towel C			

303

No 79
Egg Timer

Can you complete this puzzle in the time it takes to hard-boil an egg? The answers to the clues are anagrams of the words immediately above and below, plus or minus one letter.

1 Very hard rock, often pink in color

2 Precious stone

3 Representative

4 Orderly, tidy

5 Stolen, removed

6 Leg ornament

7 Most limp and dull

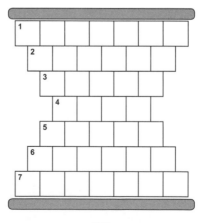

No 80

Latin Square

The grid should be filled with numbers from 1 to 6, so that each appears just once in every row and column. The clues refer to the digit totals in the squares, eg B C D 4 = 8 means that the numbers in squares B4, C4 and D4 add up to 8.

1 A 4 5 6 = 11   **6** D E 1 = 3

2 B C D 4 = 8   **7** D E 5 = 11

3 C 3 4 = 4   **8** D E F 2 = 12

4 C D E 6 = 9   **9** E 3 4 5 = 11

5 D 5 6 = 9   **10** E F 4 = 10

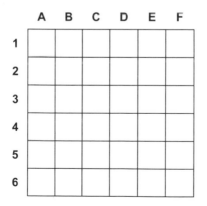

Fallen Idols

The letters in the vertical columns belong in the squares immediately beneath them, but not necessarily in the given order. When entered correctly, they reveal the names of four well-known film stars.

B	A	E	I		A			C	A	A	K	H	A	M
D	A	L	N	D	A			J	A	A	L	L	E	N
G	L	R	T	D	L	A		M	C	C	S	S	O	R
W	U	V	T	E	R	M		N	C	T	T	T	U	U

↓ ↓ ↓ ↓ ↓ ↓ ↓   ↓ ↓ ↓ ↓ ↓ ↓ ↓

(empty answer grid)

No 82

Writing Letters

Starting with the letter A, add a letter to make first a two-letter word, then add another letter to these two to make a three-letter word, then add another letter to these three to make a four-letter word, etc, rearranging the letters if necessary every time, until you have an eight-letter word for which the clue is: Animal, living organism.

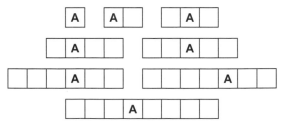

No 83
Couplets

The picture is of a central circle surrounded by shapes, linked to form six sets of three shapes apiece. Can you complete the puzzle by placing each of the two-letter groups below, one per shape, so that every set of three (the central circle, plus the two matching shapes diagonally opposite one another) forms a six-letter word? Whichever pair of letters you place in the central circle will appear in the middle of every word.

PE   MA

US   UN   TR

EN   BE

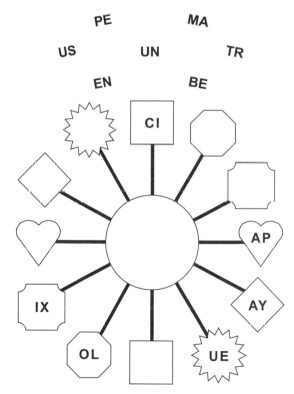

No 84

Character Assignation

Fill in the Across clues in this crossword in the normal way. Then read down the diagonal line of eight squares, to reveal: A character from Harriet Beecher Stowe's *Uncle Tom's Cabin*.

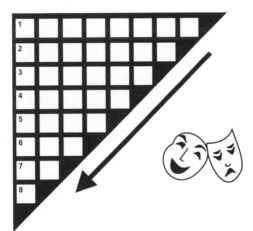

1 Provide with an incentive for action

2 Source of difficulty which needs to be resolved

3 Haphazard, depending on chance

4 Topic, subject

5 Spoken

6 Travel on runners over snow

7 Atop

8 The equivalent of MC2

Character: ___ ___ ___ ___ ___ ___ ___ ___

No 85

Alphabet Soup

Ladle the letters from the soup tureen and fit one into each of the 26 empty squares in the grid below, so that the finished result is a complete crossword containing words. All of the letters in the tureen must be used – thus no letter is used more than once.

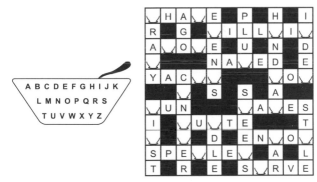

ABCDEFGHIJK
LMNOPQRS
TUVWXYZ

No 86

It Doesn't Add Up

In the grid, leave 42 of the 49 numbers exactly where they are, but change the positions of the remaining seven in such a way that in every row, column, and long diagonal line of seven squares, the seven numbers total exactly 126.

3	9	29	30	19	15	12
32	25	19	10	13	6	20
15	12	9	22	27	24	13
22	30	26	18	10	14	7
13	8	11	6	26	32	31
4	23	29	25	19	9	16
28	15	16	14	13	25	28

Leftovers

Cross off words in the box as indicated by the instructions. The remaining words will form a common saying when read from left to right and line by line.

Cross off all palindromes.

Cross off all anagrams of Elgar.

Cross off all words with two Os.

Cross off all breeds of dog.

Cross off all words with no vowels.

Cross off all synonyms of 'laugh'.

Cross off all types of fabric.

Cross off all countries.

Cross off all male forenames.

GLARE	KAYAK	CHORTLE	BEAGLE
MYTH	DENIM	BAD	TOMMY
SPAIN	FRANK	LEVEL	LARGE
NEWS	KIMONOS	ITALY	SHY
CHIFFON	GIGGLE	SPANIEL	PEEP
REFER	ROBERT	MOTOR	MEXICO
EROSION	REGAL	VELVET	TRAVELS
NYLON	FRANCE	PETER	TENET
CORGI	FAST	CIVIC	SILK
REDDER	SNICKER	CRYPT	BOOTH

No 88
Roundword

Write the answer to each clue in a clockwise direction. Every answer overlaps the next by two letters and starts in its numbered section. The solution to the final clue ends with the letter in the first section.

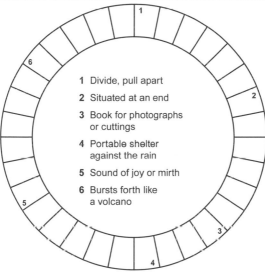

1 Divide, pull apart

2 Situated at an end

3 Book for photographs or cuttings

4 Portable shelter against the rain

5 Sound of joy or mirth

6 Bursts forth like a volcano

No 89
Word Power

Can you decide which of the four alternatives is the correct definition of the word

MUSETTE

a A species of seabird inhabiting the North Pacific

b A model made by an architect or sculptor, intended as an example

c A picture painted and inserted into a locket

d A small bagpipe formerly popular in France

Deletions

There are 11 countries and a quote from Francis Bacon hidden in this grid. Taking one letter from each box, cross off the six-letter words in the Across rows. Do the same for the five-letter words in the Down columns. When you have finished, the letters remaining will reveal a quote reading from left-to-right and row by row.

	1	2	3	4	5	6
1	E M T	E H N	E S X	I R Y	L C E	M J O
2	G E J	D O E	R P Y	E I D	I A S	N W A
3	O C Y	A P R	A S N	E A M	D B T	H P A
4	A P K	U N A	I W T	H E A	I E Y	A T D
5	B I T	L R S	A E N	A N Z	A I S	N E L

Across

1 _____

2 _____

3 _____

4 _____

5 _____

Down

1 _____

2 _____

3 _____

4 _____

5 _____

6 _____

No 91
L Shapes

Twelve L-shapes like the ones below have been inserted in the grid: each L has a hole in it. There are three pieces of each of the four kinds shown below and any piece might be turned or flipped over before being put in the grid. No two pieces of the same kind touch, even at a corner. The pieces fit together so well that you can't see the spaces: only the holes show. Can you tell where the Ls are?

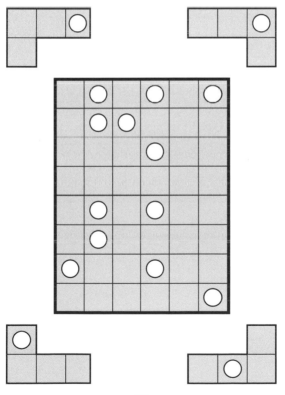

No 92

The Bottom Line

The bottom line of this grid is waiting to be filled. Every square in the solution contains only one letter from rows 1 to 5 above, although two or more squares in the solution may contain the same letter. At the end of every numbered row is a score, which shows:

1 the number of letters placed in the correct finishing position on the bottom line, as indicated by a tick; and

2 the number of letters which appear on the bottom line, but in a different position, as indicated by a cross.

Can you fill each of the four squares with the correct letter?

					Score
1	P	L	A	H	X ✓
2	Z	F	P	B	X ✓
3	T	Z	L	A	X ✓
4	B	T	L	P	X ✓
5	H	Z	A	F	X ✓
					✓✓✓✓

No 93

Digital Detection

Given just four equations, can you find the value of the letters in D-I-G-I-T-S?

Every letter should be replaced by a different digit. Use the grid to eliminate impossibilities, eg in clue 1, the square of the two-digit number DI equals the four-digit number GIST, and since no number lower than 32 has a four-digit square, D is greater than 2; and no square ends in 2, 3, 7 or 8, so T cannot be 2, 3, 7 or 8.

1 $DI^2 = GIST$

2 $G + S = I$

3 $I - D = T$

4 $T + T = S$

	D	I	G	T	S
9					
8				X	
7				X	
6					
5					
4					
3				X	
2	X			X	
1	X				
0	X				

No 94
Simple as ABC?

Each of the small squares in the table below contains either A, B or C. Every row, every column, and each of the two long diagonals contains exactly two of each letter. The information in the clues refers only to the squares in that row or column. Only those clues necessary to solve the puzzle are given below. Can you tell the letter in each square?

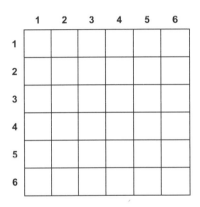

Across

1 The As are further left than the Bs

2 The Bs are further left than the Cs

3 The Bs are between the As

5 The Cs are between the As

6 The As are between the Bs

Down

1 The Bs are between the As

3 Each A is immediately next to and below a C

4 The As are lower than the Bs

6 Each A is next to and above a B

No 95

Dice-Section

Printed onto every one of the six numbered dice are six letters (one per side), which can be rearranged to form the answer to each clue; however, some sides are invisible to you. Use the clues and write every answer into the grid. When correctly filled, the letters in the shaded squares, reading in the order 1 to 6, will spell out the name of an animal.

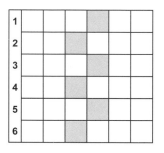

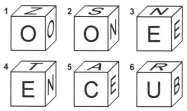

1 Take a nap

2 Extremely short time period

3 Rely (upon)

4 Soundless

5 Small recess in a room

6 Dairy product

No 96
Domino Fit

A standard set of twenty-eight dominoes has been laid out as shown. Can you draw in the edges of them all? The check-box is provided as an aid and the domino already placed may help.

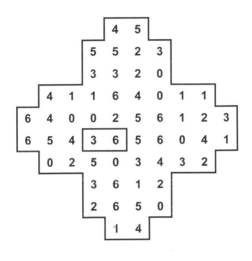

0 0	0 1	0 2	0 3	0-4	0-5	0-6	1-1	1-2

1-3	1-4	1-5	1-6	2-2	2-3	2-4	2-5	2-6	3-3

3-4	3-5	3-6	4-4	4-5	4-6	5-5	5-6	6-6
		✓						

317

No 97
Latin Square

The grid below should be filled with the numbers from 1 to 6, so that each number appears exactly once in every row and every column. The clues refer to the sum of the numbers in the squares mentioned: for example, A B C 2 = 11 would mean that the numbers in squares A2, B2 and C2 add up to 11.

1 A 2 3 = 8

2 A 4 5 6 = 10

3 A B C 2 = 11

4 B C 5 = 3

5 B C D 3 = 7

6 C 1 2 = 8

7 C 4 5 6 = 11

8 D E 6 = 8

9 D E F 5 = 14

10 E 1 2 3 = 8

11 F 2 3 = 8

12 F 4 5 = 8

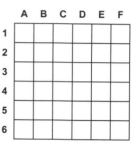

No 98
Shape Spotter

Which is the only shape to appear twice in the picture below? Some shapes overlap others.

Ring-Words

From the 32 segments below, find 16 eight-letter words by pairing one set of four letters with another. All of the segments must be used once only.

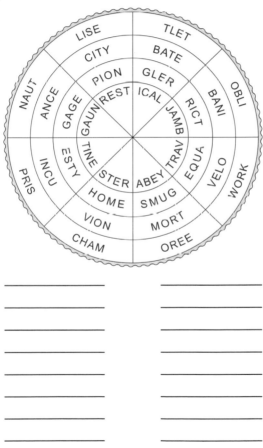

_____   _____

_____   _____

_____   _____

_____   _____

_____   _____

_____   _____

_____   _____

_____   _____

No 100
Around the Clock

Travel around the clock, one hour at a time, making 12 words all ending with the central letter. The letters to be placed in the empty squares are listed in the segment clockwise of the number to be filled. We've completed one already, in order to get you off to a timely start...

Now take the central letter of every even-numbered word and rearrange these to form another, meaning: take a trip.

_____ _____ _____ _____ _____ _____

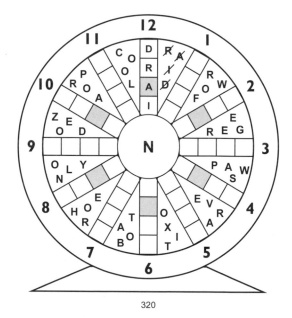

No 101
Around the Block

You won't need a starting block to get you under way, because it isn't a race! Just arrange the six-letter solutions to the clues into the six blocks around each clue number. Write the answers in a clockwise or anticlockwise direction and you'll find that the last answer fits into the first; the problem is to decide in which square to put the first letter of each word…

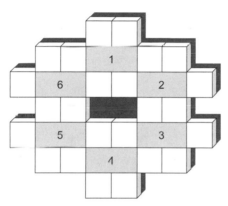

1 Look out!

2 Country in which Tel Aviv is situated

3 Precious metal, symbol Ag

4 Newspaper chief

5 Damaged by decay

6 Digit, figure

No 102
Numberfit

Can you fit all the listed numbers into the grid?

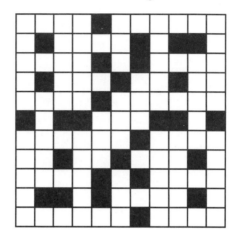

2 digits	3 digits	4 digits	5 digits	6 digits
27	212	1094	14644	312744
28	312	1601	31294	376943
41	387	2653	36784	387941
84	711	6134	49395	742537
	831	6536	54269	
	854	7435	61927	
	882	7640	63440	
	974	7897	65297	
		9032	66070	
		9220	68772	
			78903	
			92493	

Solutions

Solutions

No 1

8	9	7	6	4	2	3	1	5
5	1	4	3	9	7	6	8	2
3	6	2	5	1	8	4	7	9
6	2	9	8	7	1	5	4	3
7	3	5	4	6	9	8	2	1
4	8	1	2	5	3	9	6	7
9	4	6	1	2	5	7	3	8
2	7	3	9	8	4	1	5	6
1	5	8	7	3	6	2	9	4

No 2

9	7	1	5	3	8	4	6	2
6	5	3	9	4	2	7	1	8
4	8	2	7	1	6	5	9	3
3	2	4	6	5	1	8	7	9
8	1	7	2	9	4	6	3	5
5	6	9	3	8	7	2	4	1
1	9	6	8	7	5	3	2	4
7	4	5	1	2	3	9	8	6
2	3	8	4	6	9	1	5	7

No 3

2	5	3	4	6	9	8	7	1
7	9	4	3	1	8	6	5	2
8	1	6	5	2	7	9	3	4
6	3	5	7	8	2	1	4	9
9	2	7	6	4	1	5	8	3
4	8	1	9	5	3	2	6	7
3	7	8	2	9	5	4	1	6
5	4	2	1	7	6	3	9	8
1	6	9	8	3	4	7	2	5

No 4

1	9	8	2	4	3	6	7	5
3	7	2	5	8	6	4	9	1
4	6	5	7	1	9	8	3	2
8	2	6	3	7	5	1	4	9
9	3	4	8	6	1	5	2	7
7	5	1	9	2	4	3	6	8
2	1	9	4	3	8	7	5	6
5	8	3	6	9	7	2	1	4
6	4	7	1	5	2	9	8	3

No 5

8	9	4	7	3	1	5	2	6
2	7	1	6	5	8	9	4	3
5	3	6	9	2	4	1	8	7
9	8	3	2	6	7	4	5	1
1	6	5	4	8	9	3	7	2
7	4	2	3	1	5	8	6	9
4	1	7	5	9	6	2	3	8
6	2	9	8	4	3	7	1	5
3	5	8	1	7	2	6	9	4

No 6

7	8	1	5	3	9	4	2	6
5	6	2	4	8	1	9	7	3
9	4	3	2	6	7	1	5	8
3	1	7	6	9	5	8	4	2
8	2	9	1	4	3	5	6	7
6	5	4	8	7	2	3	9	1
1	9	8	7	5	6	2	3	4
2	7	5	3	1	4	6	8	9
4	3	6	9	2	8	7	1	5

Solutions

No 7

6	5	9	3	8	4	1	7	2
8	2	4	1	7	9	6	5	3
7	1	3	6	5	2	4	9	8
4	9	8	5	1	6	2	3	7
2	3	6	8	9	7	5	4	1
1	7	5	4	2	3	9	8	6
3	4	1	9	6	8	7	2	5
9	6	7	2	3	5	8	1	4
5	8	2	7	4	1	3	6	9

No 8

2	5	3	6	9	8	7	4	1
1	8	9	7	3	4	6	5	2
7	4	6	2	5	1	3	9	8
3	9	1	4	6	2	5	8	7
8	6	5	9	1	7	4	2	3
4	2	7	3	8	5	9	1	6
6	3	2	1	4	9	8	7	5
9	7	8	5	2	6	1	3	4
5	1	4	8	7	3	2	6	9

No 9

2	7	1	8	9	3	6	5	4
4	3	6	7	2	5	8	1	9
9	8	5	1	4	6	7	3	2
3	6	9	5	7	8	4	2	1
8	4	2	3	1	9	5	7	6
1	5	7	4	6	2	3	9	8
7	2	8	6	3	1	9	4	5
6	9	3	2	5	4	1	8	7
5	1	4	9	8	7	2	6	3

No 10

2	7	8	9	1	5	6	3	4
4	1	3	8	7	6	2	5	9
9	6	5	2	4	3	8	1	7
5	9	1	3	8	7	4	2	6
3	8	7	4	6	2	1	9	5
6	2	4	1	5	9	7	8	3
7	4	2	5	3	8	9	6	1
1	3	9	6	2	4	5	7	8
8	5	6	7	9	1	3	4	2

No 11

3	6	1	2	7	9	5	4	8
2	8	9	6	5	4	3	7	1
4	5	7	8	1	3	2	9	6
8	4	6	5	9	7	1	3	2
7	3	2	1	4	6	8	5	9
1	9	5	3	8	2	4	6	7
5	2	4	7	6	1	9	8	3
6	1	8	9	3	5	7	2	4
9	7	3	4	2	8	6	1	5

No 12

3	6	9	2	7	8	1	5	4
7	4	1	5	3	9	2	6	8
2	8	5	1	6	4	9	7	3
5	9	3	4	2	7	6	8	1
4	1	6	8	5	3	7	9	2
8	2	7	9	1	6	4	3	5
9	3	8	6	4	1	5	2	7
1	7	2	3	9	5	8	4	6
6	5	4	7	8	2	3	1	9

4	6	8
3	1	7
5	9	2

Solutions

No 13

7	3	1	9	6	2	8	5	4
9	6	5	4	8	7	3	2	1
4	8	2	5	3	1	7	9	6
6	4	9	1	5	8	2	3	7
2	5	3	6	7	4	1	8	9
8	1	7	2	9	3	4	6	5
1	7	6	3	2	5	9	4	8
3	9	8	7	4	6	5	1	2
5	2	4	8	1	9	6	7	3

No 14

3	1	9	8	5	6	7	2	4
5	8	4	2	3	7	6	1	9
7	6	2	9	1	4	5	8	3
2	3	7	1	6	8	9	4	5
8	5	6	3	4	9	1	7	2
9	4	1	5	7	2	3	6	8
6	2	5	4	9	1	8	3	7
1	9	8	7	2	3	4	5	6
4	7	3	6	8	5	2	9	1

No 15

4	9	6	5	1	8	7	3	2
8	1	3	2	4	7	5	9	6
5	7	2	3	6	9	8	1	4
6	5	8	9	3	1	2	4	7
7	2	1	8	5	4	3	6	9
9	3	4	7	2	6	1	5	8
1	8	7	6	9	3	4	2	5
3	6	5	4	7	2	9	8	1
2	4	9	1	8	5	6	7	3

No 16

4	8	3	2	5	9	1	7	6
6	1	5	8	3	7	4	2	9
2	9	7	1	4	6	8	5	3
9	3	6	4	7	2	5	8	1
7	5	8	6	1	3	9	4	2
1	4	2	5	9	8	6	3	7
3	6	9	7	8	5	2	1	4
8	7	1	9	2	4	3	6	5
5	2	4	3	6	1	7	9	8

No 17

6	8	5	3	1	4	2	7	9
9	2	1	5	7	6	4	3	8
3	4	7	9	8	2	1	6	5
5	7	3	8	2	1	9	4	6
4	1	6	7	5	9	3	8	2
2	9	8	6	4	3	7	5	1
1	6	2	4	3	5	8	9	7
8	5	4	1	9	7	6	2	3
7	3	9	2	6	8	5	1	4

No 18

5	8	1	3	4	2	9	6	7
9	2	4	8	6	7	1	3	5
3	6	7	5	1	9	8	4	2
6	4	2	9	8	5	7	1	3
7	9	8	4	3	1	2	5	6
1	3	5	7	2	6	4	9	8
8	1	6	2	5	4	3	7	9
2	5	9	1	7	3	6	8	4
4	7	3	6	9	8	5	2	1

Solutions

No 19

7	3	8	6	2	5	9	4	1
5	4	1	9	3	7	8	2	6
9	2	6	1	4	8	5	3	7
6	9	5	3	7	2	4	1	8
2	1	3	8	9	4	6	7	5
4	8	7	5	6	1	2	9	3
3	5	9	4	1	6	7	8	2
1	6	2	7	8	9	3	5	4
0	7	4	2	5	3	1	6	9

No 20

4	2	1	6	5	7	9	3	8
9	8	7	3	2	1	5	6	4
6	5	3	9	4	8	1	2	7
5	9	8	2	6	3	7	4	1
1	7	6	5	8	4	2	9	3
2	3	4	7	1	9	6	8	5
3	1	2	8	7	6	4	5	9
8	4	5	1	9	2	3	7	6
7	6	9	4	3	5	8	1	2

No 21

5	1	3	8	4	9	6	7	2
4	6	9	2	1	7	8	5	3
8	7	2	5	6	3	9	4	1
1	9	6	4	3	8	5	2	7
2	3	4	9	7	5	1	6	8
7	8	5	6	2	1	4	3	9
9	2	1	3	5	4	7	8	6
3	4	7	1	8	6	2	0	5
6	5	8	7	9	2	3	1	4

No 22

4	5	9	7	3	8	2	1	6
3	6	7	1	2	5	4	8	9
8	2	1	6	9	4	3	7	5
6	1	8	5	7	2	9	4	3
7	3	5	4	6	9	1	2	8
2	9	4	3	8	1	6	5	7
5	8	6	2	4	3	7	9	1
9	4	3	8	1	7	5	6	2
1	7	2	9	5	6	8	3	4

No 23

9	5	7	1	4	2	8	6	3
4	8	2	6	3	5	9	1	7
6	3	1	8	9	7	5	4	2
5	2	8	7	1	4	3	9	6
7	1	9	3	5	6	4	2	8
3	4	6	9	2	8	7	5	1
8	9	5	2	7	1	6	3	4
2	7	3	4	6	9	1	8	5
1	6	4	5	8	3	2	7	9

No 24

7	4	3	6	9	1	8	2	5
6	2	5	8	4	3	9	7	1
8	9	1	2	5	7	3	6	4
3	6	9	4	1	8	2	5	7
2	8	7	3	6	5	4	1	9
1	5	4	9	7	2	6	3	8
5	3	6	7	8	4	1	9	2
9	1	8	5	2	6	7	4	3
4	7	2	1	3	9	5	8	6

4	6	8
3	1	7
5	9	2

Solutions

No 25

2	1	9	4	3	5	8	6	7
6	4	8	7	1	9	3	2	5
5	3	7	6	2	8	9	1	4
1	9	6	2	8	7	4	5	3
8	7	2	5	4	3	6	9	1
3	5	4	9	6	1	2	7	8
4	6	1	3	5	2	7	8	9
7	8	3	1	9	6	5	4	2
9	2	5	8	7	4	1	3	6

No 26

2	6	9	1	3	5	8	4	7
3	7	1	8	6	4	2	9	5
5	4	8	9	7	2	6	3	1
4	5	3	2	1	7	9	6	8
9	2	7	6	4	8	5	1	3
1	8	6	5	9	3	4	7	2
6	1	2	3	8	9	7	5	4
7	3	5	4	2	6	1	8	9
8	9	4	7	5	1	3	2	6

No 27

4	1	9	3	6	2	5	7	8
7	8	6	1	4	5	3	9	2
2	3	5	8	7	9	1	4	6
9	5	4	6	8	3	7	2	1
3	6	2	7	9	1	8	5	4
1	7	8	2	5	4	6	3	9
8	4	3	5	2	6	9	1	7
6	2	1	9	3	7	4	8	5
5	9	7	4	1	8	2	6	3

No 28

6	4	2	5	3	7	9	1	8
5	7	1	2	9	8	4	3	6
8	3	9	4	6	1	5	2	7
9	1	8	3	5	2	7	6	4
2	5	4	6	7	9	3	8	1
3	6	7	1	8	4	2	9	5
4	8	3	9	1	5	6	7	2
1	9	5	7	2	6	8	4	3
7	2	6	8	4	3	1	5	9

No 29

3	9	8	1	4	5	2	6	7
2	5	7	9	8	6	3	1	4
1	4	6	2	7	3	9	5	8
5	8	2	3	6	9	4	7	1
4	6	9	7	1	8	5	3	2
7	1	3	4	5	2	8	9	6
8	2	5	6	9	7	1	4	3
9	7	1	8	3	4	6	2	5
6	3	4	5	2	1	7	8	9

No 30

3	2	7	8	6	1	4	9	5
9	6	5	4	2	7	3	8	1
4	1	8	3	9	5	2	7	6
1	9	2	7	4	8	6	5	3
7	8	6	2	5	3	1	4	9
5	3	4	9	1	6	8	2	7
2	4	3	1	7	9	5	6	8
8	5	9	6	3	2	7	1	4
6	7	1	5	8	4	9	3	2

5	1	4
8	3	6
9	2	7

Solutions

No 31

9	5	2	4	7	1	3	6	8
8	1	3	6	2	5	4	7	9
4	6	7	3	8	9	2	1	5
2	7	8	9	3	6	1	5	4
5	3	6	1	4	8	7	9	2
1	9	4	7	5	2	6	8	3
6	2	9	5	1	3	8	4	7
3	4	1	8	9	7	5	2	6
7	8	5	2	6	4	9	3	1

No 32

5	6	9	7	1	3	2	4	8
2	7	8	5	4	6	1	3	9
1	4	3	9	8	2	7	5	6
8	9	2	4	7	1	5	6	3
4	1	6	3	9	5	8	7	2
7	3	5	6	2	8	4	9	1
3	5	1	2	6	4	9	8	7
6	2	7	8	5	9	3	1	4
9	8	4	1	3	7	6	2	5

No 33

2	9	6	4	7	8	3	1	5
3	8	7	2	1	5	6	4	9
4	5	1	6	3	9	8	7	2
1	2	4	9	8	3	5	6	7
6	3	9	5	4	7	1	2	8
8	7	5	1	2	6	4	9	3
7	4	2	8	5	1	9	3	6
5	6	3	7	9	4	2	0	1
9	1	8	3	6	2	7	5	4

No 34

1	3	5	4	2	0	7	8	6
7	6	9	3	1	8	2	4	5
8	2	4	5	7	6	1	3	9
9	8	7	6	5	1	3	2	4
6	4	1	2	8	3	5	9	7
3	5	2	9	4	7	6	1	8
4	1	3	7	9	5	8	6	2
5	9	6	8	3	2	4	7	1
2	7	8	1	6	4	9	5	3

No 35

3	1	2	8	7	9	5	4	6
6	8	9	5	2	4	3	7	1
4	5	7	1	3	6	9	8	2
1	7	8	6	5	3	2	9	4
5	2	4	7	9	8	1	6	3
9	3	6	4	1	2	7	5	8
8	9	5	2	6	1	4	3	7
7	4	1	3	8	5	6	2	9
2	6	3	9	4	7	8	1	5

No 36

7	9	3	8	1	2	5	6	4
5	6	2	4	3	7	1	8	9
4	8	1	5	9	6	7	3	2
6	7	4	3	5	9	2	1	8
1	5	9	2	8	4	3	7	6
2	3	8	6	7	1	9	4	5
3	2	5	7	4	8	6	9	1
8	1	6	9	2	3	4	5	7
9	4	7	1	6	5	8	2	3

4	6	8
3	1	7
5	9	2

Solutions

No 37

1	8	9	5	2	3	7	6	4
4	7	5	6	9	8	3	1	2
3	6	2	4	1	7	8	5	9
8	2	4	7	3	1	6	9	5
9	3	6	8	5	2	1	4	7
5	1	7	9	6	4	2	3	8
7	4	1	3	8	9	5	2	6
6	9	3	2	7	5	4	8	1
2	5	8	1	4	6	9	7	3

No 38

1	3	4	7	5	8	6	9	2
5	6	7	2	3	9	4	8	1
2	8	9	6	4	1	5	7	3
8	9	3	4	7	2	1	6	5
7	2	5	8	1	6	3	4	9
4	1	6	3	9	5	8	2	7
6	5	1	9	2	4	7	3	8
3	4	2	1	8	7	9	5	6
9	7	8	5	6	3	2	1	4

No 39

1	6	9	8	4	7	3	2	5
4	7	5	9	2	3	1	6	8
2	8	3	6	5	1	9	7	4
8	3	2	4	7	5	6	9	1
5	4	7	1	6	9	8	3	2
6	9	1	2	3	8	4	5	7
9	2	4	5	1	6	7	8	3
7	1	6	3	8	2	5	4	9
3	5	8	7	9	4	2	1	6

No 40

5	4	2	1	8	6	7	3	9
7	3	9	2	4	5	6	8	1
6	8	1	9	3	7	5	4	2
4	2	6	7	1	8	3	9	5
8	1	7	5	9	3	4	2	6
3	9	5	6	2	4	8	1	7
1	7	3	4	5	9	2	6	8
2	6	8	3	7	1	9	5	4
9	5	4	8	6	2	1	7	3

No 41

7	6	3	8	9	5	1	4	2
8	4	2	3	6	1	9	7	5
9	5	1	2	4	7	3	8	6
3	1	5	4	8	2	6	9	7
4	8	6	7	1	9	2	5	3
2	7	9	6	5	3	4	1	8
5	2	4	1	3	8	7	6	9
6	9	7	5	2	4	8	3	1
1	3	8	9	7	6	5	2	4

No 42

1	3	9	8	6	5	4	2	7
5	7	8	2	1	4	3	9	6
4	2	6	7	3	9	5	1	8
3	8	2	6	4	1	9	7	5
9	5	1	3	7	2	8	6	4
6	4	7	5	9	8	2	3	1
8	1	3	4	2	7	6	5	9
7	6	4	9	5	3	1	8	2
2	9	5	1	8	6	7	4	3

Solutions

No 43

3	4	7	1	8	5	2	9	6
9	8	6	7	2	3	1	5	4
5	2	1	6	4	9	3	8	7
8	7	5	4	3	6	9	1	2
2	1	4	8	9	7	5	6	3
6	3	9	2	5	1	4	7	8
4	6	2	5	1	8	7	3	9
1	9	8	3	7	4	6	2	5
7	5	3	9	6	2	8	4	1

No 44

6	8	2	7	3	1	5	9	4
7	5	4	9	8	6	3	2	1
1	3	9	5	4	2	6	8	7
5	7	1	6	2	8	9	4	3
3	2	8	4	7	9	1	5	6
4	9	6	1	5	3	2	7	8
2	1	7	3	9	4	8	6	5
8	6	5	2	1	7	4	3	9
9	4	3	8	6	5	7	1	2

No 45

7	5	9	1	8	4	6	2	3
6	8	1	9	2	3	7	5	4
3	4	2	7	6	5	8	1	9
4	9	3	2	1	6	5	8	7
5	1	7	3	4	8	2	9	6
8	2	6	5	9	7	4	3	1
9	6	4	8	5	1	3	7	2
1	3	8	6	7	2	9	4	5
2	7	5	4	3	9	1	6	8

No 46

3	0	2	9	4	1	7	5	6
7	1	5	3	6	2	8	4	9
9	4	6	7	8	5	3	1	2
2	9	1	4	7	6	5	8	3
6	3	4	2	5	8	9	7	1
5	7	8	1	3	9	6	2	4
4	6	7	5	2	3	1	9	8
8	5	9	6	1	4	2	3	7
1	2	3	8	9	7	4	6	5

No 47

2	5	4	6	8	3	7	1	9
7	8	9	2	1	4	6	3	5
6	1	3	7	5	9	8	4	2
3	9	6	5	4	2	1	7	8
8	2	5	1	3	7	9	6	4
4	7	1	8	9	6	5	2	3
1	3	2	9	7	8	4	5	6
9	4	7	3	6	5	2	8	1
5	6	8	4	2	1	3	9	7

No 48

7	9	6	1	2	5	3	4	8
4	1	8	7	3	9	5	2	6
5	3	2	6	8	4	7	1	9
3	8	7	2	6	1	9	5	4
9	2	4	3	5	7	8	6	1
6	5	1	9	4	8	2	7	3
2	4	9	8	7	6	1	3	5
8	6	3	5	1	2	4	9	7
1	7	5	4	9	3	6	8	2

4 6 8
3 1 7
5 9 2

Solutions

No 49

2	6	7	1	8	9	4	5	3
5	8	1	3	2	4	9	7	6
9	3	4	6	5	7	1	8	2
6	4	2	5	7	3	8	9	1
1	7	5	8	9	6	2	3	4
8	9	3	2	4	1	5	6	7
4	1	8	7	6	5	3	2	9
7	5	9	4	3	2	6	1	8
3	2	6	9	1	8	7	4	5

No 50

3	2	8	7	1	9	5	4	6
7	6	5	3	4	2	8	1	9
9	1	4	8	6	5	2	7	3
5	7	6	1	9	4	3	2	8
1	4	9	2	3	8	7	6	5
8	3	2	6	5	7	1	9	4
2	9	3	5	7	6	4	8	1
6	8	1	4	2	3	9	5	7
4	5	7	9	8	1	6	3	2

No 51

5	4	8	2	7	1	3	9	6
1	2	9	3	6	8	4	5	7
6	3	7	4	5	9	1	2	8
3	8	2	9	1	7	6	4	5
9	5	1	6	2	4	8	7	3
7	6	4	5	8	3	2	1	9
4	9	5	8	3	2	7	6	1
8	1	6	7	4	5	9	3	2
2	7	3	1	9	6	5	8	4

No 52

4	2	9	6	7	1	3	5	8
5	1	3	8	9	2	7	4	6
7	8	6	5	4	3	1	2	9
1	6	2	3	8	5	9	7	4
9	4	8	2	1	7	6	3	5
3	5	7	9	6	4	8	1	2
2	9	5	7	3	6	4	8	1
8	3	1	4	5	9	2	6	7
6	7	4	1	2	8	5	9	3

No 53

5	6	2	7	9	3	1	8	4
7	9	1	6	4	8	2	5	3
4	3	8	1	5	2	9	7	6
6	8	9	2	7	5	4	3	1
3	4	5	9	1	6	8	2	7
1	2	7	8	3	4	5	6	9
9	5	6	4	8	7	3	1	2
8	7	4	3	2	1	6	9	5
2	1	3	5	6	9	7	4	8

No 54

5	1	7	6	9	4	8	2	3
8	2	3	7	1	5	6	4	9
4	9	6	8	2	3	1	7	5
7	4	2	5	3	1	9	6	8
9	8	5	4	6	2	7	3	1
3	6	1	9	8	7	4	5	2
1	3	4	2	7	8	5	9	6
6	7	8	3	5	9	2	1	4
2	5	9	1	4	6	3	8	7

Solutions

No 55

3	9	5	1	8	4	6	2	7
7	8	4	9	2	6	5	3	1
1	6	2	5	7	3	9	8	4
6	2	7	3	9	5	4	1	8
9	5	8	7	4	1	2	6	3
4	3	1	8	6	2	7	5	9
5	7	9	2	1	8	3	4	6
2	1	6	4	3	7	8	9	5
8	4	3	6	5	9	1	7	2

No 56

2	7	5	3	9	8	6	1	4
9	8	1	6	5	4	2	7	3
3	6	4	7	2	1	8	9	5
4	9	6	5	1	7	3	8	2
7	5	2	9	8	3	4	6	1
8	1	3	4	6	2	9	5	7
5	2	9	1	3	6	7	4	8
6	4	8	2	7	5	1	3	9
1	3	7	8	4	9	5	2	6

No 57

4	3	1	9	5	2	6	7	8
7	2	5	4	8	6	1	9	3
8	6	9	1	3	7	5	4	2
1	7	3	2	9	4	8	6	5
2	9	4	8	6	5	7	3	1
5	8	6	7	1	3	9	2	4
9	4	2	5	7	1	3	8	6
3	1	7	6	4	8	2	5	9
6	5	8	3	2	9	4	1	7

No 58

9	5	6	8	1	3	4	7	2
4	3	2	6	9	7	5	1	8
1	7	8	4	5	2	3	9	6
5	1	4	9	2	6	8	3	7
2	9	7	1	3	8	6	5	4
6	8	3	7	4	5	1	2	9
7	2	5	3	6	4	9	8	1
3	4	1	2	8	9	7	6	5
8	6	9	5	7	1	2	4	3

No 59

5	2	1	4	7	6	8	9	3
9	8	4	3	1	2	5	6	7
6	7	3	9	8	5	1	2	4
1	4	6	5	9	7	2	3	8
7	3	9	2	4	8	6	5	1
8	5	2	6	3	1	7	4	9
3	1	5	8	6	9	4	7	2
2	9	8	7	5	4	3	1	6
4	6	7	1	2	3	9	8	5

No 60

2	3	1	8	5	9	6	4	7
6	4	8	2	3	7	1	5	9
9	7	5	6	1	4	2	3	8
3	8	7	4	6	1	9	2	5
5	2	9	7	8	3	4	6	1
1	6	4	5	9	2	7	8	3
8	9	6	1	4	5	3	7	2
7	5	3	9	2	6	8	1	4
4	1	2	3	7	8	5	9	6

4	6	8
3	1	7
5	9	2

Solutions

No 61

2	6	9	7	5	3	8	1	4
1	7	5	4	6	8	9	3	2
4	8	3	2	9	1	6	7	5
3	5	7	9	8	2	1	4	6
6	4	1	5	3	7	2	9	8
8	9	2	1	4	6	7	5	3
5	1	4	8	2	9	3	6	7
9	3	8	6	7	5	4	2	1
7	2	6	3	1	4	5	8	9

No 62

3	1	2	5	9	7	8	4	6
9	8	6	1	3	4	5	2	7
4	7	5	8	6	2	1	9	3
6	3	8	2	7	9	4	5	1
1	4	9	3	5	8	6	7	2
2	5	7	6	4	1	3	8	9
7	9	3	4	1	5	2	6	8
5	2	1	9	8	6	7	3	4
8	6	4	7	2	3	9	1	5

No 63

6	2	8	3	4	5	7	1	9
3	7	5	6	1	9	4	8	2
9	1	4	2	7	8	6	5	3
7	8	2	9	3	4	1	6	5
4	5	3	8	6	1	9	2	7
1	6	9	5	2	7	8	3	4
5	4	6	7	8	2	3	9	1
2	3	7	1	9	6	5	4	8
8	9	1	4	5	3	2	7	6

No 64

8	6	3	2	5	7	1	4	9
4	7	1	9	3	6	5	8	2
2	5	9	1	8	4	6	3	7
3	8	5	4	7	1	2	9	6
1	4	6	3	9	2	7	5	8
9	2	7	8	6	5	3	1	4
7	9	8	6	1	3	4	2	5
5	1	4	7	2	9	8	6	3
6	3	2	5	4	8	9	7	1

No 65

4	6	8	2	7	5	3	9	1
3	5	9	4	6	1	8	2	7
2	1	7	8	9	3	5	4	6
8	4	2	3	1	6	7	5	9
1	7	3	5	8	9	4	6	2
6	9	5	7	2	4	1	3	8
5	2	1	9	4	8	6	7	3
9	8	4	6	3	7	2	1	5
7	3	6	1	5	2	9	8	4

No 66

1	4	3	5	6	7	8	9	2
6	2	7	9	8	4	3	1	5
9	8	5	2	1	3	6	4	7
2	6	4	8	3	9	5	7	1
3	9	1	7	4	5	2	6	8
7	5	8	6	2	1	9	3	4
8	3	9	1	7	2	4	5	6
4	7	2	3	5	6	1	8	9
5	1	6	4	9	8	7	2	3

Solutions

No 67

7	8	2	4	5	9	1	3	6
1	9	5	6	3	2	4	7	8
4	6	3	1	7	8	5	9	2
6	1	7	8	4	5	9	2	3
5	2	8	9	1	3	6	4	7
3	4	9	2	6	7	8	1	5
2	3	6	5	9	4	7	8	1
9	7	1	3	8	6	2	5	4
8	5	4	7	2	1	3	6	9

No 68

9	2	1	6	4	5	8	3	7
3	4	8	9	2	7	1	6	5
5	7	6	8	3	1	4	2	9
1	6	5	4	9	2	3	7	8
8	3	7	1	5	6	9	4	2
4	9	2	7	8	3	6	5	1
2	1	4	3	7	8	5	9	6
6	5	3	2	1	9	7	8	4
7	8	9	5	6	4	2	1	3

No 69

5	6	1	7	4	2	3	8	9
2	3	4	8	9	1	6	5	7
8	7	9	6	3	5	1	4	2
9	5	6	2	7	3	4	1	8
3	4	2	1	8	9	7	6	5
7	1	8	4	5	6	2	9	3
6	8	5	3	2	4	9	7	1
1	2	7	9	6	8	5	3	4
4	9	3	5	1	7	8	2	6

No 70

6	2	1	8	7	3	9	4	5
4	9	3	1	5	2	7	6	8
7	8	5	9	4	6	3	1	2
2	5	4	3	6	7	8	9	1
9	1	7	2	8	5	6	3	4
3	6	8	4	9	1	2	5	7
1	7	9	6	2	4	5	8	3
5	4	6	7	3	8	1	2	9
8	3	2	5	1	9	4	7	6

No 71

6	7	2	1	4	3	5	8	9
5	4	1	8	9	6	3	7	2
9	3	8	5	2	7	6	4	1
7	2	5	6	3	1	8	9	4
1	6	3	4	8	9	2	5	7
4	8	9	2	7	5	1	3	6
3	1	6	7	5	4	9	2	8
2	5	7	9	6	8	4	1	3
8	9	4	3	1	2	7	6	5

No 72

5	9	6	8	1	2	7	3	4
2	1	7	4	9	3	6	5	8
4	8	3	7	5	6	9	1	2
9	2	1	5	6	8	3	4	7
6	5	8	3	4	7	2	9	1
7	3	4	1	2	9	5	8	6
1	7	9	6	8	5	4	2	3
8	6	2	9	3	4	1	7	5
3	4	5	2	7	1	8	6	9

Solutions

No 73

3	4	8	5	9	1	6	2	7
6	7	1	4	8	2	9	3	5
9	5	2	6	7	3	4	8	1
2	8	7	9	3	5	1	6	4
5	6	4	7	1	8	2	9	3
1	3	9	2	4	6	5	7	8
7	2	3	1	5	9	8	4	6
8	1	6	3	2	4	7	5	9
4	9	5	8	6	7	3	1	2

No 74

5	3	6	9	7	1	4	2	8
1	4	7	3	8	2	9	6	5
9	2	8	5	4	6	7	3	1
2	8	9	7	1	4	6	5	3
7	1	4	6	5	3	8	9	2
3	6	5	8	2	9	1	7	4
8	7	3	4	6	5	2	1	9
6	5	1	2	9	8	3	4	7
4	9	2	1	3	7	5	8	6

No 75

5	8	1	9	2	3	7	4	6
6	4	7	1	8	5	9	3	2
2	9	3	4	6	7	5	8	1
7	3	6	2	4	9	8	1	5
4	1	9	5	7	8	6	2	3
8	5	2	6	3	1	4	9	7
3	7	5	8	9	2	1	6	4
1	6	8	3	5	4	2	7	9
9	2	4	7	1	6	3	5	8

No 76

1	4	7	9	2	5	8	3	6
2	6	5	3	8	1	9	7	4
8	9	3	4	6	7	5	2	1
4	7	8	5	9	6	3	1	2
5	2	6	1	3	8	7	4	9
3	1	9	2	7	4	6	8	5
7	3	4	6	5	2	1	9	8
9	5	1	8	4	3	2	6	7
6	8	2	7	1	9	4	5	3

No 77

1	3	9	7	6	8	4	2	5
6	2	7	5	4	9	1	8	3
8	4	5	1	2	3	6	7	9
3	9	1	6	7	4	8	5	2
5	7	6	8	3	2	9	1	4
2	8	4	9	1	5	3	6	7
9	1	2	3	8	7	5	4	6
7	5	8	4	9	6	2	3	1
4	6	3	2	5	1	7	9	8

No 78

6	5	3	7	2	9	8	4	1
4	1	7	8	6	5	2	3	9
2	9	8	1	3	4	6	7	5
5	7	9	3	4	8	1	2	6
1	8	6	9	7	2	3	5	4
3	4	2	5	1	6	7	9	8
8	3	1	4	5	7	9	6	2
7	2	4	6	9	1	5	8	3
9	6	5	2	8	3	4	1	7

Solutions

No 79

3	8	1	9	4	2	6	5	7
4	7	5	8	1	6	3	9	2
9	2	6	7	5	3	4	1	8
5	1	2	6	9	4	7	8	3
8	9	4	5	3	7	1	2	6
7	6	3	1	2	8	5	4	9
2	3	9	4	6	5	8	7	1
6	4	8	2	7	1	9	3	5
1	5	7	3	8	9	2	6	4

No 80

5	7	8	6	4	9	1	2	3
6	4	2	3	1	7	9	5	8
3	9	1	2	8	5	7	6	4
7	8	3	4	5	2	6	1	9
2	1	6	8	9	3	5	4	7
9	5	4	1	7	6	3	8	2
4	3	9	5	6	8	2	7	1
1	6	7	9	2	4	8	3	5
8	2	5	7	3	1	4	9	6

No 81

6	1	2	5	4	7	9	3	8
3	5	9	8	1	6	7	4	2
4	8	7	3	9	2	6	5	1
1	7	4	2	3	8	5	9	6
5	3	8	7	6	9	1	2	4
2	9	6	1	5	4	3	8	7
7	6	5	4	2	3	8	1	9
9	4	1	6	8	5	2	7	3
8	2	3	9	7	1	4	6	5

No 82

6	4	9	1	5	8	7	3	2
8	2	3	9	4	7	1	6	5
5	1	7	6	3	2	9	8	4
3	8	4	5	6	1	2	9	7
2	9	1	8	7	3	4	5	6
7	6	5	4	2	9	3	1	8
1	5	2	3	8	4	6	7	9
9	7	6	2	1	5	8	4	3
4	3	8	7	9	6	5	2	1

No 83

6	1	5	8	4	2	3	9	7
9	8	3	5	1	7	4	2	6
2	7	4	3	9	6	8	5	1
4	5	6	7	2	8	9	1	3
8	9	1	4	5	3	7	6	2
7	3	2	9	6	1	5	8	4
5	6	9	1	3	4	2	7	8
3	2	8	6	7	5	1	4	9
1	4	7	2	8	9	6	3	5

No 84

4	8	2	7	3	5	6	1	9
9	5	6	1	2	8	4	3	7
1	7	3	4	6	9	5	8	2
3	2	9	5	8	7	1	4	6
5	4	1	6	9	3	2	7	8
7	6	8	2	1	4	9	5	3
6	9	7	3	4	1	8	2	5
2	3	4	8	5	6	7	9	1
8	1	5	9	7	2	3	6	4

4 6 8
3 1 7
5 9 2

Solutions

No 85

1	7	4	2	6	5	9	3	8
2	6	3	1	8	9	7	4	5
5	9	8	3	4	7	2	1	6
3	2	5	7	9	8	4	6	1
7	4	9	6	5	1	3	8	2
8	1	6	4	3	2	5	7	9
9	3	1	8	2	4	6	5	7
6	5	7	9	1	3	8	2	4
4	8	2	5	7	6	1	9	3

No 86

2	5	1	6	9	8	4	3	7
6	8	9	3	4	7	5	1	2
4	3	7	5	2	1	6	8	9
8	9	6	7	3	4	1	2	5
3	7	4	1	5	2	8	9	6
5	1	2	8	6	9	3	7	4
7	4	3	2	1	5	9	6	8
1	2	5	9	8	6	7	4	3
9	6	8	4	7	3	2	5	1

No 87

7	9	1	6	8	5	4	2	3
4	8	6	3	2	7	1	5	9
3	2	5	1	4	9	8	7	6
1	5	8	2	7	3	9	6	4
2	3	7	4	9	6	5	8	1
6	4	9	8	5	1	2	3	7
9	7	4	5	3	8	6	1	2
5	6	3	9	1	2	7	4	8
8	1	2	7	6	4	3	9	5

No 88

3	1	4	6	5	9	8	2	7
7	9	5	3	2	8	1	6	4
8	2	6	4	7	1	3	9	5
5	3	8	9	6	2	4	7	1
1	4	2	8	3	7	6	5	9
9	6	7	1	4	5	2	3	8
6	5	3	7	1	4	9	8	2
4	7	9	2	8	3	5	1	6
2	8	1	5	9	6	7	4	3

No 89

1	7	2	8	9	4	6	5	3
8	4	5	3	6	1	7	2	9
6	9	3	7	2	5	4	8	1
4	3	6	2	7	8	1	9	5
2	1	7	5	3	9	8	4	6
5	8	9	1	4	6	2	3	7
9	2	4	6	1	3	5	7	8
7	6	8	9	5	2	3	1	4
3	5	1	4	8	7	9	6	2

No 90

2	9	3	6	5	7	4	1	8
7	4	8	1	3	2	9	6	5
5	1	6	9	4	8	7	3	2
8	5	7	4	1	3	2	9	6
9	6	1	2	8	5	3	7	4
3	2	4	7	6	9	8	5	1
4	3	5	8	9	1	6	2	7
6	7	9	5	2	4	1	8	3
1	8	2	3	7	6	5	4	9

Solutions

No 91

8	7	5	2	3	6	4	9	1
9	2	3	8	1	4	7	5	6
1	6	4	9	5	7	2	8	3
4	3	6	7	8	1	9	2	5
2	5	8	4	9	3	6	1	7
7	1	9	6	2	5	8	3	4
5	9	7	1	4	8	3	6	2
3	4	2	5	6	9	1	7	8
6	8	1	3	7	2	5	4	9

No 92

2	5	4	1	3	8	6	9	7
3	9	7	6	2	4	1	5	8
6	8	1	5	7	9	4	3	2
8	1	5	2	4	3	9	7	6
7	6	9	8	1	5	2	4	3
4	2	3	7	9	6	5	8	1
5	3	2	9	6	7	8	1	4
1	7	8	4	5	2	3	6	9
9	4	6	3	8	1	7	2	5

No 93

9	8	6	1	4	2	7	5	3
4	3	5	9	6	7	8	2	1
2	1	7	3	8	5	6	4	9
1	5	8	6	3	4	9	7	2
7	9	3	2	5	8	1	6	4
6	4	2	7	1	9	3	8	5
8	7	9	5	2	1	4	3	6
5	6	4	8	9	3	2	1	7
3	2	1	4	7	6	5	9	8

No 94

4	1	7	6	8	2	5	9	3
8	2	6	9	3	5	7	4	1
5	9	3	1	7	4	8	2	6
1	7	4	8	2	6	9	3	5
9	3	5	7	4	1	2	6	8
2	6	8	3	5	9	4	1	7
3	5	9	4	1	7	6	8	2
7	4	1	2	6	8	3	5	9
6	8	2	5	9	3	1	7	4

No 95

4	6	3	5	9	7	8	1	2
5	1	7	4	2	8	6	9	3
9	2	8	3	6	1	4	5	7
7	5	6	8	4	9	3	2	1
2	8	9	1	3	6	7	4	5
1	3	4	2	7	5	9	8	6
8	4	1	6	5	3	2	7	9
6	9	2	7	1	4	5	3	8
3	7	5	9	8	2	1	6	4

No 96

6	9	3	5	8	2	1	7	4
7	8	4	1	6	3	2	9	5
1	2	5	9	7	4	6	3	8
5	6	8	7	1	9	3	4	2
3	7	2	8	4	5	9	1	6
9	4	1	2	3	6	8	5	7
4	5	9	3	2	8	7	6	1
2	3	7	6	5	1	4	8	9
8	1	6	4	9	7	5	2	3

4	6	8
3	1	7
5	9	2

Solutions

No 97

3	8	2	5	6	1	7	9	4
1	6	4	8	9	7	3	2	5
7	5	9	4	3	2	8	1	6
4	7	1	2	8	3	5	6	9
5	3	8	6	4	9	2	7	1
2	9	6	7	1	5	4	8	3
8	4	5	9	7	6	1	3	2
6	1	7	3	2	4	9	5	8
9	2	3	1	5	8	6	4	7

No 98

9	8	7	5	3	2	4	6	1
3	5	6	7	4	1	8	2	9
4	2	1	6	8	9	5	3	7
5	9	2	4	6	8	1	7	3
6	4	3	1	2	7	9	5	8
7	1	8	3	9	5	6	4	2
2	7	4	8	1	6	3	9	5
1	6	9	2	5	3	7	8	4
8	3	5	9	7	4	2	1	6

No 99

6	5	1	4	7	3	2	9	8
9	3	8	5	1	2	6	4	7
2	4	7	6	8	9	5	1	3
5	1	4	9	6	7	8	3	2
8	2	6	1	3	4	7	5	9
3	7	9	2	5	8	1	6	4
1	9	3	8	2	6	4	7	5
4	6	2	7	9	5	3	8	1
7	8	5	3	4	1	9	2	6

No 100

6	7	8	9	4	2	3	5	1
1	5	2	3	6	8	7	4	9
9	3	4	7	1	5	8	6	2
7	9	3	4	2	6	5	1	8
8	6	5	1	7	9	4	2	3
4	2	1	5	8	3	6	9	7
5	1	6	8	9	7	2	3	4
3	8	9	2	5	4	1	7	6
2	4	7	6	3	1	9	8	5

No 101

3	1	6	9	2	5	4	7	8
9	8	4	3	6	7	2	5	1
2	5	7	8	1	4	3	9	6
1	6	2	4	9	8	5	3	7
8	4	3	5	7	6	9	1	2
5	7	9	2	3	1	6	8	4
7	9	1	6	4	3	8	2	5
4	2	8	7	5	9	1	6	3
6	3	5	1	8	2	7	4	9

No 102

6	7	1	2	3	5	9	4	8
9	2	3	1	4	8	5	7	6
5	4	8	6	9	7	3	1	2
8	6	7	9	1	4	2	3	5
2	1	5	8	7	3	4	6	9
4	3	9	5	2	6	1	8	7
7	9	2	3	8	1	6	5	4
1	8	6	4	5	2	7	9	3
3	5	4	7	6	9	8	2	1

Solutions

No 103

9	1	8	2	7	5	4	6	3
4	7	3	1	9	6	8	2	5
6	5	2	4	3	8	7	9	1
7	2	6	8	5	3	1	4	9
1	8	9	6	4	7	3	5	2
3	4	5	9	1	2	6	7	8
2	3	1	7	6	9	5	8	4
5	9	7	3	8	4	2	1	6
8	6	4	5	2	1	9	3	7

No 104

9	2	7	8	1	6	3	4	5
3	4	1	2	5	7	9	8	6
8	5	6	3	4	9	1	2	7
6	3	8	1	2	4	5	7	9
5	1	9	6	7	8	4	3	2
2	7	4	5	9	3	8	6	1
1	6	3	9	8	2	7	5	4
7	8	5	4	6	1	2	9	3
4	9	2	7	3	5	6	1	8

No 105

9	4	1	7	6	3	5	2	8
6	3	2	5	8	4	7	1	9
5	7	8	1	2	9	6	3	4
8	1	9	6	5	2	3	4	7
7	2	6	3	4	8	1	9	5
3	5	4	9	7	1	2	8	6
1	6	3	8	9	5	4	7	2
2	8	5	4	3	7	9	6	1
4	9	7	2	1	6	8	5	3

No 106

6	9	3	1	2	7	4	8	5
4	8	7	9	5	3	1	6	2
1	5	2	6	4	8	3	7	9
5	2	4	3	6	9	8	1	7
9	3	1	8	7	2	6	5	4
8	7	6	4	1	5	2	9	3
2	1	8	5	9	4	7	3	6
7	6	5	2	3	1	9	4	8
3	4	9	7	8	6	5	2	1

No 107

8	2	7	9	5	4	1	3	6
9	4	5	1	6	3	7	8	2
6	1	3	8	7	2	5	4	9
3	7	6	5	2	1	4	9	8
1	8	9	3	4	6	2	5	7
2	5	4	7	9	8	3	6	1
7	9	8	4	1	5	6	2	3
5	6	1	2	3	9	8	7	4
4	3	2	6	8	7	9	1	5

No 108

4	9	6	5	2	3	1	8	7
3	7	1	4	8	6	9	2	5
8	2	5	7	1	9	4	3	6
5	4	7	1	6	2	8	9	3
9	3	2	8	4	7	6	5	1
6	1	8	3	9	5	2	7	4
7	6	4	9	5	8	3	1	2
1	5	9	2	3	4	7	6	8
2	8	3	6	7	1	5	4	9

4 6 8
3 1 7
5 9 2

Solutions

No 109

8	2	6	7	9	4	1	5	3
3	5	7	1	6	8	2	4	9
4	1	9	2	3	5	8	7	6
7	9	1	3	8	6	4	2	5
2	3	8	4	5	1	6	9	7
5	6	4	9	7	2	3	1	8
1	7	5	6	4	3	9	8	2
9	4	3	8	2	7	5	6	1
6	8	2	5	1	9	7	3	4

No 110

4	9	2	8	7	1	6	3	5
1	8	6	9	3	5	2	4	7
7	3	5	2	4	6	1	8	9
9	6	3	5	2	8	4	7	1
5	7	8	6	1	4	9	2	3
2	4	1	7	9	3	5	6	8
6	2	9	1	8	7	3	5	4
3	1	7	4	5	2	8	9	6
8	5	4	3	6	9	7	1	2

No 111

6	8	7	9	3	2	1	5	4
4	1	2	5	6	8	9	3	7
5	3	9	4	1	7	6	8	2
3	6	5	7	4	9	8	2	1
9	4	1	8	2	3	5	7	6
7	2	8	1	5	6	3	4	9
8	7	4	6	9	5	2	1	3
2	5	6	3	7	1	4	9	8
1	9	3	2	8	4	7	6	5

No 112

2	3	6	7	4	5	1	9	8
9	8	4	6	1	2	7	5	3
7	1	5	3	8	9	6	4	2
4	5	3	8	2	6	9	7	1
1	9	7	4	5	3	2	8	6
8	6	2	1	9	7	4	3	5
3	4	1	2	7	8	5	6	9
5	2	8	9	6	4	3	1	7
6	7	9	5	3	1	8	2	4

No 113

6	2	8	4	7	9	3	1	5
4	1	9	3	6	5	2	7	8
3	5	7	2	8	1	9	6	4
1	4	5	6	9	3	8	2	7
9	3	2	7	5	8	6	4	1
7	8	6	1	4	2	5	9	3
2	6	1	5	3	4	7	8	9
5	9	4	8	2	7	1	3	6
8	7	3	9	1	6	4	5	2

No 114

3	5	4	1	2	8	9	7	6
7	8	6	9	3	4	1	2	5
1	9	2	5	6	7	3	4	8
5	3	8	4	9	1	2	6	7
2	4	9	7	8	6	5	3	1
6	1	7	3	5	2	8	9	4
8	6	1	2	4	9	7	5	3
9	7	3	6	1	5	4	8	2
4	2	5	8	7	3	6	1	9

Solutions

No 115

8	4	9	2	6	3	7	1	5
7	2	6	5	9	1	3	8	4
5	1	3	8	4	7	9	2	6
2	9	4	1	7	8	5	6	3
6	5	7	9	3	2	1	4	8
3	8	1	6	5	4	2	9	7
9	3	2	4	8	5	6	7	1
4	6	5	7	1	9	8	3	2
1	7	8	3	2	6	4	5	9

No 116

5	9	8	7	4	3	2	1	6
4	1	7	6	2	9	8	3	5
2	3	6	5	1	8	7	4	9
3	5	4	8	9	6	1	2	7
6	8	2	1	3	7	5	9	4
9	7	1	4	5	2	6	8	3
7	6	3	9	8	1	4	5	2
8	4	9	2	6	5	3	7	1
1	2	5	3	7	4	9	6	8

No 117

6	1	2	3	9	5	4	7	8
8	5	4	7	1	2	9	3	6
9	7	3	8	4	6	1	5	2
1	8	9	5	3	7	2	6	4
2	3	6	9	8	4	5	1	7
7	4	5	6	2	1	3	8	9
5	2	1	4	7	8	6	9	3
3	6	8	2	5	9	7	4	1
4	9	7	1	6	3	8	2	5

No 118

6	2	5	4	9	3	1	8	7
7	4	9	1	5	8	2	6	3
8	3	1	2	7	6	9	5	4
9	1	8	5	3	4	6	7	2
3	5	7	6	8	2	4	1	9
2	6	4	7	1	9	8	3	5
1	9	3	8	4	5	7	2	6
5	8	2	9	6	7	3	4	1
4	7	6	3	2	1	5	9	8

No 119

8	6	5	4	2	3	9	7	1
4	2	7	9	1	6	8	5	3
3	9	1	5	8	7	2	6	4
7	4	9	8	3	1	5	2	6
5	8	6	2	7	4	1	3	9
1	3	2	6	9	5	4	8	7
6	5	8	7	4	9	3	1	2
9	7	3	1	5	2	6	4	8
2	1	4	3	6	8	7	9	5

No 120

7	9	5	3	8	4	2	6	1
6	1	3	9	5	2	7	4	8
8	4	2	1	6	7	5	3	9
3	5	1	4	2	9	6	8	7
4	2	8	7	1	6	9	5	3
9	6	7	5	3	8	1	2	4
2	3	6	8	7	1	4	9	5
1	8	9	6	4	5	3	7	2
5	7	4	2	9	3	8	1	6

Solutions

No 121

1	9	3	8	7	5	2	4	6
8	5	6	2	9	4	3	7	1
4	2	7	6	3	1	5	9	8
5	1	4	3	8	7	6	2	9
3	8	2	9	4	6	7	1	5
7	6	9	1	5	2	4	8	3
6	4	5	7	1	8	9	3	2
2	3	8	4	6	9	1	5	7
9	7	1	5	2	3	8	6	4

No 122

1	7	5	9	2	6	4	8	3
6	4	9	8	3	7	5	1	2
3	8	2	5	1	4	6	9	7
4	1	3	6	7	5	8	2	9
9	5	7	1	8	2	3	6	4
2	6	8	3	4	9	7	5	1
8	2	1	4	6	3	9	7	5
7	9	4	2	5	8	1	3	6
5	3	6	7	9	1	2	4	8

No 123

2	6	1	7	8	5	9	4	3
7	3	8	1	4	9	2	6	5
4	5	9	3	6	2	1	7	8
3	8	4	2	5	6	7	1	9
9	7	2	8	1	3	4	5	6
5	1	6	9	7	4	8	3	2
8	4	3	5	9	1	6	2	7
1	9	5	6	2	7	3	8	4
6	2	7	4	3	8	5	9	1

No 124

8	2	6	4	5	7	3	9	1
3	1	4	2	8	9	5	7	6
7	9	5	6	3	1	2	4	8
9	3	7	1	2	8	4	6	5
4	5	1	7	9	6	8	2	3
6	8	2	3	4	5	9	1	7
2	7	8	5	6	4	1	3	9
5	6	3	9	1	2	7	8	4
1	4	9	8	7	3	6	5	2

No 125

9	6	4	2	5	3	1	8	7
7	8	3	4	9	1	6	5	2
2	1	5	6	8	7	3	9	4
8	5	6	7	2	9	4	3	1
4	2	9	1	3	8	7	6	5
1	3	7	5	6	4	8	2	9
3	4	2	8	7	5	9	1	6
6	7	8	9	1	2	5	4	3
5	9	1	3	4	6	2	7	8

No 126

5	4	6	9	2	1	3	7	8
8	1	9	7	3	5	4	2	6
2	3	7	6	4	8	5	1	9
4	5	8	2	7	9	1	6	3
1	9	2	3	5	6	8	4	7
7	6	3	1	8	4	9	5	2
6	2	1	5	9	3	7	8	4
9	7	4	8	1	2	6	3	5
3	8	5	4	6	7	2	9	1

Solutions

No 127

6	7	5	1	2	4	9	3	8
1	4	2	9	8	3	7	6	5
3	9	8	6	5	7	1	4	2
8	6	7	2	3	1	4	5	9
5	2	3	7	4	9	8	1	6
9	1	4	5	6	8	2	7	3
4	5	9	3	1	2	6	8	7
7	3	1	8	9	6	5	2	4
2	8	6	4	7	5	3	9	1

No 128

6	4	2	1	5	7	3	9	8
1	9	7	4	8	3	2	5	6
3	8	5	9	6	2	7	1	4
9	6	4	5	2	1	8	3	7
5	3	8	7	9	4	1	6	2
7	2	1	8	3	6	5	4	9
8	5	3	6	7	9	4	2	1
4	7	6	2	1	5	9	8	3
2	1	9	3	4	8	6	7	5

No 129

1	2	8	4	3	7	6	5	9
7	6	9	8	2	5	1	4	3
4	3	5	9	6	1	2	8	7
2	4	3	5	1	9	8	7	6
5	8	7	2	4	6	9	3	1
9	1	6	3	7	8	5	2	4
8	7	1	6	5	3	4	9	2
3	5	4	1	9	2	7	6	8
6	9	2	7	8	4	3	1	5

No 130

9	7	5	4	3	1	8	6	2
2	8	6	5	7	9	3	4	1
4	3	1	2	8	6	7	9	5
6	2	9	7	1	3	5	8	4
8	5	3	9	2	4	1	7	6
1	4	7	6	5	8	9	2	3
7	1	8	3	4	2	6	5	9
5	6	4	1	9	7	2	3	8
3	9	2	8	6	5	4	1	7

No 131

4	5	8	6	9	3	1	2	7
1	6	2	5	8	7	9	3	4
7	3	9	4	2	1	5	6	8
3	2	1	8	5	6	4	7	9
8	7	4	9	3	2	6	5	1
6	9	5	7	1	4	2	8	3
5	4	3	1	6	8	7	9	2
9	8	7	2	4	5	3	1	6
2	1	6	3	7	9	8	4	5

No 132

7	9	6	2	8	3	4	1	5
3	5	4	6	9	1	7	8	2
8	1	2	7	4	5	6	3	9
6	3	5	9	1	8	2	4	7
9	7	8	4	2	6	3	5	1
2	4	1	3	5	7	9	6	8
4	8	3	5	7	9	1	2	6
1	2	9	8	6	4	5	7	3
5	6	7	1	3	2	8	9	4

4	6	8
3	1	7
5	9	2

Solutions

No 133

6	7	2	4	1	3	9	5	8
9	3	8	2	5	6	7	4	1
5	4	1	7	9	8	2	6	3
2	6	9	5	8	1	3	7	4
1	5	3	9	7	4	8	2	6
7	8	4	6	3	2	1	9	5
8	9	5	3	4	7	6	1	2
4	1	6	8	2	9	5	3	7
3	2	7	1	6	5	4	8	9

No 134

9	8	7	1	5	6	3	2	4
6	1	4	3	9	2	8	5	7
3	2	5	8	7	4	1	9	6
5	9	8	4	1	3	6	7	2
7	4	3	2	6	9	5	1	8
2	6	1	5	8	7	4	3	9
1	3	6	7	2	8	9	4	5
8	5	2	9	4	1	7	6	3
4	7	9	6	3	5	2	8	1

No 135

5	8	6	1	2	4	3	7	9
7	1	9	6	3	5	4	8	2
4	3	2	8	9	7	6	5	1
8	9	1	5	4	3	7	2	6
3	6	5	7	1	2	9	4	8
2	4	7	9	8	6	1	3	5
6	7	3	2	5	1	8	9	4
1	2	8	4	7	9	5	6	3
9	5	4	3	6	8	2	1	7

No 136

5	7	4	6	1	2	3	8	9
3	8	6	4	7	9	1	2	5
9	1	2	8	5	3	6	4	7
2	6	5	7	4	8	9	1	3
7	4	3	9	2	1	8	5	6
8	9	1	3	6	5	4	7	2
6	5	7	1	3	4	2	9	8
4	2	9	5	8	6	7	3	1
1	3	8	2	9	7	5	6	4

No 137

9	4	8	2	5	6	1	3	7
7	2	5	1	3	8	4	9	6
3	6	1	9	4	7	8	5	2
1	9	6	5	8	4	7	2	3
5	7	2	3	6	1	9	4	8
8	3	4	7	9	2	6	1	5
6	8	9	4	2	3	5	7	1
4	1	3	8	7	5	2	6	9
2	5	7	6	1	9	3	8	4

No 138

8	5	1	4	7	9	3	6	2
4	9	7	2	3	6	8	5	1
6	2	3	8	5	1	7	9	4
9	6	4	1	2	7	5	8	3
7	3	2	5	4	8	9	1	6
5	1	8	6	9	3	4	2	7
3	4	6	9	8	2	1	7	5
2	8	5	7	1	4	6	3	9
1	7	9	3	6	5	2	4	8

Solutions

No 139

1	4	7	9	2	8	3	6	5
6	9	5	3	1	7	4	2	8
8	3	2	6	5	4	9	7	1
4	1	8	7	6	3	5	9	2
2	7	3	5	4	9	1	8	6
5	6	9	1	8	2	7	3	4
9	2	1	4	7	6	8	5	3
7	5	6	8	3	1	2	4	9
3	8	4	2	9	5	6	1	7

No 140

5	7	9	2	4	8	6	3	1
6	2	1	3	5	7	9	8	4
4	3	8	9	1	6	2	7	5
2	8	3	6	9	4	5	1	7
9	5	6	8	7	1	4	2	3
7	1	4	5	3	2	8	6	9
8	4	7	1	6	5	3	9	2
3	6	5	7	2	9	1	4	8
1	9	2	4	8	3	7	5	6

No 141

8	2	3	4	5	7	6	9	1
1	6	5	8	9	3	2	7	4
9	4	7	6	1	2	5	3	8
3	8	1	9	2	6	4	5	7
5	9	2	7	3	4	1	8	6
6	7	4	5	8	1	9	2	3
7	5	6	2	4	8	3	1	9
4	3	9	1	7	5	8	6	2
2	1	8	3	6	9	7	4	5

No 142

2	8	4	3	9	5	1	7	6
1	3	5	7	6	2	8	9	4
7	6	9	8	1	4	5	3	2
3	5	2	9	8	6	7	4	1
6	9	7	1	4	3	2	8	5
8	4	1	5	2	7	3	6	9
5	2	8	4	7	9	6	1	3
9	7	6	2	3	1	4	5	8
4	1	3	6	5	8	9	2	7

No 143

2	8	3	1	5	4	6	9	7
5	7	9	8	6	3	1	4	2
6	4	1	7	9	2	8	5	3
4	3	8	2	1	7	5	6	9
1	6	2	5	3	9	4	7	8
7	9	5	6	4	8	2	3	1
9	5	4	3	8	1	7	2	6
8	2	6	9	7	5	3	1	4
3	1	7	4	2	6	9	8	5

No 144

9	4	8	3	5	7	6	2	1
7	5	1	8	2	6	4	9	3
6	3	2	4	9	1	5	7	8
3	1	7	5	8	9	2	6	4
5	8	4	6	1	2	9	3	7
2	9	6	7	3	4	8	1	5
4	2	3	1	6	5	7	8	9
8	6	5	9	7	3	1	4	2
1	7	9	2	4	8	3	5	6

4 6 8
3 1 7
5 9 2

Solutions

No 145

3	2	8	5	6	9	1	4	7
6	4	5	1	7	2	8	3	9
7	1	9	4	8	3	6	5	2
2	9	7	8	3	5	4	6	1
8	3	6	9	4	1	2	7	5
4	5	1	7	2	6	9	8	3
1	8	2	3	5	4	7	9	6
9	7	3	6	1	8	5	2	4
5	6	4	2	9	7	3	1	8

No 146

1	5	3	9	6	8	7	2	4
4	8	6	2	7	3	9	5	1
7	2	9	4	5	1	6	3	8
9	3	4	6	2	5	1	8	7
2	1	7	8	9	4	5	6	3
8	6	5	3	1	7	2	4	9
5	9	8	1	3	6	4	7	2
3	7	1	5	4	2	8	9	6
6	4	2	7	8	9	3	1	5

No 147

2	1	4	8	7	5	3	9	6
5	9	3	4	6	2	1	7	8
8	6	7	3	9	1	5	2	4
3	4	6	2	1	8	7	5	9
9	5	2	7	3	6	8	4	1
1	7	8	9	5	4	2	6	3
7	2	9	6	8	3	4	1	5
6	3	5	1	4	7	9	8	2
4	8	1	5	2	9	6	3	7

No 148

1	8	4	7	2	6	3	5	9
3	2	9	5	8	4	1	7	6
7	5	6	3	1	9	4	8	2
5	4	3	1	6	8	9	2	7
8	9	1	2	7	3	5	6	4
2	6	7	4	9	5	8	3	1
4	7	2	8	5	1	6	9	3
9	3	5	6	4	2	7	1	8
6	1	8	9	3	7	2	4	5

No 149

2	3	4	8	5	9	1	6	7
7	1	5	6	4	3	8	9	2
6	9	8	1	2	7	3	5	4
5	4	7	9	8	1	6	2	3
1	6	3	5	7	2	9	4	8
9	8	2	4	3	6	7	1	5
8	2	1	7	6	4	5	3	9
3	5	9	2	1	8	4	7	6
4	7	6	3	9	5	2	8	1

No 150

4	1	3	5	2	8	9	7	6
9	2	7	4	3	6	8	1	5
6	5	8	1	7	9	4	2	3
3	8	1	2	6	5	7	4	9
5	7	9	3	4	1	2	6	8
2	4	6	8	9	7	3	5	1
1	9	4	6	8	2	5	3	7
8	3	5	7	1	4	6	9	2
7	6	2	9	5	3	1	8	4

Solutions

No 1

No 2

No 3

No 4

No 5

No 6

Solutions

No 7

No 8

No 9

No 10

No 11

No 12

Solutions

No 13

No 14

No 15

No 16

No 17

No 18

Solutions

No 19

No 20

No 21

No 22

No 23

No 24

Solutions

No 25

No 26

No 27

No 28

No 29

No 30

Solutions

No 31

No 32

No 33

No 34

No 35

No 36

Solutions

No 37

No 38

No 39

No 40

No 41

No 42

Solutions

No 43

No 44

No 45

No 46

No 47

No 48

Solutions

No 49

No 50

No 51

No 52

No 53

No 54

Solutions

No 55

No 56

No 57

No 58

No 59

No 60

Solutions

No 61

No 62

No 63

No 64

No 65

No 66

Solutions

No 67

No 68

No 69

No 70

No 71

No 72

Solutions

No 73

```
C L F T S E P M E T E H T X M
A M S E C A R G E E R H T Y O
L A M E N T A T I O N H X R N
V E Q C T I S A P S E Z O E A
A R T R O B A X E D R O A H L L
R C X S I E N W E E K C C G I
Y S W K T W W P Y Y L I T G S
S E E J I N U O C A E N A U A
C H T N K B X S T L H R W J L
T T D F L Z L A I P D E T E L
S O A I D U N E S D G U H H E
W P C S B A T H E R S G G T R
N A N D R O M E D A U L I A B
P A R A D I S E W C S U N K M
S U M S A R E E D D K V F N U
```

No 74

```
Q I J Z S N Y J T A T O R L
C L L U I O J P N N H F H S B
O H L R G R I Z I Y C T J Q K
T K I N T F Z M M O R U Q Y A
R P D V X F R E R Y O O Y C I
K N C W E A M I E B X R I I C
V D W H E S A J P A E P S L J
O O A P G N R Y P L L Z E A B
C J S Y D R O S E M A R Y N L
L A V E L D J C P L V P E T I
E C R S C E R A N I S E E K V
N O G A R R A T L F Y R G O R
N E O J W S M F M L O V A G E
E U P G B A S I L C I D S P H
F B O W P T Y R O V A S P H C
```

No 75

```
C W R E T N E P R A C S W E V
U T C E T I H C R A O U T A D
B O V R S A L E S M A N L B E
A Q X E T S I G O L O E G L C
S C G G C T E R M B T K E S O
P J I A S E J R E I A C U U R
W L U N R Z P A D T T R M R A
K B U A A G O T N R S V B V T
H K L M Z H E U I I F W F U I
E G A P B A C C K O T A R Y R
L C W O C E X E N E N O H O N
U F I R J A R K W V E I R K U
K U E E N U R S E H I P S M I
S R R D W E I N K U C U E T R
M N Z W A I T R E S S M O R D
```

No 76

```
S R E T S Y O N B E U N C G H
G O L E N T A T R O U G H J A
M Z O L Y B O X W M Q N C B J
Y A V L R F I N M I L A N S M
J R E U L M X U E L L U O P F
M X T M T E L H E L Q T C G X
D X I U R H X H F F I I K W P
V Y N R T U S S C P M L N Y W
U P I E Z E S P N Q Q U Y I A
S C H X L U M M G R A S N S I
V O C D M T V Y O I O K E Z R
U K C O U S H II T L II A B W
X E T I N O M M A F N C T S H
N A R Q F T X Y U H V E F U R
R F Z M S H Z N Q N U W I K S
```

No 77

```
K V Z U Y E I H K N S F O E O
G B Z I N A Y A M I N C A N Q
A X A H C H X I R A E B T L Z
P V L B F T N R C T P J G S X
P Q W C Y O W D Z H O U U T V
B E C H A L D A E A N M Y D V
H E R N M B O H V A E A S S I
B I T S J X N N E R G A M S Z
T Y T A I A N A I L B G H O H
S M D T X M A M A I A L A D P R
I O Q O I A N S T R N E W N D
Y P T D R T T A L G Y J N Y G
R T Y A N A E A N I M S X I A
O L T P N A I T P Y G E S U C
P V S E N S S Y S A B A E A N
```

Solutions

No 1

Across: 1 Stupid, 5 Costly, 8 Groped, 9 Really, 10 Ode, 11 Could, 13 Overcast, 15 Asbestos, 16 Smock, 19 Orb, 21 Albino, 22 Annual, 23 Blooms, 24 Easter.

Down: 2 Terrorism, 3 Pupil, 4 Dodo, 5 Careless, 6 Staunch, 7 Yo-yo, 12 Associate, 13 Outdoors, 14 Vertigo, 17 Minus, 18 Lamb, 20 Bake.

No 2

Across: 1 Assiduous, 8 Ample, 9 Twine, 10 Drama, 11 Sweet, 12 Chaser, 13 Agenda, 17 Recto, 20 Sewer, 22 Banal, 23 Swiss, 24 Evergreen.

Down: 1 Ached, 2 Sultana, 3 Dictate, 4 Oblige, 5 Saves, 6 Apace, 7 Regatta, 12 Carouse, 14 Gosling, 15 Nowhere, 16 Bangle, 18 Cabin, 19 Obese, 21 Reign.

No 3

Across: 1 Mange, 7 Lunatic, 8 Tableau, 9 Essence, 12 Idealize, 14 Ever, 16 Lure, 18 Blessing, 20 Withers, 23 Elevate, 24 Pensive, 25 Sleet.

Down: 1 Material, 2 Nibble, 3 Epee, 4 Glue, 5 Paleness, 6 Circle, 10 Sweden, 11 Timber, 13 Amethyst, 15 Regiment, 17 United, 19 Ice age, 21 Seer, 22 Begs.

No 4

Across: 1 Cobweb, 4 Smells, 7 Lifelong, 8 Hard, 9 Skein, 10 Ascetic, 12 Muslin, 13 Vendor, 15 Nearest, 18 Roses, 20 Iran, 21 Exterior, 22 Dither, 23 Astray.

Down: 1 Cells, 2 Buffers, 3 Eglantine, 4 Sighs, 5 Leant, 6 Sidecar, 11 Cheerless, 12 Mankind, 14 Dossier, 16 Adapt, 17 Shear, 19 Sorry.

No 5

Across: 1 Seesaw, 4 Lucent, 7 Anti, 8 Notified, 10 Solder, 12 Parish, 14 Nimbus, 17 Smooth, 19 Lavender, 21 Tall, 22 Redeem, 23 Turtle.

Down: 1 Seal, 2 Shield, 3 Winner, 4 Laptop, 5 Confer, 6 Necessity, 9 Dominance, 11 Emu, 13 Arm, 15 Bye-bye, 16 Sodium, 17 Script, 18 Oyster, 20 Floe.

No 6

Across: 1 Tacit, 4 Airmail, 8 Arabesque, 9 Lists, 10 Transpire, 13 Sprang, 14 Made up, 16 Platitude, 19 Ready, 20 Reinforce, 22 Hundred, 23 Tiers.

Down: 1 Tablets, 2 Consternation, 3 Toast, 4 Aba, 5 Reeds, 6 Acquired taste, 7 Liege, 11 Right, 12 Named, 15 Papyrus, 16 Parch, 17 Infer, 18 Erect, 21 Rid.

No 7

Across: 1 Beat, 3 Subsists, 9 Contour, 10 Apron, 11 Hyena, 12 Leeway, 14 Nether, 16 Raisin, 18 Safari, 19 Argot, 22 Mufti, 23 Teenage, 24 Nickname, 25 Coda.

Down: 1 Backhand, 2 Annie, 4 Unruly, 5 Stage manager, 6 Surpass, 7 Sand, 8 Nonagenarian, 13 Anathema, 15 Traffic, 17 Victim, 20 Guano, 21 Omen.

Solutions

No 8

Across: 1 Grapple, 5 Addle,
8 Second-guess, 9 Run-in,
11 Tempest, 13 Cut out, 14 Annals,
17 Coinage, 18 Elope, 19 Ill-
informed, 22 Annoy, 23 Shatter.

Down: 1 Gastric, 2 Arc, 3 Peninsula,
4 Eighty, 5 Ave, 6 Desperado,
7 Erupt, 10 Nutrition, 12 Minnesota,
15 Slender, 16 Beings, 17 Copra,
20 Lay, 21 Met

No 9

Across: 1 Ordeal, 5 Cacti,
9 Analgesia, 10 Title, 11 Testament,
13 Nuance, 15 Crypts, 19 Pot-pourri,
21 Reins, 22 Triennial, 24 Satan,
25 Either.

Down: 2 Roads, 3 Egg, 4 Lessee,
5 Chatter, 6 Cloth, 7 Irresistible,
8 Cantankerous, 12 Ten, 14 Capstan,
16 You, 17 Strive, 18 Liszt, 20 Raise,
23 Nit.

No 10

Across: 4 Samovar, 7 Chronic,
8 Bulls, 9 Sinai, 10 Moa, 11 Yearn,
12 Andantino, 14 Calibrate,
17 Drive, 18 Aft, 19 Sidle, 21 Arson,
22 Examine, 23 Inhaler.

Down: 1 Ices, 2 Pruned, 3 Indian
Ocean, 4 Scampi, 5 Vulgar,
6 Resonate, 8 Bay of Biscay, 12 Abu
Dhabi, 13 Kirsch, 15 Litter, 16 Aldrin,
20 Eked.

No 11

Across: 1 Shoulder blade,
7 Hand, 8 Agrees, 9 Upend,
10 Ogle, 12 Magyar, 13 Scrub,
15 Power, 18 Astral, 20 Bevy,
21 Agape, 22 Spoilt, 23 Four,
24 Misunderstand.

Down: 1 School, 2 Undue,
3 Defer, 4 Road map, 5 Acetylene,
6 Ensure, 11 Locations, 14 Belated,
16 Hansom, 17 Hybrid, 19 Wafer,
20 Befit.

No 12

Across: 1 Squib, 5 Rash, 7 Unwise,
8 Chair, 9 Satellite, 10 Lee,
11 Recovered, 15 Pedometer, 19 Rip,
20 Momentous, 21 Scone, 22 Evolve,
23 Magi, 24 Truss.

Down: 1 Sickle, 2 Unaged, 3 Bursar,
4 Tiresome, 5 Replies, 6 Sauteed,
12 Electron, 13 Segovia, 14 Lorelei,
16 Russet, 17 Ormolu, 18 Speeds.

No 13

Across: 1 Chaps, 4 Faux pas, 8 Eye,
9 Grotesque, 10 Seine, 11 Protege,
13 Cayman Islands, 15 Tangelo,
17 Viola, 19 Incognito, 21 Oak,
22 Earplug, 23 Style.

Down: 1 Chess, 2 Amenity,
3 Segregate, 4 Food poisoning,
5 Use, 6 Pique, 7 Shekels,
12 Oblivious, 13 Citrine, 14 Neology,
16 Nicer, 18 Ankle, 20 Gel.

No 14

Across: 1 Stopped, 5 Fluid,
8 Contentment, 9 Eased,
11 Charmer, 13 Divine, 14 Posted,
17 Caramel, 18 Gamma,
19 Investigate, 22 Sinew,
23 Amended.

Down: 1 Succeed, 2 Own,
3 Pseudonym, 4 Detach, 5 Fee,
6 Ultimatum, 7 Deter, 10 Sovereign,
12 Alongside, 15 Dead end,
16 Plasma, 17 Cross, 20 Vow,
21 Add.

Solutions

No 15

Across: 1 Beginning, 5 Men,
7 Choose, 8 Summon, 10 Heir,
11 Balance, 13 Placate, 17 Slipper,
19 Poet, 21 Cygnet, 22 Doctor,
23 Lie, 24 Eternally.
Down: 1 Buck, 2 Gloves, 3 Nostril,
4 Gruel, 5 Moment, 6 Nonsense,
9 Obscure, 12 Physical, 14 Typhoon,
15 Single, 16 Lentil, 18 Piece,
20 Prey.

No 16

Across: 1 Liable, 5 Change, 8 Kill,
9 Complete, 10 Miser, 11 Massive,
14 Fleece, 15 Galore, 17 Mystery,
19 Nasal, 21 Assemble, 23 Hail,
24 Sphere, 25 Nudged.
Down: 2 Initially, 3 Believe, 4 Each,
5 Campaign, 6 Atlas, 7 Get,
12 Versatile, 13 Terrible, 16 Loathed,
18 Theme, 20 Seen, 22 Sap.

No 17

Across: 1 Restriction, 7 Ace,
8 Adventure, 9 History, 11 Lilac,
14 Stress, 15 Chosen, 16 Gusto,
19 Buoyant, 21 Catamaran, 23 See,
24 Perspective.
Down: 1 Reach, 2 Tie, 3 Interest,
4 Ideal, 5 Navel, 6 Lexicon, 10 Theft,
12 Ivory, 13 Accurate, 14 Suggest,
17 Sleep, 18 Occur, 20 Tense,
22 Apt.

No 18

Across: 1 Find, 3 Quantity,
7 Indicate, 8 Oval, 9 Heater,
10 Danger, 11 Pedal, 12 Ample,
15 Sought, 18 Treble, 19 Tine,
20 Bachelor, 21 Persuade, 22 Defy.
Down: 1 Fright, 2 Drifted, 3 Quarrel,
4 Ahead, 5 Thorn, 6 Trapeze,
11 Provide, 12 Article, 13 Pretend,
14 Yearly, 16 Guess, 17 Tibia.

No 19

Across: 1 Etch, 3 Fugitive,
9 Trainee, 10 Taste, 11 Ankle,
12 Servant, 13 Travel, 15 Better,
18 Asunder, 19 Trail, 21 Often,
22 Trouble, 23 Exceeded, 24 True.
Down: 1 Extract, 2 Crack, 4 Uneasy,
5 Intersection, 6 Instant, 7 Elect,
8 Independence, 14 Aquatic,
16 Relieve, 17 Writhe, 18 Alone,
20 Amber.

No 20

Across: 1 Refuge, 7 Reverse,
8 Fabric, 9 Antenna, 10 Seemed,
13 Order, 15 Gear, 16 Saga,
17 Credo, 18 Palate, 21 Tornado,
23 Singer, 24 Repress, 25 Debate.
Down: 2 Erase, 3 Guile, 4 Vein,
5 Rehearsal, 6 Retaliate,
10 Signature, 11 Mercenary,
12 Doze, 14 Drop, 19 Abide,
20 Treat, 22 Dish.

No 21

Across: 1 Separate, 5 Past,
7 Glisten, 8 Triumph, 9 Texture,
11 Sketch, 14 Theory, 16 Blanket,
18 Related, 21 Advance, 22 Dune,
23 Strength.
Down: 1 Spot, 2 Praise, 3 Room,
4 Tight, 5 Positive, 6 Tendency,
10 Edit, 11 Scabbard, 12 Truncate,
13 Hide, 15 Opting, 17 Treat, 19 Like,
20 Dash.

No 22

Across: 1 Seldom, 7 Employee,
8 Has, 9 Saliva, 10 Quit, 11 Lunar,
13 Reliant, 15 Emotion, 17 Lotus,
21 Brat, 22 Sierra, 23 Vat,
24 Boldness, 25 Twelve.
Down: 1 School, 2 Lessen, 3 Merit,
4 Apparel, 5 Mosquito, 6 Region,
12 Altitude, 14 Holster, 16 Mirror,
18 Travel, 19 Subtle, 20 Feast.

Solutions

No 23

Across: 1 Submit, 5 Ground, 8 Icon, 9 Action, 10 Owner, 11 Ever, 12 Able, 13 Liking, 15 Drop, 17 Earn, 19 Absent, 20 Veer, 21 Ramp, 22 Gecko, 24 Loosen, 25 Bunk, 26 Paella, 27 Better.

Down: 2 Uncover, 3 Minor, 4 Turn, 5 Guardian, 6 Outrage, 7 Dungeon, 14 Insignia, 15 Develop, 16 Parasol, 18 Romance, 21 Robot, 23 Club

No 24

Across: 1 Weak, 3 Vocation, 9 Tuition, 10 Topic, 11 Disentangled, 14 Arc, 16 Frown, 17 See, 18 Inaccessible, 21 Again, 22 Agitate, 23 Motherly, 24 Holy.

Down: 1 Withdraw, 2 Alias, 4 Own, 5 Antagonistic, 6 Impress, 7 Nice, 8 Significance, 12 Anode, 13 Cemetery, 15 Contact, 19 Bravo, 20 Calm, 22 All.

No 25

Across: 1 Class, 4 Residue, 8 Lie, 9 Extra, 10 Amble, 11 Dedication, 13 Stairs, 15 Fresco, 18 Evaluation, 22 Larva, 23 Butte, 24 Ago, 25 Sweater, 26 Wedge.

Down: 1 Crevasse, 2 Acted, 3 Slander, 4 Reject, 5 Start, 6 Dubious, 7 Even, 12 Complete, 14 Adverse, 16 Rainbow, 17 Hangar, 19 Leapt, 20 Noted, 21 Plus.

No 26

Across: 1 Fabric, 7 Amicable, 8 Akin, 10 Lancet, 11 Kind, 12 Digit, 13 Drifter, 16 Laundry, 18 Rapid, 21 Brig, 23 Crater, 25 Dump, 26 Peerless, 27 Expert.

Down: 1 Framed, 2 Boil, 3 Catch, 4 Jittery, 5 Mask, 6 Blonde, 9 Nation, 14 Feared, 15 Trachea, 17 Agreed, 19 Despot, 20 False, 22 Girl, 24 Rule.

No 27

Across: 1 Apprehensive, 9 Claim, 10 Basic, 11 Oil, 12 Enter, 13 Overall, 14 Elated, 16 Settle, 20 Skittle, 22 Right, 24 Spa, 25 Llano, 26 Trait, 27 Disagreement.

Down: 2 Plant, 3 Remorse, 4 Hollow, 5 Noble, 6 Instant, 7 Excel, 8 Scheme, 15 Animals, 17 Erratum, 18 Estate, 19 Beside, 20 Solid, 21 Thong, 23 Grain.

No 28

Across: 1 Redeem, 4 Giving, 7 Pledge, 9 Deadline, 11 Damp, 14 Unclean, 15 Poor, 16 Iota, 17 Cutlass, 18 Tart, 21 Macaroon, 22 Toupee, 24 Neural, 25 Deceit.

Down: 1 Rapid, 2 Dream, 3 Egg, 4 Greasepaint, 5 Violinist, 6 Gale, 8 Educational, 10 Nectar, 12 Amoeba, 13 Purchaser, 19 Apple, 20 Tweet, 21 Main, 23 Ode.

No 29

Across: 1 Stardom, 8 Examine, 9 Chalice, 10 Raider, 12 Source, 13 Penultimate, 17 Appear, 20 Escape, 23 Apostle, 24 Glacier, 25 Desired.

Down: 1 Secure, 2 Avarice, 3 Drive, 4 Meet, 5 Cargo, 6 Viper, 7 Beaten, 11 Ruler, 12 Spite, 14 Traitor, 15 Savage, 16 Behead, 18 Papal, 19 Avoid, 21 Shoes, 22 Hard.

Solutions

No 30

Across: 4 Display, 8 Ahead,
9 Landscape, 10 There,
11 Retreated, 13 Needed, 16 Storey,
20 Retaliate, 23 Visor, 24 Clearance,
25 Niece, 26 Respect.

Down: 1 Pattern, 2 Reverse, 3 Idler,
4 Donate, 5 Suspect, 6 Least,
7 Yield, 12 Eve, 14 Eye, 15 Enlarge,
17 Rooster, 18 Yearned, 19 Magnet,
20 Recur, 21 Tress, 22 Event.

No 31

Across: 1 Blessed, 5 Tired, 8 One,
9 Realistic, 10 Sinus, 12 Easy,
13 Stanza, 15 Mild, 17 Drab,
20 Amulet, 22 Fuss, 23 Easel,
25 Oblivious, 26 Urn, 27 Deign,
28 Endorse.

Down: 1 Blossom, 2 Eternal,
3 Stress, 4 Drag, 6 Instead, 7 Decay,
11 Knee, 14 Thus, 16 Dashing,
18 Rescuer, 19 Balance, 21 Teased,
22 Flood, 24 More.

No 32

Across: 1 Shifty, 3 Cartel,
7 Inspiration, 10 Chaplain, 11 Ogee,
13 Berne, 14 Malta, 18 Skew,
19 Calabash, 21 Sister-in-law,
22 Embryo, 23 Devoid.

Down: 1 Stitch, 2 Trifling, 4 Arid,
5 Larder, 6 Gamin, 8 Shapeless,
9 Nightfall, 12 Parasite, 15 Ashore,
16 Cakes, 17 Thawed, 20 Espy.

No 33

Across: 1 Subtract, 5 Near,
8 Relevant, 10 Earnest, 11 Noose,
12 Witticism, 15 Reduction, 18 Agile,
19 Ostrich, 22 Template, 23 Ever,
24 Fondness.

Down: 1 Strong, 2 Bellowed,
3 Review, 4 Cane, 6 Edge,
7 Rhythm, 9 Tattoo, 13 Intact,
14 Indicate, 15 Rookie, 16 Napped,
17 Recess, 20 Tune, 21 Hero.

No 34

Across: 1 Instant, 7 Fabric,
9 Leonine, 10 Taken, 11 Then,
12 Proof, 16 Vault, 17 Tome,
21 Above, 22 Shampoo, 23 Polite,
24 Without.

Down: 1 Inflate, 2 Stroked,
3 Avoid, 4 Cartoon, 5 Drake,
6 Scent, 8 Heartless, 13 Magenta,
14 Torpedo, 15 Deposit, 18 Happy,
19 World, 20 Faint.

No 35

Across: 1 Beside, 4 Fitted, 9 Prairie,
10 Pollute, 11 Shiny, 12 Tepid,
14 Haste, 15 Pasta, 17 Cache,
18 Attempt, 20 Exclude, 21 Dangle,
22 Faulty.

Down: 1 Bypass, 2 Spacious,
3 Dirty, 5 Isolate, 6 Tutu, 7 Defend,
8 Represented, 13 Punctual,
14 Harmful, 15 Placid, 16 Merely,
17 Cocoa, 19 Turn.

No 36

Across: 1 Faint, 4 Abscond,
8 Unclear, 9 Rants, 10 Denim,
11 Shelter, 12 Mainly, 13 Canopy,
16 Cherish, 18 Cross, 20 Brawl,
21 Sterile, 22 Ejected, 23 Total.

Down: 1 Found, 2 Inconsiderate,
3 Thermal, 4 Arrest, 5 Serve,
6 Ornithologist, 7 Destroy,
12 Macabre, 14 Ancient, 15 Chased,
17 Inlet, 19 Spell.

Solutions

No 37

Across: 1 Consequence, 9 Beast, 10 Owe, 11 Erode, 12 Actor, 13 Peerless, 16 Occupant, 18 Leash, 21 Throb, 22 Ear, 23 Larva, 24 Decelerated.

Down: 2 Opposed, 3 Soberly, 4 Qualms, 5 Extra, 6 Clout, 7 Sleepwalker, 8 Regrettable, 14 Sultana, 15 Caprice, 17 Charge, 19 Agree, 20 Halve.

No 38

Across: 1 Dressed, 6 Cut, 8 Error, 9 Platoon, 10 Plant, 11 Familiar, 13 Gemini, 15 Bridge, 18 Onlooker, 19 Draft, 21 Unalike, 22 Cling, 23 Ash, 24 Hitting.

Down: 2 Release, 3 Spoiling, 4 Denial, 5 Wrap, 6 Created, 7 Tactile, 12 Arrogant, 13 Gondola, 14 Monarch, 16 Gherkin, 17 Enough, 20 Trip.

No 39

Across: 1 Withdraw, 5 Roll, 9 Impasse, 10 Point, 11 Wanderlust, 14 Deceit, 15 Scared, 17 Artificial, 20 Crime, 21 Raising, 22 Digs, 23 Recently.

Down: 1 Wait, 2 Type, 3 Dissatisfied, 4 Agenda, 6 Obituary, 7 Latitude, 8 Appreciative, 12 Advanced, 13 Scathing, 16 Scarce, 18 Fist, 19 Ugly.

No 40

Across: 1 Deposed, 5 Bless, 7 Stall, 8 Glasses, 9 Retinue, 10 Trait, 11 Dieter, 13 Edible, 18 Asset, 20 Adverse, 21 Dentist, 22 Tiara, 23 Stalk, 24 Present.

Down: 1 Desired, 2 Prattle, 3 Silence, 4 Dagger, 5 Blast, 6 Special, 12 Inspect, 14 Devotee, 15 Barrage, 16 Elegant, 17 Laptop, 19 Think.

No 41

Across: 1 Nought, 4 Finish, 7 Divine, 8 Bulletin, 12 Trudge, 14 Larynx, 15 Aviary, 16 Memory, 18 Bachelor, 22 Driver, 23 Mailed, 24 Remove.

Down: 1 Node, 2 Gained, 3 Treble, 4 Foal, 5 Name, 6 Hymn, 9 Lease, 10 Ignore, 11 Trivia, 13 Gorge, 16 Murder, 17 Medium, 18 Balm, 19 Hull, 20 Land, 21 True.

No 42

Across: 1 Flood, 4 Captive, 7 Pause, 8 Tactless, 9 Width, 11 Serenity, 15 Basement, 17 Carol, 19 Temporal, 20 Mirth, 21 Essence, 22 Tatty.

Down: 1 Fantastic, 2 Obscure, 3 Decline, 4 Closet, 5 Tragic, 6 Visit, 10 Hostility, 12 Respect, 13 Retreat, 14 Goatee, 16 Avenue, 18 Aries.

No 43

Across: 1 Probability, 7 Numerous, 8 Glue, 9 Sandal, 11 Outfit, 13 Evict, 14 Stool, 17 Helmet, 20 Cygnet, 22 Also, 23 Prudence, 24 Retribution.

Down: 1 Punish, 2 Breed, 3 Booklet, 4 Lasso, 5 Tight, 6 Sleuth, 10 Navel, 12 Frown, 14 Succumb, 15 Thrash, 16 Strewn, 18 Moose, 19 Taper, 21 Greet.

No 44

Across: 1 Sign, 3 Belittle, 9 Precede, 10 Chart, 11 Issue, 12 Panacea, 13 Tomato, 15 Meteor, 17 Convent, 18 Cacti, 20 Trade, 21 Amnesia, 22 Dressing, 23 Very.

Solutions

Down: 1 Sophisticated, 2 Guess, 4 Exempt, 5 Incandescent, 6 Tranche, 7 Extraordinary, 8 Nevertheless, 14 Montage, 16 Strain, 19 Caste.

No 45

Across: 1 Attach, 8 Adequate, 9 Bishop, 10 Position, 11 Starve, 12 Newcomer, 16 Lavender, 18 Rumble, 21 Cowardly, 23 Invent, 24 Magician, 25 Greedy.
Down: 2 Twist, 3 Abhor, 4 Happened, 5 Less, 6 Auction, 7 Stroke, 11 Soil, 13 Worrying, 14 Rare, 15 Ceramic, 17 Anorak, 19 Movie, 20 Lined, 22 Dais.

No 46

Across: 1 Dreadful, 5 Long, 8 Swell, 9 Boulder, 10 Average, 12 Payment, 14 Curious, 16 Slender, 18 Adorned, 19 State, 20 Eyed, 21 Needless.
Down: 1 Dish, 2 Energy, 3 Delivered, 4 Upbeat, 6 Ordeal, 7 Gorgeous, 11 Engrossed, 12 Persuade, 13 Become, 14 Cradle, 15 Ornate, 17 News.

No 47

Across: 7 Maintain, 8 Clad, 9 Late, 10 Grin, 11 Lit, 13 Terse, 14 Zoology, 16 Spanner, 18 Snack, 21 Pip, 22 Gene, 23 Suit, 25 Hero, 26 Abundant.
Down: 1 Savage, 2 Incessant, 3 Cargo, 4 Incisor, 5 Act, 6 Saying, 12 Alongside, 15 Several, 17 Prized, 19 Client, 20 Femur, 24 Hog.

No 48

Across: 1 Force, 7 Abandon, 8 Rot, 9 Loathsome, 11 Eerie, 12 Marriage, 16 Snapshot, 20 Inept, 21 Erroneous, 23 Owl, 24 Tourist, 25 Entry.

Down: 1 Forfeit, 2 Return, 3 Emblem, 4 Saga, 5 Unusual, 6 Under, 10 Torso, 13 Aisle, 14 Masonry, 15 Totally, 17 Tissue, 18 Revolt, 19 Death, 22 Oath.

No 49

Across: 1 Floral, 7 Appeared, 8 Marvel, 10 Roller, 11 Large, 13 Western, 16 Illegal, 17 Vixen, 20 Assess, 22 Averse, 24 Dominoes, 25 Allege.

Down: 1 Formal, 2 Over, 3 Ladle, 4 Spurned, 5 Hail, 6 Rehearse, 9 Vague, 12 Allusion, 14 Twice, 15 Mansion, 18 Needle, 19 Salsa, 21 Exit, 23 Rude.

No 50

Across: 1 Drifted, 7 Imagine, 8 Vocal, 10 Utensil, 11 Linen, 12 Energetic, 16 Tarpaulin, 18 Irate, 20 Aladdin, 23 Gulch, 24 Trident, 25 Holiday.

Down: 1 Dwell, 2 Inventor, 3 Dilute, 4 Gave, 5 Miss, 6 Deflect, 9 Cinema, 13 Genial, 14 Thrashed, 15 Stealth, 17 Length, 19 Ebony, 21 Aria, 22 Drew.

No 51

Across: 1 Victor, 5 System, 8 Listen, 9 Breeze, 10 Get, 11 Rifle, 13 Fragrant, 15 Pleasant, 16 Magma, 19 Mob, 21 Jungle, 22 Adopts, 23 Repent, 24 Effect.

Down: 2 Initially, 3 Total, 4 Rung, 5 Subtract, 6 Steward, 7 Meet, 12 Enigmatic, 13 Fragment, 14 Fatigue, 17 Aloof, 18 Ajar, 20 Bare.

Solutions

No 52

Across: 1 Technique, 8 Learn, 9 Per, 10 Torso, 11 Cheer, 12 Write, 14 Battle, 16 Hamper, 20 Stoop, 23 Sweat, 25 Raise, 26 Age, 27 Clean, 28 Excellent.

Down: 1 Topic, 2 Current, 3 Neutral, 4 Quarry, 5 Elbow, 6 Cacti, 7 Unclear, 13 Rim, 14 Beseech, 15 Two, 17 Arsenal, 18 Prepare, 19 Clinic, 21 Often, 22 Prune, 24 Theft.

No 53

Across: 1 Awful, 7 Antenna, 8 Adapted, 9 Emerged, 12 Showdown, 14 Byte, 16 Shun, 18 Standing, 20 Patella, 23 Portend, 24 Steeple, 25 Water.

Down: 1 Analysis, 2 Fiasco, 3 Late, 4 Fade, 5 Disrobed, 6 Invent, 10 Manual, 11 Morsel, 13 Wondered, 15 Engender, 17 Health, 19 Insect, 21 Apex, 22 Grow.

No 54

Across: 1 Scream, 4 Nought, 7 Ascended, 8 Bear, 9 Study, 10 Written, 13 Potent, 13 Vanity, 15 Replete, 18 Cupid, 20 Part, 21 Stubborn, 22 Treaty, 23 Recede.

Down: 1 Seats, 2 Recruit, 3 Annoyance, 4 Nadir, 5 Greet, 6 Tyranny, 11 Irascible, 12 Parapet, 14 Improve, 16 Purse, 17 Tasty, 19 Dense.

No 55

Across: 1 Cravat, 4 Depict, 7 Peer, 8 Protrude, 10 Raised, 12 Trendy, 14 Amused, 17 Beauty, 19 Innocent, 21 Over, 22 Mainly, 23 Meddle.

Down: 1 Copy, 2 Versus, 3 Tripod, 4 Devout, 5 Pierce, 6 Candidate, 9 Harmonica, 11 Ewe, 13 Rye, 15 Stolen, 16 Deeply, 17 Bottom, 18 Abroad, 20 Free.

No 56

Across: 1 Wiped, 4 Discuss, 8 Expletive, 9 Rapid, 10 Spectator, 13 Riddle, 14 Branch, 16 Succeeded, 19 Ozone, 20 Enlighten, 22 Torrent, 23 Relay.

Down: 1 Warrior, 2 Perpendicular, 3 Deeds, 4 Dip, 5 Spent, 6 Unintentional, 7 Sheer, 11 Piece, 12 Cable, 15 Honesty, 16 Slept, 17 Eagle, 18 Donor, 21 Tot.

No 57

Across: 1 Oath, 3 Accident, 9 Extreme, 10 Cheap, 11 Canoe, 12 Stream, 14 Safety, 16 Needle, 18 Gateau, 19 Alpha, 22 Range, 23 Blessed, 24 Molasses, 25 Land.

Down: 1 Overcast, 2 Titan, 4 Crease, 5 Incarcerated, 6 Emerald, 7 Type, 8 Nevertheless, 13 Regarded, 15 Flannel, 17 Mumble, 20 Pasta, 21 From.

No 58

Across: 1 Address, 5 Guard, 8 Conditioned, 9 Album, 11 Grouchy, 13 Mighty, 14 Sleigh, 17 Council, 18 Venom, 19 Grasshopper, 22 Ledge, 23 Desires.

Down: 1 Acclaim, 2 Don, 3 Enigmatic, 4 Stingy, 5 Gun, 6 Abduction, 7 Deity, 10 Begrudged, 12 Oblivious, 15 Humerus, 16 Closed, 17 Carol, 20 Ape, 21 Per.

Solutions

No 59

Across: 1 Lodger, 5 Aroma,
9 Encounter, 10 Igloo, 11 Irritated,
13 Quench, 15 Recall, 19 Epidermis,
21 Spine, 22 Platitude, 24 Diner,
25 Dieter.

Down: 2 Occur, 3 Gnu, 4 Rotate,
5 Abridge, 6 Oddly, 7 Accomplished,
8 Relinquished, 12 Inn, 14 Creeper,
16 Car, 17 Wizard, 18 Vixen,
20 Mauve, 23 Ice.

No 60

Across: 4 Related, 7 Enlarge,
8 Prize, 9 Notes, 10 Era, 11 Relic,
12 Endowment, 14 Ridiculed,
17 Avert, 18 Hat, 19 Pixie, 21 Glory,
22 Caterer, 23 Retreat.

Down: 1 Keen, 2 Slated,
3 Trustworthy, 4 Revere, 5 Trifle,
6 Drenched, 8 Participate,
12 Endanger, 13 Report, 15 Detect,
16 Luxury, 20 Earl.

No 61

Across: 1 Disrespectful,
7 Flag, 8 Secret, 9 Haiku,
10 Chat, 12 Refuse, 13 Asset,
15 Dread, 18 Reside, 20 Here,
21 Azure, 22 Abided, 23 Also,
24 Argumentative.

Down: 1 Defect, 2 Right, 3 Strip,
4 Ensured, 5 Fortunate, 6 Letter,
11 Assisting, 14 Treadle, 16 Armada,
17 Become, 19 Built, 20 Heart.

No 62

Across: 1 Worth, 5 Area, 7 Expose,
8 Natal, 9 Postponed, 10 Err,
11 Reinforce, 15 Monitored, 19 Her,
20 Unpopular, 21 Inane, 22 Tannin,
23 Tome, 24 Guest.

Down: 1 Wanted, 2 Return, 3 Helper,
4 Continue, 5 Aerosol, 6 Essence,
12 Eloquent, 13 Tornado, 14 Riposte,
16 Daring, 17 Phrase, 18 Priest.

No 63

Across: 1 Sharp, 4 Captain, 8 Emu,
9 Innermost, 10 Fungi, 11 Tactful,
13 Miscellaneous, 15 Taffeta,
17 Light, 19 Horrified, 21 Icy,
22 Discern, 23 Digit.

Down: 1 Shelf, 2 Alumnus,
3 Privilege, 4 Constellation, 5 Par,
6 Aloof, 7 Nettles, 12 Concluded,
13 Matched, 14 Ongoing, 16 Firms,
18 Tryst, 20 Ire.

No 64

Across: 1 Rampant, 5 Gapes,
8 Permanently, 9 Award, 11 Inbuilt,
13 Extent, 14 Alpine, 17 Swindle,
18 Ounce, 19 Disturbance, 22 Lorry,
23 Foxtrot.

Down: 1 Replace, 2 Mar,
3 Abandoned, 4 Thesis, 5 Gut,
6 Physician, 7 Saint, 10 Attainder,
12 Ballot box, 15 Everest, 16 Rebuff,
17 Skill, 20 Spy, 21 Nor.

No 65

Across: 1 Ambiguous, 5 Sue,
7 Hating, 8 Babied, 10 Lets,
11 Rambler, 13 Useless, 17 Tremble,
19 Ajar, 21 Reborn, 22 Ignite,
23 Ace, 24 Laborious.

Down: 1 Ache, 2 Bother, 3 Genesis,
4 Swarm, 5 Stifle, 6 El Dorado,
9 Trolley, 12 Hysteria, 14 Swagger,
15 Feeble, 16 Calico, 18 Beryl,
20 Bees.

Solutions

No 66

Across: 1 Isobar, 5 Swathe, 8 Taps, 9 Flamingo, 10 Cruet, 11 Segment, 14 Raceme, 15 Alpaca, 17 Pension, 19 Dryad, 21 Vagabond, 23 Lair, 24 Months, 25 Sextet.

Down: 2 Staircase, 3 Besiege, 4 Rife, 5 Space bar, 6 Axiom, 7 Hag, 12 Nectarine, 13 Venomous, 16 Perplex, 18 Shaft, 20 Odds, 22 Ago.

No 67

Across: 1 Citrus fruit, 7 Hue, 8 Grumbling, 9 Routine, 11 Slain, 14 Defame, 15 Spread, 16 Sways, 19 Housing, 21 Rectitude, 23 Tan, 24 Expenditure.

Down: 1 Cigar, 2 Ram, 3 Splinter, 4 Urges, 5 Theta, 6 Learned, 10 Toady, 12 Lurks, 13 Assorted, 14 Dispute, 17 Alone, 18 Strop, 20 Geese, 22 Tot.

No 68

Across: 1 Bald, 3 Handsome, 7 Newlywed, 8 Arch, 9 Gustav, 10 Reflex, 11 Cider, 12 Puree, 15 Arrays, 18 Ripple, 19 Abet, 20 Tortilla, 21 Currency, 22 Acid.

Down: 1 Benign, 2 Diluted, 3 However, 4 Nadir, 5 Scarf, 6 Machete, 11 Caribou, 12 Portray, 13 Replica, 14 Remand, 16 Alter, 17 Satin.

No 69

Across: 1 Pane, 3 Couscous, 9 Atheist, 10 Abide, 11 Equip, 12 Old hand, 13 Oxygen, 15 Trying, 18 Airsick, 19 Tibia, 21 Gland, 22 Timpani, 23 Overdose, 24 Cove.

Down: 1 Placebo, 2 Nehru, 4 Option, 5 Standard time, 6 Origami, 7 Steed, 8 Simple-minded, 14 Yardage, 16 Granite, 17 Skates, 18 Anglo, 20 Bravo.

No 70

Across: 1 Object, 7 Antenna, 8 Itched, 9 Remodel, 10 Astern, 13 Egret, 15 Comb, 16 Isle, 17 Rondo, 18 Tights, 21 Sausage, 23 Adjure, 24 Overlap, 25 Lament.

Down: 2 Baths, 3 Cheer, 4 Knee, 5 Revolting, 6 Faultless, 10 Ascension, 11 Embrasure, 12 Neon, 14 Root, 19 India, 20 Turin, 22 Grab.

No 71

Across: 1 Chrysler, 5 Abed, 7 Philter, 8 Breathe, 9 Launder, 11 Catnap, 14 Possum, 16 Stirrup, 18 Unstrap, 21 Wistful, 22 Year, 23 Begrudge.

Down: 1 Curb, 2 Revert, 3 Salt, 4 Expel, 5 Atlantis, 6 Darkroom, 10 Atop, 11 Causeway, 12 Narrator, 13 Peru, 15 Shroud, 17 Pulse, 19 Stir, 20 Pile.

No 72

Across: 1 Abduct, 7 Universe, 8 Ran, 9 Income, 10 Dual, 11 Ended, 13 Rustler, 15 Psychic, 17 Waste, 21 Free, 22 Clever, 23 Via, 24 Reversal, 25 Meddle.

Down: 1 Arrive, 2 Denied, 3 Tutor, 4 Hideous, 5 Vendetta, 6 Escape, 12 Exceeded, 14 Discuss, 16 Street, 18 Served, 19 Enrage, 20 Realm.

Solutions

No 73

Across: 1 Lauded, 5 Reduce, 8 Ogre, 9 Castle, 10 Atone, 11 Firm, 12 Urge, 13 Shiver, 15 Aged, 17 Best, 19 Remedy, 20 Type, 21 Rued, 22 Ratio, 24 Studio, 25 Beta, 26 Exodus, 27 Detach.

Down: 2 Angling, 3 Dream, 4 Dodo, 5 Received, 6 Disturb, 7 Element, 14 Humorous, 15 Artiste, 16 Dreaded, 18 Skeptic, 21 Robot, 23 Trod.

No 74

Across: 1 Team, 3 Marooned, 9 Angered, 10 Thorn, 11 Questionable, 14 Ice, 16 Fated, 17 Sea, 18 Replenishing, 21 Abode, 22 Reliant, 23 Pleasant, 24 Pear.

Down: 1 Tranquil, 2 Argue, 4 Aid, 5 Outlandishly, 6 Noodles, 7 Done, 8 Truthfulness, 12 Often, 13 Daughter, 15 Eyesore, 19 Image, 20 Damp, 22 Run.

No 75

Across: 1 Fatal, 4 Believe, 8 Ate, 9 Alien, 10 Depth, 11 Gluttonous, 13 Embody, 15 Breeze, 18 Sanctioned, 22 Actor, 23 Leave, 24 Cue, 25 Radiate, 26 Trade.

Down: 1 Featured, 2 Tying, 3 Languid, 4 Beauty, 5 Laden, 6 Espouse, 7 Echo, 12 Reprieve, 14 Boasted, 16 Ringlet, 17 Pierce, 19 Circa, 20 Drama, 21 Pair.

No 76

Across: 1 Despot, 7 Overture, 8 Gift, 10 Tasted, 11 Pick, 12 Truly, 13 Another, 16 Neutral, 18 Brief, 21 Vast, 23 Girder, 25 Dull, 26 Verified, 27 Extend.

Down: 1 Digest, 2 Soft, 3 Tooth, 4 Verdant, 5 Stop, 6 Oracle, 9 Tablet, 14 Turned, 15 Bargain, 17 Erased, 19 Fooled, 20 Crude, 22 Twig, 24 Rule.

No 77

Across: 1 Discourteous, 9 Amaze, 10 Price, 11 Aye, 12 Sheen, 13 Excited, 14 Decide, 16 Middle, 20 Gorilla, 22 Patch, 24 Toe, 25 Frank, 26 Trial, 27 Extinguished.

Down: 2 Irate, 3 Cleaned, 4 Upkeep, 5 Topic, 6 Omitted, 7 Speed, 8 Passed, 15 Currant, 17 Impetus, 18 Exhale, 19 Gateau, 20 Gaffe, 21 Liken, 23 Twine.

No 78

Across: 1 Please, 4 Enigma, 7 Ignite, 9 Shortage, 11 Epic, 14 Against, 15 Coop, 16 Unit, 17 Tallest, 18 Ease, 21 Crevasse, 22 Danger, 24 Legend, 25 Stated.

Down: 1 Pride, 2 Ennui, 3 Set, 4 Encountered, 5 Institute, 6 Ante, 8 Established, 10 Genius, 12 Proper, 13 Captivate, 19 Angst, 20 Erred, 21 Cowl, 23 Apt.

No 79

Across: 1 Distant, 8 Improve, 9 Tangled, 10 Siesta, 12 Secret, 13 Resemblance, 17 Ascent, 20 Equine, 23 Abiding, 24 Galleon, 25 Delight.

Down: 1 Detest, 2 Sincere, 3 Allot, 4 Tidy, 5 Spine, 6 Boxer, 7 Wealth, 11 Admit, 12 Salve, 14 Chiding, 15 Manage, 16 Weight, 18 Child, 19 Nicer, 21 Quill, 22 Land.

Solutions

No 1

1 Parcel, 2 Flower, 3 August,
4 Regret, 5 Sahara, 6 Person.
The animal is: COUGAR.

No 2

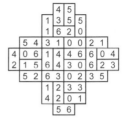

No 3

4	3	5	6	1	2
1	6	2	3	4	5
6	4	1	5	2	3
5	2	3	1	6	4
3	1	4	2	5	6
2	5	6	4	3	1

No 4

The shape which
appears twice is:

No 5

ASSEMBLY, BOTANIST,
CAJOLERY, DIAGNOSE,
EXEMPTED, FUGITIVE,
GLOVEBOX, HORSEFLY,
KEEPSAKE, LABURNUM,
MOISTURE, POTHOLER,
QUAGMIRE, SURPRISE,
TOBOGGAN, YOUNGEST.

No 6

1 Abacus, 2 Assess, 3 Severn, 4 Raisin,
5 Aisles, 6 Saucer.

No 7

1 Error, 2 Sugar, 3 Stair or sitar, 4 Prior,
5 Flair, 6 Safer, 7 Scour, 8 Lunar, 9 Floor,
10 Mayor, 11 Rotor, 12 Molar.
The word is: FLYING.

No 8

No 9

C and G.

No 10

1 Turquoise, 2 Entertain, 3 Normal,
4 Liberia, 5 Apologise, 6 Ecuador,
7 Replica, 8 Atmosphere,
9 Educating, 10 Glacier,
11 Rutabaga, 12 Abandoned,
13 Dressing, 14 Gargoyle.

Solutions

No 11

A	B	B	O	T
B	A	I	Z	E
B	I	S	O	N
O	Z	O	N	E
T	E	N	E	T

S	M	A	C	K
M	A	N	I	A
A	N	G	R	Y
C	I	R	C	A
K	A	Y	A	K

No 12

From top left: 1 Party, 2 Ella, 3 Gnome, 4 Lever, 5 Blot, 6 Sip, 7 Denim.
From bottom left: 1 Mined, 2 Pistol, 3 Breve, 4 Lemon, 5 Galley, 6 Trap.

No 13

8	3	1	1	14	7
9	2	15	13	14	15
12	8	14	1	5	6
5	15	7	12	7	3
1	11	11	12	13	11
10	7	15	13	4	13

No 14

4	x	7	–	9	+	2	=	21
+		–		+		+		
7	+	2	x	4	–	9	=	27
x		x		–		x		
2	x	9	–	7	+	4	=	15
–		+		x		–		
9	–	4	x	2	+	7	=	17
=		=		=		=		
13		49		12		37		

No 15

No 16

E	P	A	H	C
C	H	P	E	A
A	E	C	P	H
P	A	H	C	E
H	C	E	A	P

No 17

The nine-letter word is SEAWORTHY.

Solutions

No 18

A bucket plus a sandcastle weigh as much as a spade (scale A), so three spades weigh as much as three buckets plus three sandcastles. Thus one bucket weighs as much as six sandcastles (scale B). Seven sandcastles weigh as much as one spade (scale A), so scale C needs seven sandcastles to balance the spade and six sandcastles to balance the bucket. Thus 13 sandcastles are needed to balance scale C.

No 19

Here are some possible solutions: ROCK, sock, sack, sank, SAND, WORK, pork, port, pert, pest, REST, WARM, wars, bars, bats, bets, sets, SEAS.

No 20

Cast, Step, Lead, Tour, Frog, Time, Spin, Bath.
The word is: STARFISH.

No 21

b – Having the end rounded and slightly indented.

No 22

I must go down to the seas again, to the lonely sea and the sky, And all I ask is a tall ship and a star to steer her by...

No 23

The time should be 10.20, since each clock advances by one hour and 52 minutes every time.

No 24

A=7, B=3, C=9, D=6, E=2, F=10, G=12, H=15, I=8, J=22, K=27, L=23, M=49, N=50 and O=99.

No 25

In clue 7, S+H+O+E=22, so T=5 (clue 1). In clue 6, T+H+E+S+E=22, so E=4 (clue 3). Since T+E+E+E=5+4+4+4, S+H=9 (clue 3), so O=9 (clue 1) and G=1 (clue 4). N+M=9 (clue 5) and S+H=9 (clue 3), so (since G=1) neither N, M, S nor H is 8. Thus I=8. Since T+O+E=5+9+4 (above), S+N=10 (clue 2); thus S and N are 3 and/or 7. So H and M are 2 and/or 6. S+M=5 (clue 8), so S=3 and M=2. Thus N=7 and H=6.
Thus:
S=3, O=9, M=2, E=4, T=5, H=6, I=8, N=7 and G=1.

No 26

Comparing columns 1 and 4, a spade is worth 1, so (row 3) a club is worth 8, a diamond is worth 10 and (column 2) a heart is worth 3.
Thus:
Heart = 3, club = 8, diamond = 10 and spade = 1.

Solutions

No 27

16731 x 3 = 50193
RIDER x E = HORSE

No 29

S	T	I	T	C	H		S		N
P		C	H		P	I	L	O	T
E	L	E	V	A	T	O	R		I
E		C		L		S		U	S	E
C	A	R	E	L	E	S	S	L	Y
H		E		E		E		T		A
	T	A	R	N	I	S	H	I	N	G
G	E	M		G		S		M		R
	R		D	E	L	I	C	A	T	E
A	S	K	E	D		O		T		E
	E		N		I	N	T	E	N	D

No 31

5	4	1	3	6	2
6	5	3	2	1	4
1	2	6	5	4	3
2	3	4	1	5	6
3	6	5	4	2	1
4	1	2	6	3	5

No 34

Orlando Bloom, John Travolta, Charlie Sheen and Marlon Brando.

No 35

A, At, Ate, Rate, Stare, Grates, Gyrates, STRATEGY.
(Alternatives and anagrams of the above words are also acceptable.)

No 28

No 30

B

No 32

1 Sundial, 2 Island, 3 Snail, 4 Nail, 5 Final, 6 Finial, 7 Failing.

No 33

The couple on the first floor aren't surnamed Taylor (clue 1) or Jones (clue 3), so Brown. Judy is Mrs Brown (2). Rose's husband is Colin (4). John's wife isn't Ann (4), so Judy. Ann's husband is thus Steven. They aren't on the third floor (3), so the second floor, and Mr and Mrs Jones are on the third. By elimination, Colin and Rose are Mr and Mrs Jones and Steven and Ann are Mr and Mrs Taylor.
Thus:
Colin, Rose, Jones, third floor; Steven, Ann, Taylor, second floor; John, Judy, Brown, first floor.

Solutions

No 36

The words are: Cobalt, Embark, Rebate, Ribald, Tabard and Urbane.

No 37

1 Telegram, 2 Propose, 3 Hangar, 4 Blanc, 5 Tutu, 6 Rot, 7 Hi, 8 O. The character is: MERCUTIO.

No 38

E	X	A	C	T		S	Q	U	A	T
D		G		E	G	O		G		O
I	C	E		L		V	A	L	E	T
F		D	E	L	H	I		I		E
Y		M		E		E	L	M		
	J	U	P	I	T	E	R			
S	H	E		R		A				B
C		R		A	Z	U	R	E		E
A	S	K	E	W		R		C	A	R
R	E		N	A	G		H			R
F	A	D	E	S		E	B	O	N	Y

No 39

The numbers which have moved are heavily outlined.

15	22	9	11	17	4	27
2	26	14	23	8	12	20
10	20	4	27	14	22	8
23	7	11	19	3	27	15
28	14	22	7	12	20	2
20	4	28	15	22	6	10
7	12	17	3	29	14	23

No 40

The saying is: GREAT MINDS THINK ALIKE.

No 41

1 Dove, 2 Velodrome, 3 Message, 4 Genuine, 5 Negative, 6 Verified.

No 42

c – Having numerous small branches.

No 43

Across: 1 Badger, 2 Weasel, 3 Cougar, 4 Possum, 5 Rabbit.
Down: 1 Koala, 2 Tiger, 3 Otter, 4 Camel, 5 Hyena, 6 Moose.
Quote: No wise man ever wished to be younger.

No 44

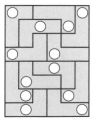

No 45

F	B	S	B

No 46

S=5, Q=4, U=2, A=9, R=1 and E=6.

377

Solutions

No 47

C	B	A	C	A	B
B	A	C	B	A	C
C	C	B	A	B	A
A	B	C	A	C	B
A	C	B	C	B	A
B	A	A	B	C	C

No 50

5	2	1	4	3	6
3	1	4	5	6	2
1	3	5	6	2	4
6	5	3	2	4	1
2	4	6	1	5	3
4	6	2	3	1	5

No 51

The shape which
appears twice is: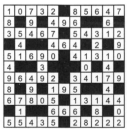

No 53

1 Gaudy, 2 Essay, 3 Lorry, 4 Annoy,
5 Beady, 6 Ivory, 7 Unity, 8 Every,
9 Glory, 10 Itchy, 11 Rusty, 12 Today.
The word is: SECOND.

No 55

ARROGANT, BRANDISH, CHUCKLED,
DOGMATIC, EIGHTEEN, FLOURISH,
GATEPOST, JOYSTICK, LOVEBIRD,
MACARONI, PHEASANT, SHOELACE,
TERRAPIN, ULTERIOR, VANGUARD,
WRECKAGE.

No 48

1 Robber, 2 Search, 3 Paddle,
4 Cygnet, 5 Jewels, 6 Persia.
The animal is: BADGER.

No 49

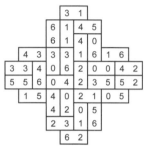

No 52

1 Privet, 2 Strive, 3 Russet,
4 Possum, 5 Simple, 6 Prison.

No 54

1	0	7	3	2		8	5	6	4	7
8		9		4	9	6			6	
3	5	4	6	7		5	4	3	1	2
	4			4	6	4		2		9
5	1	6	9	0		4	1	3	1	0
4			3			0		4		
9	6	4	9	2		3	4	1	7	9
8		9		1	9	5			4	
6	7	8	0	5		1	3	1	4	4
	1			6	6	6		8		0
5	5	4	3	5		2	8	2	2	2

Solutions

No 56

C and D.

No 57

1 Argentina, 2 Azores, 3 Savannah, 4 Hudson, 5 Nile,
6 Edmonton, 7 Norway, 8 Yosemite, 9 Euphrates,
10 Sahara, 11 Adelaide, 12 Everglades, 13 Syria.
The state is: WYOMING.

No 58

D	E	V	I	L
E	L	I	D	E
V	I	O	L	A
I	D	L	E	S
L	E	A	S	H

M	A	R	C	H
A	F	I	R	E
R	I	V	A	L
C	R	A	W	L
H	E	L	L	O

No 59

From top left: 1 Dahlia,
2 Feta, 3 Tsetse, 4 Matron,
5 Etna, 6 Traps.
From bottom left:
1 Spartan, 2 Tenor,
3 Tamest, 4 Estate, 5 Fail,
6 Had.

No 60

6	x	4	–	7	+	9	=	26
+		x		–		+		
9	–	7	x	6	+	4	=	16
–		+		x		x		
4	x	6	–	9	+	7	=	22
x		–		+		–		
7	+	9	x	4	–	6	=	58
=		=		=		=		
77		25		13		85		

No 61

2	8	3	15	6	1
7	12	10	7	11	9
13	3	10	1	14	2
12	7	12	3	5	6
6	10	1	2	8	1
2	6	14	13	11	14

No 62

The nine-letter word is
BAROMETER.

No 63

A	N	C	D	Y
N	Y	A	C	D
Y	C	D	N	A
C	D	Y	A	N
D	A	N	Y	C

No 64

A bucket plus a spade weigh as much as a
sandcastle (scale A), so three spades weigh
as much as one sandcastle (scale B), and one
bucket weighs as much as two spades (scale
A). Thus four sandcastles weigh the same as
12 spades and 12 spades weigh the same as six
buckets. So six buckets are needed to balance
scale C.

Solutions

No 65

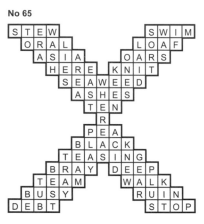

No 66

Here are some possible solutions:
WIND, wand, rand, raid, RAIN,
BEEF, reef, reek, peek, perk, PORK,
GOOD, food, fond, find, fine, tine, TIME.

No 67

1 Aberrant, 2 Bacteria, 3 Rhythmic, 4 Cyclical, 5 Ointment, 6 Gnarlier, 7 Salivate, 8 Inaction.

No 68

a – A heavy type of fabric used especially in upholstery.

No 69

A perfect summer day is when the sun is shining, the breeze is blowing, the birds are singing, and the lawn mower is broken.

No 70

Adding together all of the numbers in the top left segments gives a total of 154; and adding together all of the numbers in the bottom segments gives a total of 154. The numbers showing in the top right segments give a total of 138, so the missing number is 16.

No 71

A=8, B=9, C=2, D=3, E=4, F=17, G=11, H=5, I=7, J=28, K=16, L=12, M=44, N=28 and O=72.

No 72

In clue 5, G+R+I+N=27, so A=4 (clue 1). In clue 7, C+A+R+T=20, so K=1 (clue 2), thus I+N+G=18 (clue 4) and R=9 (clue 5). C+T=7 (clue 2). Since A=4 and K=1 (above), the values of C and T are 2 and/or 5. If T=5, then C=2 and (clue 3) H+L=9: but then H+A+L+T=18, which isn't possible (clue 9). So C=5 and T=2. G+N=15 (clue 8), so I=3 (clue 4). H+L=6 (clue 9), so their values are 0 and/or 6. If H=0, then N=14 (clue 6), which isn't possible. Thus H=6 and L=0. N=8 (clue 6), so G=7.

Thus:
C=5, R=9, I=3, T=2, A=4, L=0, H=6, N=8, K=1 and G=7.

Solutions

No 73

Comparing rows 2 and 4, a spade is worth 8 and a diamond is worth 4. A club is thus worth 6 (row 3), so (row 1) a heart is worth 3.

Thus:
Heart = 3, club = 6, diamond = 4 and spade = 8.

No 74

32058 X 3 = 96174
MATCH x M = BOXES

No 75

No 76

T	A	X	I		A	R	O	U	N	D
A			N	O	T			S		Y
K	I	N	D		E	N	D	U	R	E
E		I			A		A		I	
	O	R	A	L		N	Y	L	O	N
D		E		I	N	N		L		G
O	F	T	E	N		Y	O	Y	O	
U		U		E			W			A
R	O	R	I	N	G		N	E	W	S
L		N			U	S	E			I
E	A	S	I	L	Y		D	A	T	A

No 77

D

No 78

Kate's bikini isn't lemon or pink (clue 2), so blue. She doesn't own towels A (clue 2) or B (clue 3), so C. Towel A is lemon (2). Towel C isn't blue (1), so pink. The woman on towel A hasn't a lemon bikini (1), so pink. Thus towel B is blue and the woman who owns it has a lemon bikini. Towel A doesn't belong to Sharon (1), so Pauline. Sharon owns towel B.

Thus:

Towel A, Pauline, pink bikini, lemon towel;

Towel B, Sharon, lemon bikini, blue towel;

Towel C, Kate, blue bikini, pink towel.

No 79

1 Granite, 2 Garnet, 3 Agent, 4 Neat, 5 Taken, 6 Anklet, 7 Lankest.

No 80

4	6	5	1	2	3
1	2	6	3	5	4
5	4	3	6	1	2
3	5	1	2	4	6
2	3	4	5	6	1
6	1	2	4	3	5

Solutions

No 81

Glenda Jackson, Burt Lancaster, David McCallum and Walter Matthau.

No 82

A, At, Cat, Cart, React, Create, Terrace, CREATURE.
(Alternatives and anagrams of the above words are also acceptable.)

No 83

The words are: Betray, Citrus, Entrap, Matrix, Petrol and Untrue.

No 84

1 Motivate, 2 Problem, 3 Random, 4 Theme, 5 Oral, 6 Ski, 7 On, 8 E. The character is: EMMELINE.

No 85

No 86

The numbers which have moved are heavily outlined.

12	9	29	30	19	15	12
32	25	19	10	13	7	20
15	16	9	22	27	24	13
22	30	26	18	10	14	6
13	8	11	6	25	32	31
4	23	29	26	19	9	16
28	15	3	14	13	25	28

No 87

The saying is:
BAD NEWS TRAVELS FAST.

No 88

1 Separate, 2 Terminal, 3 Album, 4 Umbrella, 5 Laughter, 6 Erupts.

No 89

d – A small bagpipe formerly popular in France

Solutions

No 90

Across: 1 Mexico, 2 Jordan, 3 Canada,
4 Kuwait, 5 Brazil.
Down: 1 Egypt, 2 Nepal, 3 Spain, 4 Yemen,
5 Libya, 6 Japan.
Quote: The remedy is worse than the disease.

No 91

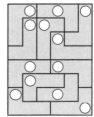

No 92

T	F	A	P

No 93

D=8, I=9, G=7,
S=2 and T=1.

No 94

A	A	C	B	B	C
B	B	A	C	A	C
C	A	C	B	B	A
B	C	A	A	C	B
A	B	B	C	C	A
C	C	B	A	A	B

No 95

1 Snooze, 2 Second, 3 Depend, 4 Silent,
5 Alcove, 6 Butter.
The animal is: OCELOT.

No 96

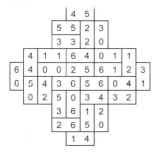

No 97

3	1	5	6	2	4
2	6	3	4	1	5
6	4	2	1	5	3
1	5	6	3	4	2
4	2	1	5	3	6
5	3	4	2	6	1

Solutions

No 98

The shape which appears twice is:

No 99

ABEYANCE, BANISTER, CHAMPION, EQUALISE, GAUNTLET, HOMEWORK, INCUBATE, JAMBOREE, MORTGAGE, NAUTICAL, OBLIVION, PRISTINE, RESTRICT, SMUGGLER, TRAVESTY, VELOCITY.

No 100

1 Frown, 2 Green, 3 Spawn,
4 Raven, 5 Toxin, 6 Baton, 7 Heron,
8 Nylon, 9 Dozen, 10 Apron,
11 Colon, 12 Drain.
The word is: TRAVEL.

No 101

Beware, 2 Israel, 3 Silver,
4 Editor, 5 Rotten, 6 Number.

No 102

6	5	3	6		3	7	6	9	4	3
1		1	6	0	1		8			6
9	2	2	0		2		7	8	9	7
2		9	7	4		2	7		2	8
7	6	4	0		3	1	2	7	4	4
	3			8	8	2			9	
7	4	2	5	3	7		6	1	3	4
8	4		4	1		8	5	4		9
9	0	3	2		7		2	6	5	3
0			6		1	0	9	4		9
3	8	7	9	4	1		7	4	3	5